Leading and Managing Open and Distance e-Learning (ODeL) Institutions in Africa

Edited by

Cuthbert Majoni
Zimbabwe Open University, Zimbabwe

Series in Education

VERNON PRESS

In the Americas:	*In the rest of the world:*
Vernon Press	Vernon Press
1000 N West Street, Suite 1200,	C/Sancti Espiritu 17,
Wilmington, Delaware 19801	Malaga, 29006
United States	Spain

Series in Education

Library of Congress Control Number: 2022939784

ISBN: 978-1-64889-652-1

Also available: 978-1-64889-352-0 [Hardback]; 978-1-64889-543-2 [PDF, E-Book]

Cover design by Vernon Press.

Cover image by macrovector on Freepik.

Table of Contents

List of figures and tables   vii

Acronyms   ix

Editor   xi

Acknowledgments   xiii

Dedication   xv

Preamble   xvii

Foreword   xix

Ignatius Isaac Dambudzo
Zimbabwe Open University

Contributors   xxi

Preface   xxiii

Chapter 1
Leadership in a Decentralised ODeL Institution   1
Cuthbert Majoni
Zimbabwe Open University

Chapter 2
Managing Staff and Training in an ODeL Institution   11
Moffat Chitapa Tarusikirwa
Zimbabwe Open University

Chapter 3
**Leading Open, Distance and E-Learning Organisations
in a Virtual Environment: Leader mindset**   29
Chrispen Chiome
Zimbabwe Open University

Chapter 4
Effective marketing in ODeL   43
Felix Chikosha
Zimbabwe Open University

Chapter 5
Managing Student Affairs in Distance Education   59
Cuthbert Majoni
Zimbabwe Open University

Chapter 6
Effective Library Services in ODL Institutions   69
Kudzayi Chiwanza
Zimbabwe Open University

Chapter 7
Performance Management in an ODeL Institution   87
Rittah Kasowe
Zimbabwe Open University

Chapter 8
ODeL and Inclusion of Vulnerable Students in Higher
Education Institutions   105
Gilliet Chigunwe
Zimbabwe Open University

Chapter 9
Innovation and Industrialisation in ODeL Institutions   123
Cuthbert Majoni
Zimbabwe Open University

Felix Chikosha
Zimbabwe Open University

Chapter 10
Organisational Climate and Development in ODeL
Institutions   143
Rittah Kasowe
Zimbabwe Open University

Chapter 11
Programme Management, Implementation and
Evaluation Practices in ODeL Universities   165
Richard Bukaliya
Zimbabwe Open University

Chapter 12
Quality Assurance Practices in Open and Distance
e-Learning (ODeL) Institutions   193
Tichaona Mapolisa
Zimbabwe Open University

Index   219

List of figures and tables

Figures

Figure 8.1: Students in the Rural Areas and Access to Internet 110

Figure 8.2: Mobile Phones and Access to Tertiary Education 111

Figure 8.3: ODeL through Radio Broadcasting of HEI Programmes and Courses 114

Figure 8.4: Digital Accessibility 115

Figure 8.5: Students with Disabilities and Online Learning 116

Figure 10.1: Mechanisms of Shaping Organisational Climate in ODeL Institutions 146

Figure 11.1: Roles of the Coordinator in ODeL Programmes 177

Tables

Table 4.1: Social Media Usage in ODeL 54

Table 10.1: Past and Emerging Forms of the Employment Relationship 153

Acronyms

ACRL	Association of College and Research Libraries
AIDS	Acquired Immune Deficiency Syndrome
AVU	African Virtual University
BEAM	Basic Education Assistance Module
CCRTVU	China Central Radio and Television University
CLT	Complexity Leadership Theory
COVID19	Corona Virus Disease
CTVTC	China Television Teachers College
DE	Distance Education
DEATA	Distance Education Association of Tanzania
DL	Distance Learning
DLTF	Distance Learning Task Force
EDA	Exploratory Data Analysis
HEIs	Higher Education Institutions
HIV	Human Immunodeficiency Virus
ICDE	International Council for Open Distance Learning
ICT	Information Communication Technology
IP	Intellectual Property
IPR	Intellectual Property Rights
IT	Information Technology
MBKs	Massive Open Online Courses
MOOCs	Massive Open Online Courses
My VISTA	Zimbabwe Open University Electronic Learning Systems
NACADA	National Academic Advisory Association Technology in Advisory Commission
NGO	Non-Governmental Organisation
NOUN	National Open University of Nigeria
NYU	New York University
ODeL	Open and Distance e-learning
ODL	Open Distance Learning
OECD	Organisation for Economic Cooperation and Development
OPAC	Online Public Access Catalogue
PM	Performance Management
PMS	Performance Management System
PR	Public Relations
PVC	Pro Vice-Chancellor
PWD	Persons with Disabilities

QA	Quality Assurance
R&D	Research and Development
ROI	Return for Investment
SDGs	Sustainable Development Goals
SMART	Specific, Measurable, Achievable, Relevant, Timebound
SMEs	Small Scale Enterprises
STEM	Science Technology Engineering and Mathematics
STP	Segmentation Targeting and Positioning
UCDE	University College of Distance Education
UFE	Utilisation Focused Evaluation
UNESCO	United Nations Economic and Scientific Organisation
UNICEF	United Nations International Children's Emergency Fund
UNISA	University of South Africa
UZ	University of Zimbabwe
VC	Vice Chancellor
VEE	Values Engaged Evaluation
WIFI	Wireless Technology
ZIMSTAT	Zimbabwe Statistics
ZOU	Zimbabwe Open University

Editor

Cuthbert Majoni is an Associate Professor of Educational Management at the Zimbabwe Open University. He holds a Ph.D. in Educational Management. He is the Regional Director of Mashonaland Central Regional Campus of the Zimbabwe Open University He has experience in teaching at tertiary and university level as a lecturer. He has published in multiple refereed journals and has presented papers at international conferences. He is an external examiner for PhD theses engaged by several universities in South Africa. He is also a content reviewer, an external assessor, and an academic module writer. His research interest is in the areas of Leadership and Management in Higher Education, Teacher Development, and Open and Distance Learning.

Acknowledgments

Acknowledgements go to Professor Mapolisa, who suggested the idea of coming up with a book focusing on e-learning. He wrote the initial chapter outlines and suggested that we flight a call for writers for those who might be interested to contribute chapters for the book. I want to thank academic colleagues who assisted in cleaning up the manuscript: Dr Felix Chikosha, Zimbabwe Open University, and Mr Tarwirei, Zimbabwe Open University, who volunteered to work on the technical elements of the manuscript as well as editorial aspects; thank you for taking time to ensure this book is published. I want to thank Prof Dambudzo for the foreword of this book.

Dedication

This book is dedicated to all the academic colleagues in Zimbabwe and Africa who are making e-learning a reality in the absence of common continental and national approaches to e-learning, absence of financial and technical support in terms of data bundles, and teaching/learning platforms and other related ICT support; but they are soldiering on. The advent of COVID-19 forced all institutions in Africa to embrace e-learning without the dedicated e-platforms to ensure effective teaching and learning. This book is dedicated to rural students who must travel long distances to access e-learning resources and upload assignments. Yet some drop out of programmes because they cannot cope with the demands of e-learning. I also dedicate this book to my Regional Mashonaland Central staff for their encouragement and support. And most of all, to my family, for creating a conducive environment to work at home.

Preamble

This book focuses on e-learning, especially in developing countries in Africa. The outbreak of COVID-19 forced most educational institutions, including conventional institutions in higher education, to embrace e-learning as a tool to not only ensure education is not paralysed but continues to thrive. However, the major challenge has been the need to shift focus from the conventional face-to-face mode to the e-learning mode. This calls for a change of mindset and a review of practices to ensure success in the implementation of e-learning. This book has 12 chapters that explore the leadership theories and approaches that influence administrative practices in Open and Distance e-Learning (ODeL) institutions. It also presents the types of leadership required for organisational effectiveness. The training approaches and needs of staff as they apply to ODeL institutions are outlined. Student support in Open and Distance e-Learning (ODeL) is discussed in chapters focusing on library and information services, student affairs, and inclusion of students with special needs to ensure successful completion of studies under challenging environments. The contemporary issues of innovation and industrialisation are also dealt with, as is effective marketing in ODeL institutions, which is critical for the survival and growth of tertiary institutions. This book will be useful to senior and middle managers in both conventional and ODeL institutions. It is hoped that the recipients of this book can acquire the theoretical and practical knowledge relevant to the successful implementation and management of e-learning. Moreso, students studying for post-graduate studies will benefit from the well-researched literature that contributes to the body of knowledge in e-learning. The book will add value to the already-existing literature on e-learning, which is a new development in education.

Foreword

Ignatius Isaac Dambudzo

Zimbabwe Open University

The book covers a wide range of topics relevant to any Higher Education Institution wherever it may be located. They include Leadership in Decentralised ODeL Institutions, Managing staff, Leading in a Virtual Environment, Effective Marketing, Managing Students, Library Services, Performance Management, Inclusion of Vulnerable students, Innovation and Industrialisation, Organisational Climate and Development, Programme Management, Implementation and Evaluation Practices, and Quality Assurance Practices. All the chapters are topical and of interest to any Higher Education leader and manager. From the book title, one gets the impression of a handbook for leaders and managers in ODeL Higher Education Institutions. The content and presentation provide guidance to existing and future leaders of ODeL institutions to help them lead and manage their organisations more effectively.

The presentation of different chapters is quite detailed and informative. Chapter One presents the concept of leadership and leadership styles. It creates an awareness in the reader about the different leadership styles displayed in the workplace. It enables one to reflect on one's leadership style. Chapter Two presents the management of staff and training in an ODeL institution using a case study approach. Chapter Three examines leadership in a virtual environment. The discussion is quite detailed. Chapter Four presents marketing. Every organisation needs to market itself for survival. Different methods and strategies for marketing their benefits and effectiveness are presented. This is an informative chapter on the marketing of an educational institution. Chapter Five examines the management of student affairs in ODeL institutions. This is another detailed chapter that informs the readers of students' needs. Chapter Six presents effective management of the Library Services in an ODeL institution. Performance management is presented in Chapter Seven. The role of leadership and management need to be brought out clearly to sharpen the focus of the book title. Chapter Eight deals with inclusive education in an ODeL institution. Some relevant illustrations have been presented to support the text and how leaders should deal with an inclusive teaching and learning environment. Innovation and industrialisation are presented in Chapter Nine, showing recent additions to Education 3.0 to make Education 5.0. Every leader and manager in Higher Education should be aware of the concept and philosophy of Education 5.0. This chapter articulates the role of universities in innovation and industrialisation. Organisational Climate and Development is presented in Chapter Ten. This chapter reflects leadership and management influence organisational climate and its development. Chapter Eleven focuses on Programme Management, Implementation, and Evaluation Practices. The chapter contextualises leadership and management roles in an ODeL institution. The book concludes with Chapter Twelve on Quality Assurance Practices in ODeL institutions. The content is pertinent and is contextualised to leadership and management in ODeL institutions. Individual chapters are informative on the relevant topics, giving informative and detailed content. For information that links leadership and management in ODeL institutions, Chapter Eleven is the bus stop.

Prof. Ignatius Isaac Dambudzo

Contributors

Richard Bukaliya teaches at the Zimbabwe Open University as part of the Faculty of Education. He is the Regional Programme Coordinator at the Mashonaland East Regional Campus, Department of Teacher Development, responsible for the Postgraduate Diploma in Education, Bachelor of Education in Early Childhood Development, Bachelor of Education (Secondary), and Diploma in Education (Primary). He holds a Doctor of Philosophy in Educational Management. His research interests include issues in the educational management of primary and secondary education and distance education.

Dr **Gilliet Chigunwe** is a Senior Lecturer in the Department of Special Needs Education at Zimbabwe Open University. She holds a Ph.D. in Special Education and is a qualified teacher. She holds a Master in Educational Foundation (Psychology), Master of Science in Special Education, Bachelor of Education in Hearing Impairment, Bsc in Special Education, Diploma in Special Education (Hearing Impairment), Certificate in Education, Certificate in Leadership & Management of Higher Education, and Certificate in Multimedia Enhanced Learning. She is an executive member of the Zimbabwean Academic and Non-Fiction Authors Association (ZANA). Her research interests include special needs education and inclusive education. Dr Gilliet Chigunwe has published several research articles in peer-reviewed journals and has presented papers at international conferences. She is a consultant in special needs education and inclusive education.

Felix Chikosha is currently Regional Programme Coordinator for the Faculty of Commerce and Law at the Zimbabwe Open University Mashonaland Central Regional Campus. He specialises in Marketing, with a specific interest in Green Marketing. He holds a Bachelor of Commerce (Hons) Marketing, MBA, and PhD degrees. He has vast experience in university teaching, research, and community services. His research work directly contributes to the promotion of sustainable business practices and use of environmentally friendly products.

Chrispen Chiome is a Professor of Educational Leadership in the Zimbabwe Open University. He holds a Ph.D. in Educational Leadership and Policy. He has published 11 books, 16 book chapters, and 53 research articles in refereed journals. He has presented over 73 papers at local, regional, and international conferences. He is a member of the Distance Education Association of Southern Africa, (DEASA); World Social Science Forum (WSSF); African Council for Distance Education (ACDE), and E-infrastructures for Africa (eI4Africa) among others.

Kudzayi Chiwanza, an information management academic, specialist, and administrator, has vast experience in leading and managing programs and teams. She is a Senior Lecturer in the Department of Information Sciences and Records Management. She holds an MSc in Library and Information Science from the National University of Science and Technology, a BA Degree in Media Studies from ZOU, and a Diploma and Certificate in Library and Information Science (HEXCO). She is also currently enroled with the University of South Africa (UNISA) for a DPhil. She has been a Board of Trustee Member of the Humanitarian Development Trust (HUDET) and a member of the Zimbabwe Library Association.

Rittah Kasowe is a Senior Lecturer in the Department of Educational Studies at Zimbabwe Open University. She holds a PhD in Educational Management and is a qualified teacher who has been in Open and Distance learning for 12 years. She has a certificate in Technology Enabled Learning. She is a member of the Zimbabwean Academic and Non-Fiction Authors Association (ZANA) and a member of the Zimbabwe Evaluation Society (ZES). Her research interests include teachers' training, teaching and learning effectiveness, organisational effectiveness, personal effectiveness, open and distance learning, leadership and management, policy implementation in education, and performance management. Dr. Rittah Kasowe has published several research articles in peer-reviewed journals. She participated and continues to participate in various community and university service projects.

Tichaona Mapolisa is a Full Professor in Educational Management and holds a PhD in educational management. Currently, he is the Director of the Directorate of Research, Innovation and Technology at the Zimbabwe Open University. He has vast experience teaching at various levels of education, namely primary school, high school, teacher education, and university. His areas of research interest are quality assurance and students' retention in private and public universities.

Moffat Chitapa Tarusikirwa is an Associate Professor who holds a Ph.D. in Comparative Education from the University of the Western Cape. Currently, he is the Chairperson of the Department of Teacher Development at Zimbabwe Open University. He has held several positions in the Education Ministry in Zimbabwe. He has presented papers at international conferences and has published in several refereed journals. He is a member of the African Network for Internationalization of Education (ANIE) and the Zimbabwe Academic and Non-Fiction Writers Association (ZANA) inter alia.

Preface

The development in information and communication technology has revolutionised higher education in general and has also impacted on distance education delivery. This book was motivated by this development; on the other hand, the outbreak of COVID-19 has heavily impacted the education sector for distance education institutions and conventional institutions. Social distancing resulted in limited face-to-face teaching and learning; hence, most staff and students now rely on e-teaching and e-learning. This book is all about e-learning, especially in developing countries where institutions are embracing it. The book will contribute to effective implementation of e-learning and focuses on various critical success factors such as leadership management, quality assurance, staff training, student affairs and students with special needs among other factors. This book will assist senior management, administrators, and academics in the implementation of e-learning in their respective institutions. We wrote to write this book because there is currently scanty literature written on e-learning, especially in the context of developing countries in Africa.

Chapter 1

Leadership in a Decentralised ODeL Institution

Cuthbert Majoni

Zimbabwe Open University

Abstract

This chapter presents the concept of leadership in higher education and the related theoretical perspectives. The focus is on theories, namely the systems, situational, complexity, and transformational leadership theories and how they can be applied in ODeL institutions. The virtual environment and how virtual methods can promote effective administration of ODeL institutions are also discussed.

Keywords: Leadership, Open and Distance e-learning, virtual

***

1.0 Introduction

Technological advancement has contributed immensely to the development of Distance Education (DE) (Cornford & Pollock, 2003; Portugal, 2006). The transformation of distance education has created new challenges, such as a diverse student body and increased competition. Students have new demands, such as the need for high-quality education and individualised instruction (Milligan & Buckenmeyer, 2008; Folkers, 2005). The new shift from campus-based to a virtual education model of delivery has called for new leadership for the success of virtual or distributed administration of distance education institutions. This chapter discusses the concept of leadership in the context of open and distance e-learning (ODeL) and institutional positions of responsibility considered to have leadership functions in academic institutions. This chapter also presents leadership theories and practices deemed relevant to the effective delivery of distance e-learning, drawing examples from institutions in Southern Africa. Application of the leadership theories and the virtual approaches to leadership administration are discussed as to how they can be applied to distance e-learning.

1.1 Concept of Leadership

A distance education leader is a person in higher education administration who oversees distance education programmes and activities. These include Vice-Chancellors, Pro-Vice Chancellors, Deans and Directors of Distance Education units and departments. Leadership has been defined as a set of attitudes and behaviours that create conditions for innovative changes that enable individuals and organisations to share a vision, move in the same direction, and contribute to the management and operationalisation of ideas (Beaudion, 2003). A leader creates things, innovates ways to accomplish goals, mobilises resources as well as sets direction. The leader bears all responsibility for the overall outputs and outcomes and ensures subordinates achieve set goals (Halder, 2010).

In DE institutions, leaders are expected to direct and coordinate employees' work and contribute to individual and organisational growth and renewal. Distance education has entered the digitalised phase, resulting in changes in structures and systems, and as a result, there is need for new leadership approaches, styles, and practices (Bryman, 2007; Halder, 2010). There has been a paradigm shift towards e-learning, and the leadership styles and practices should promote effective virtual learning and administration. How institutions lead and manage distributed campuses requires what Kuscu and Arslan (2016) refer to as virtual leadership. The virtual environment has staff in different environments, times, and spaces. Academics can work from home attending to students who are at home and managers can manage at staff who are at home (Naktiyok, 2006; Kuscu & Arslan, 2016).

1.2 The Theoretical Perspective

1.2.1 Transformational Leadership Theory

The transformational leadership theory is premised on the assumption that leadership is based on moral ethics and equitable consideration (Northhouse, 2007). Transformational leadership defines and articulates the organisational vision, as well as how to motivate subordinates. The main characteristics of transformational leaders are self-confidence, honesty, and integrity. Other qualities include being charismatic, motivational, and intellectual (Bass & Steidelmeier, 1998). Transformational leaders can analyse the current situation in an organisation and introduce a new approach to problem-solving and decision making. They do not necessarily follow the old tradition but encourage the advancement of new ideas.

Transformational leaders inspire subordinates to achieve personal and organisational goals. They review the organisational structure to meet the current demands of the environment. Transformational leaders evaluate current organisational goals; modify them to ensure they are feasible, attainable, and acceptable to meet the organisational challenges. It leverages new technologies and research to evaluate current strategies, processes, and resources to ensure the organisation is efficient and effective (Morrill, 2010; Learning, 2007; Portugal, 2006). Transformational leaders concern themselves with continual organisational renewal and incrementally adapt to change in an organisation.

The inherent qualities of transformational leadership are applicable to distance education. The qualities of vision, trust, passion, inspiration, and commitment are required by DE leaders who are in distant campuses or centres. DE leaders must motivate and inspire their staff (Irlbeck & Pucel, 2000; Tripple, 2010; Portugal, 2006). The transformational model of leadership is relevant since leaders deal with a variety of stakeholders such as tutors, students, staff, and administrators who have different needs and expectations. In the Zimbabwe Open University (ZOU) and University of South Africa (UNISA) directors in decentralised campuses are expected to be involved in strategic planning and implementation based on their context. They are expected to handle internal and external stakeholders on behalf of the entire university. They are expected to embrace e-learning and review the delivery of e-learning with their context in mind. They need to review environmental influences in the face of competition from other higher education institutions in their location. Transformational leaders in DE institutions need to be equipped with marketing skills to ensure their programmes continually grow and attract new students.

Distance education leaders with change management abilities can anticipate unintended results of change and avoid negative results. Transformational DE leaders will be the custodian of the institutional vision they are innovative, flexible, and can adapt to the evolving organisational context (Portugal, 2006; McKenzie et al., 2005). In Zimbabwe, there has been a shift from reliance on face-to-face to the use of virtual platforms to interact and plan work. Most of the staff are working from home, using technology to accomplish tasks and give feedback while students are learning from home. relying on technology. Hence, leaders need to adapt to change.

1.2.2 Situational Leadership

The situational leadership approach proposes that leaders assess situations to determine how they can be effective in a context that has a wide variety of organisational tasks (Northhouse, 2001). This approach allows a leader to choose the right style for a specific situation. Some factors determine the appropriateness of a leadership style such as maturity of employees, the complexity of a task, competency of followers, and commitment of followers. To achieve set goals, the leader can focus on improving the relationship with followers or focus on the size of the task either increasing or decreasing it. In a change of environment, such as a change in political, social, and economic situations, the situational leader must consider the time, place, and circumstance and make the right decision. (Northouse, 2001; Hersey & Blanchard, 1990).

Leadership involves implementing change, and situational leadership adapts to those changes in the environment. They respond promptly with appropriate intervention when the conditions change in an organisation. In Zimbabwe, COVID-19 resulted in a lockdown with staff and students not allowed to travel. Leaders introduced virtual platforms for both students and staff to operate from. *WhatsApp* groups and call centres were set up to cater to students' needs as well as staff needs.

According to Tripple (2010), situational leadership is relevant in DE since its environment is constantly changing. Changes in DE have occurred mainly due to factors such as globalisation, massification, customer demands, and developments in information communication technologies. DE leaders need to respond to the environment to ensure their organisation survives. In Zimbabwe, the government directed institutions to develop their strategic plans based on results-based management (RBM) and results-based budgeting (RBB). Situational leadership can be applied when government directives are given, and compliance is expected; hence, leaders will apply the autocratic leadership style to comply with the directive. University lecturers are experts and the leader might need their expertise to implement e-learning. Therefore, a democratic leadership style is suitable. Situational leadership is useful in ensuring effective implementation of distance e-learning, whose environment and context are constantly changing.

1.2.3 Complexity Leadership Theory

Complexity Leadership Theory (CLT) is a new leadership theory that focuses more on context than the individual leader. This theory is based on the belief that the internal environment, as well as the external environment, should be considered for effective leadership. There is a need to understand the complexities of the organisational context as well as internal and external factors that affect leadership (Litchteinsten et al., 2006; Uhl-Bein et al., 2007). The complexities in the ever-changing DE environment have rendered the traditional leadership styles ineffective (Heifetz & Linsky, 2002). CLT perceives that organisational context that changes and distinguishes leadership from leaders. According to Heifetz (1994), leadership is an interactive and dynamic process that surpasses the individual abilities of the leader, hence, the basis of the analysis is the complex adaptive system (CAS). Leadership is a set of processes and conditions that influence or are influenced by organisation (Uhl-Bien et al., 2007). The relationship between parts is more important than the parts themselves. CLT promotes collaboration, flexibility, innovation, reflective thinking, and adaptability to organisational change.

The CLT is relevant to distance e-learning since DE is evolutionary and responds to changes in information communication technology. The changes that occur in embracing the new technology include pedagogy and support mechanisms that alter the DE context and affects leadership practices in the organisation. Online learning depends on technology and adoption of new technologies which alters the dynamics of DE Leadership and practices (Nworie, 2012). Knowledge of Complexity Leadership Theory by DE leaders will promote understanding of context both internal and external forces which affect their organisation as well as enable leaders successfully navigate the environment for the benefit of the institution. The result is success and achievement of organisational goals. Leaders need to empower decentralised structures or units and support them based on their context.

1.2.4 The Systems Theory

The systems theory according to Siegal (1999) is defined as an aggregation of parts that have unique functions, with goals that are connected by common information channels and paths to achieve common objectives. Systems are characterised by interrelatedness, interconnectedness and dynamism of parts that make a whole (Hutchins, 1996). The systems theory enables leaders understand the relationship between different units or of their organisation and how they interrelate to each other. The system is also dynamic and has positive and negative loops. (Sterman, 2000). The systems theory provides a better understanding of distance education. Knowledge of the system is important for leaders to understand the DE organisation and how change can be implemented. DE leaders can adopt new technologies as well as their diffusion within the decentralised units. The systems theory contextualises the implication of and adoption of technological innovation in distance education. Leaders need to consider DE as a system with subsystems that have different context and dynamics. Leaders need to solicit a solid theoretical foundation to help lead their organisation effectively. They need to be well equipped with knowledge, skills, and attitudes that will promote and embrace e-learning as well as facilitate its adoption with their departments or units.

1.3 Application of Virtual Methods in ODeL Institutions

Institutions with distributed campuses in various geographical locations need to use virtual methods of communication. They can put in place virtual teams that can be referred to as cyber teams, dispersed teams, distributed teams, or online teams (DuFrene & Lehman, 2012). Virtual teams work in different locations at different times without meeting face to face but using media, emails, telephone, or video conferencing to communicate (Akkirman, 2004). These activities have become a reality in the Zimbabwe Open University and other DE universities in Southern Africa during the COVID-19 lockdown period. Physical contact has been shelved; workshops, meetings, strategic planning workshops, staff appraisal, and attending to student needs is done online.

According to Varol and Tarcan (2000), there is a need for an institutional culture in the use of new advanced technology to establish and promote virtual methods of communication. Distance education leaders need to put in place goals, roles, responsibilities, and targets to successfully establish virtual systems. Leaders need to allow employees to work in different locations during different times but coordinate using technological gadgets or media. The advantages of virtual systems include among others removal of travel expenses, availability of personal freedom, efficiency, control of operations and quick decision making. The disadvantages include leaders and subordinates who have technological incapabilities, poor internet connectivity, and conflict of cultures, communication challenges and availability of power, especially in rural areas. In countries such as Zimbabwe and Zambia, these factors will negatively affect virtual learning and administration. Institutions also lack technological expertise and have limited bandwidth. The main question is, are leaders able to supervise employees and tell them what to do as they used to do face to face? The answer is no. Polat and Araboci (2014) propose the adoption of the open leadership concept. Open leadership emphasises that a leader should abandon staff control if he or she is to be successful. Open leaders can monitor, share, comment, produce, organize, and supervise staff wherever they are. The old model of controlling and supervising employees on the job becomes irrelevant (Polat & Araboci, 2014).

Virtual teams can work synchronously or asynchronously out of office, at home, in different provinces of a country. Zimbabwe has ten political provinces; the virtual meetings will involve participation of individuals from these distributed campuses. UNISA uses tele-conferencing as they hold meetings with campus directors from different provinces of South Africa. Leaders need to learn how to manage their subordinates using a suitable leadership style. DE leaders need skills, characteristics, and behaviours different from conventional leaders (Naktiyok, 2006). Virtual leaders need to possess the ability of selecting and using appropriate technology to promote collaboration and effective communication (Kirel, 2007). The virtual model of communication is usable and applicable in open and distance e-learning.

1.4 Summary

This chapter reveals that the changing context of distance education and the aggressive encroachment in their domain by the powerful forces of digitalisation have challenged the appropriateness of DE leadership in distance learning institutions. However, leadership practices are no longer confined to those in administrative positions but to subordinates, significantly impacting on the organisation both positively and negatively. Distance e-learning leadership calls for distinct sets of attitudes and behaviors that create conditions for change that enables the individual and the organisation to share a vision and move in one direction, as well as contribute to the effective management and implementation of ideas. The impact of leadership in distance e-learning setup cannot be overemphasised to ensure best practices in distance e-learning leadership.

References

Akkirman, A. D. (2004). *Organisational behaviour in Virtual Workplace,* Instanbul Aktuel Yayinlari.

Bass, B., & Steidelmeier, P. (1998). *Ethics, Character and Authentic Transformational Leadership Center for Leadership Studies,* NY Binghamton University http://csBinghamton/Bass Steid.

Berge, Z. (ed) (2001). *Sustaining Distance Training: Integrating Learning Technologies into the fabric of enterprise* San Francisco, Jossey-Bass.

Beaudion, M. F. (2003). Distance Education Leadership for the new century; *Online Journal for Distance Learning Administration 6(2)* Website http://www.westaga.edu/distance /oidla/summer/beadionbz html

Bryman, A. (2007). Effective Leadership in Higher Education: A Literature Review. *Studies in Higher Education, 32,* 693- 710.

Cornford, J., & Pollock, N. (2003). Putting the university online: Information, technology, and organizational change. Buckingham, England: The Society for Research into Higher Education & Open University Press.

Dixon, D. L. (1998). The Balanced CEO: A Transformational Leader and Capable Manager, *Healthcare Forum Journal, 4*(2), 26-29.

Dufrene, D. D. & Lehman, C. M. (2012). Communication Strategies for Virtual Teams USA. *Business Expert Press.*

Folkers, D. A. (2005). Competing in the marketspace: Incorporating online education into Applying Leadership Theories to Distance Education Leadership- An organizational perspective. *Information Resources Management Journal, 18*(1), 61-78.

Halder, U. K. (2010). *Leadership and Team Building.* Oxford University Press, New Dehli.

Heifetz, R. A. (1994). *Leadership Without Easy Answers.* Cambridge MA: Belnap Press of Havard University Press.

Heifetz, R. A., & Linsky, M. (2002). *Leadership Online Leadership: Staying Alive Through dangers of Leading.* Boston: Havard University Press.

Hersey, P., & Blanchard, K. H. (1990). *Management of Organization Behavior: Utilizing Human Resources.* Englewood Cliffs, NJ: Prentice-Hall.

Hutchins, C. L. (1996). *Systems Thinking.* Ourora Co Professional Development Systems.

Irlbeck, S. A., & Pucel D. J. (2000). Dimensions of Leadership in Higher Education Distance Education. In *Proceedings of international workshop on advanced learning Technology, Volume 2000*, pp. 63-64. Palmerston, North New Zealand.

Kirel, C. (2007). The Future of Organisational Behaviour in Vitrual Organisation. *Sosyal Bilimler Dergisi* (1) pp. 93-110.

Kuscu, M., & Arslan, H. (2016). Leadership at Distance Education Teams. *Turkish Journal of Distance Education, 17*(3), 136-156.

Learning, D. R. (2007). *Academic leadership: A practical guide to chairing the department 2nd Edition.* Bolton, Anker.

Lichtenstein, B., Uhl-Bien, M., Marion, R., Seers, A., Orton, D., & Schreiber, C. (2006). Complexity leadership theory: An interactive perspective on leading in complex adaptive systems. *Emergence: Complexity and Organization, 8*(4), 2-12.

Marion, R. (1999). *The Edge of Organisational Chaos and Complacency Theories of Formal Social Systems.* Newbury Park CA: Sage.

McKenzie, B., Ozkan, B., & Layton, K. (2005). Distance Leadership Practices: What works in Higher Education. In G. Richards (ed.) *Proceedings of World conference on E-learning in Corporate and Government Health Care and Higher Education,* pp. 926-931.

Milligan, A. T., & Buckenmeyer, J. A. (2008). Assessing Students for Online Learning. *International Journal on E-learning 7*(3), 449-461.

Morrill, R. L. (2007). *Strategic Leadership: Interacting and leadership in colleges and universities.* Westport, Praceger Publishers.

Naktiyok, A. (2006). E-leadership. A research on examining of E-leadership characteristics. *Istetme Fakultesi Degisi 7*(1), pp. 19-40.

Northouse, P.G. (2001). *Leadership Theory and Practice.* Thousand Orks, CA: Sage.

Northouse, P.G. (2007). *Leadership: Theory and Practice (4th ed).* Thousand Oaks, CA: Sage.

Nowrie, J., Houghton, N., & Oparandi, S. (2012). Leadership in Distance Education: Qualities and Qualifications sought by Higher Education Institutions. *American Journal for Distance Education, 26*(3), 180-199.

Polat, M., & Araboci, I. B. (2014). Open Leadership and Social Network Education. *Journal of World Turks 6*(1), 257-275.

Portugal, L. M. (2006). Emerging Leadership Roles in Distance Education: Current State of Affairs and Forecasting Future Trends. *Online Journal for Distance Learning Admiration, 9*(111).

Siegal, M. E. (1999). Instructional Structure Planning Innovation Theory Systems Theory and Computer Modelling. https://www.horizon.unc.edu.projects/monogragh/siegal.asp

Sterman, J. D. (2000). *Business dynamics: Systems thinking and modeling for a complex world.* Boston: Irwin McGraw Hill.

Tierney, P., Farmer, S. M., & Graen, G. B. (1999). An examination of leadership and employee creativity: The relevance of traits and relations. *Personnel Psychology, 52*(3), 591-620.

Tripple, R. (2010). Effective Leadership of Online Adjunct Faculty. *Online Journal of Distance Learning, 13*(1).

Uhl-Bien, M., Marion, R., & McKelney, B. (2007). Complexity Leadership Theory: Shifting leadership from the industrial age to the knowledge era. *The Leadership Quarterly 18*(4), 298-318.

Varol, E. S. & Tarcan, E. (2000). Real Producers Who work Virtual. *Virtual Organisation Yonetim 11*(36), pp. 25-32.

Chapter 2

Managing Staff and Training in an ODeL Institution

Moffat Chitapa Tarusikirwa

Zimbabwe Open University

Abstract

In this chapter, Open and Distance Learning (ODL) is defined in addition to provision of a background to ODL. Additionally, the chapter discusses leadership and the role of innovative leadership in the shift from ODL to Open and Distance e -Learning (ODeL). Moreover, the chapter discusses 21st-century working and learning environments in ODL vis-à-vis the skills requirements. Additionally, leadership vis-à-vis institutional cultures is discussed followed by the training of staff and students in an ODeL institutional setup. Furthermore, the chapter covers issues of training such as needs identification, theory, and training of types that ODeL institutions may carry out during transition from ODL to ODeL.

Keywords: Managing staff, Training, ODeL Institution, Skills

***

2.0 Introduction

Open and Distance Learning (ODL) or Distance Education (DE), the precursor of ODeL, started way back in the 1940s as a way of training teachers. The 21st century brought with it a rapid advancement in technology, coupled with a high demand for the educational service. There was an unprecedented massification of education. Such a view is espoused by Mama, 2003, 2005; Maunde, 2003; Tlali et al., 2019, & Noui, 2020, among others. In the view of Gaidzanwa (2007), in Zimbabwe, the single University of Zimbabwe (UZ) at the time failed to cope with the many school leavers that demanded university education. It was clear from the onset that the solution lay in the introduction of ODL as a way of university educational provision as it had the capacity to school thousands of students at the same time and at a low cost. It was not business as usual, the situation called for a new type of institutional leader. This chapter is based on the researcher's experiences as a seasoned Open and Distance Learning) practitioner over many years spanning over two decades. Moreover, the chapter benefits from the findings of past field research work by the author and desk research in the field of ODL inclusive of Higher Education Leadership and Management.

2.1. Open and Distance Education Background

Distance education has been defined as an educational process in which a significant proportion of the teaching is conducted by someone removed in space and time from the learner (Brown & Brown, 1994). Open learning, in turn, has been defined as an organised educational activity based on the use of teaching materials in which constraints on the study are minimised in terms either of access, time, place, pace, method of study, or any combination of these (UNESCO, 2001). The term 'open and distance learning' is used as an umbrella term to cover educational approaches of this kind that reach teachers in their schools, provide learning resources for them, or enable them to qualify without attending college in person, or open new opportunities for keeping up to date no matter where or when they want to study (UNESCO, 2001). The flexibility inherent in Open and Distance Learning, and the fact that it can be combined with a full or near full-time job, makes it particularly appropriate for the often widely distributed force of teachers and school managers.

Historically, on the African continent, the University of South Africa (UNISA) has been a major provider of distance education and teacher education at the tertiary level throughout the southern African region since the 1940s (see UNESCO, 1998, 2000, 2001). In the early 1980s and 1990s, UNISA's main role in distance and teacher education was to provide upgrading programmes for serving primary and secondary teachers at the diploma and graduate levels (UNESCO, 1998, 2000). From the mid-1990s, UNISA has undergone a period of change in attempting to respond to new national priorities in distance and teacher education and to improve the quality of some of its services (such as learner support). Since 1998, UNISA has offered two teacher education programmes at the bachelor's degree level for primary and secondary teachers (BPrimEd and BSecEd) (see UNESCO, 2001) among other programmes. These can be taken as in-service or pre-service programmes by students with appropriate levels of entry qualifications. The main medium used was print. These print materials were complemented by face-to-face contact sessions (discussion classes), practical work, and some online learning activities. UNISA is in the process of integrating Computer Mediated Communication (CMC) and World Wide Web (WWW) technologies into their programmes, and this is expected to grow (see UNESCO, 2000, 2001). In the case of China, the provision of large-scale teacher education through a national distance teaching institution, the China Television

Teachers College (CTVTC), a part of the China Central Radio and Television University (CCRTVU), had been done since 1994. Distance education is included in China's strategic planning for teacher education and plays a significant role in initial teacher education and continuing professional development (see UNESCO, 2001).

Several other countries on a global basis also offered Education through Distance Learning as revealed by several case studies contracted by UNESCO (2001). For example, Chile, Brazil, Burkina Faso, India, Nigeria, Mongolia, and the United Kingdom. According to UNESCO (2001), the studies represent an interesting mix of applications of different modes of distance learning. According to UNESCO (2001), globally, there is still the need for more and better teachers. UNESCO (2001) recognised that there were still more than 100 million children out of school who needed teachers as the world moved towards 2015, targeted as the year of education for all. According to UNESO (2001), the world needs to raise the skills of the existing 60 million teachers, too many of whom are untrained and unqualified. UNESCO (2001) points out that beyond 2015, the skills and knowledge needed by all teachers are no longer fixed and familiar targets but moving ones. Hence, they say, teachers need more opportunities than ever before going on learning throughout their careers. According to UNESO (2000, 2001), one of the ways of strengthening the teaching profession is to use distance education or open and distance learning. From the leadership side, UNESCO (2000) looked at organisational structures, the kinds of organisations that provide teacher-education programmes, and the different patterns of funding. They also looked at the technologies, ranging from print to computers, and the relationship between work done through the technologies and work done face-to-face, including all-important issues about classroom practice. According to UNESCO (2000), many countries still do not have enough teachers.

Moreover, in some countries, the expansion needed in the teaching force is far beyond the capacity of traditional colleges. The supply of teachers is also adversely affected in countries where retention rates are low for newly trained teachers or where significant numbers of teachers are being lost through HIV and AIDS or in rural areas that have difficulties in recruiting and retaining teachers (UNESCO, 2000, 2001; OECD, 2001). Teacher quality is an issue in most countries. Many teachers are untrained or underqualified or teaching subjects in which they are not qualified or trained. In addition, teachers face a widening range of demands and roles (UNESCO, 2000, 2001; OECD, 2001).

Additionally, national governments, international organisations, and specific circumstances continually set new goals: gender parity by 2005 and universal basic education by 2015; inclusive education; education for democracy, peace and social cohesion; multi-grade teaching; increased accountability for achieving learning targets; the development of learners who are self-managing and independent, skilled in critical thinking and problem solving, equipped with life-skills; the preparation of learners who are competent for knowledge-based economies, capable in the use of information technology; and the expansion of teachers' roles to include social work in communities where child-headed households and orphans are common as a result of HIV and AIDS (UNESCO, 2001). In the light of the foregoing, distance education has been used to teach, support, and develop teachers for many years.

Furthermore, the history of distance education for teachers, especially in developing countries, is littered with the bones of short-term projects which have served their purpose and been discarded (until the next crisis in teacher education) (UNESCO, 2000, 2001). The established distance teaching universities here have provided teacher education programmes alongside others. Through their regional infrastructures, they have increased access to programmes and professional development opportunities for teachers (UNESCO, 2000, 2001).

Over the years, UNESCO-funded case studies show that distance education for teachers receives funds from all four of the most usual sources of funds for education: from government budgets, student fees, the private sector, and NGOs, as well as from funding agencies. Several programmes receive funding from a combination of sources so that, for example, the programmes in both China and Nigeria are funded partly by government and partly by student fees (UNESCO, 2000). The birth of the African Virtual University brought about e-learning/ ODel.

2.2 The African Virtual University

The African Virtual University provides online and distance education services to many existing universities across Africa. The AVU has more than 50 academic partner institutions in more than 27 countries in Africa. It helps partner institutions set up local study centres in different countries, where programmes from numerous partner institutions, learner support and guidance, and access to e-learning technologies are made available. To date, there are 10 such centres in 10 different countries. The focus now is on teacher education, with four bachelor programmes for teachers of mathematics, physics, chemistry, and biology offered through a consortium of 12 universities in 10 African countries. Delivery is mixed mode, through online learning and attendance at local centres. AVU also offers or facilitates a wide range of webinars, self-learning programmes, workshops, and certificate/diploma programmes in collaboration with the partner institutions. AVU also offers student scholarships (UNESCO, 2000, 2001; OECD, 2001). In the view of Bozkurt (2019), Distance Education has evolved over the years and keeps changing.

2.3 Leadership

Leadership has been defined by scholars in many ways. For example, leadership can be regarded collectively as the individuals who are the leaders in an organisation or the activity of leading a group of people or an organisation or the ability to do this. It involves establishing a clear vision, sharing that vision with others so that they will follow willingly, providing the information, knowledge and methods to realise that vision, and coordinating and balancing the conflicting interests of all members and stakeholders. Van Schalkwyk (2011) defined leadership as the mobilisation and influencing of people to work towards a common goal through the building of interpersonal relationships and the breaking of tradition to achieve the organisation's objectives despite risk and uncertainty. In the view of Kouzes and Posner (2007), this is achieved by engaging in the following leadership practices: modelling the way, inspiring a shared vision, challenging the process, enabling others to act, and encouraging the heart. Such views on leadership, as espoused by scholars above, are also echoed by Morgan (2020).

Moreover, in the views of some scholars, a leader steps up in times of crisis and can think and act creatively in difficult situations. Unlike management, leadership cannot be taught, although it may be learned and enhanced through coaching or mentoring. Leaders inspire subordinates to perform and engage in achieving a goal. Leadership has been described in many ways, for example, authoritarian, laissez-faire, chaotic, inter alia. Some scholars have argued that there is a leadership continuum from laissez-faire to authoritarian, with other forms such as democratic falling in the middle. In the academic setup, the colleagueship model of leadership was propounded by scholars like Gonzales and Terosky (2016), among others.

2.3.1 The Shift from ODL to ODeL Vis-À-Vis Innovative Leadership

The 21st Century brought with it a rapid advancement in technology which ushered in many opportunities for communication. The distance education provider now had the opportunity to offer service in many cost-effective ways. Instead of the print module, the mode of delivery can now be in electronic form. For example, many distance education providers migrated to e-learning among other web-based teaching and learning platforms. Nevertheless, there were significant challenges experienced by the ICDE membership. Some of the challenges had to do with academic recognition. However, over time, open distance and online learning have become more accepted and MOOCs (Massive Open Online Courses) have propelled this acceptance even further (see Robinson, 1997).

At the same time, ODL institutions have major challenges from conventional universities, particularly for the open and online space despite having much to offer, particularly in terms of cost-effectiveness, flexibility, and quality. Conventional institutions have invaded the ODL market space with a variety of semi or near ODL modes of delivery to deliver courses competitively with ODL institutions (see Burns, 2011). For example, in Zimbabwe, some conventional universities are now offering courses on Block release and parallel evening programmes. The Block release system is a way in which conventional institutions of Higher Education offer learning programmes to people who are employed on a full-time basis in other organisations through an arrangement in which the employer releases the employee for a limited period, say one month at a time, to study for their degree as well as for writing examinations. Such study periods are interspaced with stints at work and at the university until the end of the study programme. That way, employed people get developed while the organisations benefit from the skills gained and the work input by the employee. Another way, that of parallel programmes run by universities in the evening for employed people as opposed to day programmes for the unemployed, is often used by universities to cater to large student numbers requiring an educational service. Such a development has brought about stiff completion for students between conventional and ODL institutions. Further challenges, particularly in developing countries arise from funds available for equipment purchase, poor internet network systems, infrastructure (particularly in rural areas), poverty among students, computer literacy skills among both students and lecturers, and accessibility to technological equipment, inter alia (see Rai, 2019).

Moreover, with the advent of managerialism, universities have grown into large bureaucratic structures with professional managers (Perkin, 2007; Kogan & Teichler, 2007). The bureaucratisation of universities, as the need for professional management and bureaucratic systems of control come into effect globally, put academic freedom at risk as academic faculty autonomy was lost (Perkin, 2007; Kogan & Teichler, 2007). Academic freedom is important for academics to be able to debate, research, and publish important social, political, and other issues without any hindrance or interference from the government. In this manner, the conditions for knowledge production are created.

Furthermore, in the past, for most workers the key job skills were: knowing the job, following instructions, keeping good relations with others, hard work, being professional, efficient, timely, honest, and fair. Although still needed today and taught very well in the school system, the 21st Century work environment, demands a different set of work skills suited for the fast-changing technologies and mass information overload (see The Partnership for 21st Century SkillsP21, 2011).

In this new information age, the work environment demands new skills. There is need for workers who are: critical, innovative, creative problem-solvers, team workers, communicators through multimedia, and adaptable to the ever-changing technological landscape through fast learning (see The Partnership for 21st Century SkillsP21, 2011).

Institutional leadership at any level in the 21st century educational environment therefore demands for a smart leadership that communicates and is informed, solution-seeking, critical thinking, creative, well-networked both locally and globally, team workers capable of collaboration and partnership formation, as well as multimedia fluent. The skills demanded should now match the job requirements for effective and efficient leadership. The leadership should also be aware of national and global education goals such as the Sustainable Development Goals (SDG's) and STEM. The leadership should be aware of the student skills required for the 21st Century and offer relevant programmes to students. There is need for students to know enough about Science, Technology, Engineering and Mathematics to contribute significantly to or fully benefit from the knowledge-based economy of the 21st developmental landscape. Educational leaders should avoid disparity of skills between work and learning by providing students with skills that are relevant for this period. Hence, accountable leadership is called for in the 21st century education environment (see The Partnership for 21st Century SkillsP21, 2011).

Shahmandi et al. (2011) urged university leaders to improve their leadership competencies to enable their institutions to survive and continuously develop. These competencies include leadership skills, communication skills, persuasive skills, and professional skills. Additionally, Yang (2005) identified four categories of leadership competencies: personality and disposition, personal knowledge and skill, administrative competency, and social responsibility competency that can aid leadership. However, Bargh et al. (1996) and Rowley (1997) observed that university Vice-Chancellors that were appointed were usually prominent academics who did not possess any formal training beyond their academic credentials, achievements, and experiences in academia. In the face of the challenges in higher education today, there is need for a paradigm shift for appointing a new breed of university leaders capable of navigating a new complex environment. As alluded to earlier, the advent of managerialism and the bureaucratisation of the university management landscape call for such leadership instalment in the universities.

Briefly, ODL leadership at whatever level in the 21st century, learning environments are required to produce graduates with a unique set of abilities for them to succeed in this digital age. Students should have learning skills as follows: critical thinking, creative thinking, collaborating, communication, information literacy, media literacy, technology literacy, flexibility, initiative, social skills, productivity, and leadership (see The Partnership for 21st Century Skills P21, 2011).

2.4 The Twenty-First Century Working and Learning Environment in ODL

ODL institutional leadership must evolve to suit the new work environment. From my close observations and work as a researcher into leadership in open and distance learning, I have learned several things over the years. For example, the key movers in post-high school education have shifted due to several factors as follows:

- With the massification of education provision, access to post-secondary education has increased in conventional institutions. Therefore, for most ODL institutions, the question of access is no longer a vantage point for student recruitment purposes. It is now more about affordability. How much does it cost for a student to acquire an education? With massification of higher education, issues of quality come to the fore. However, in some developing countries, access to conventional institutions remains an issue. ODL leadership can therefore leverage on quality of offering as well as targeting the marginalised and poorly paid groups in society through the offering of affordable courses to them.

- For socio-economic development purposes, as alluded to earlier, the 21st century has brought about a paradigm shift towards the development of workers who are knowledgeable, critical thinkers, innovators, and collaborators/team workers, imbued in modern-day communication skills such as multi-media literacy, communication skills, including technical literacy. The 21st century ODL leadership should therefore move away from the mainly text and other less-digitalised pedagogical models adopted by large ODL institutions to develop the skills as required in the 21st century workplace. They need to steer their management teams towards the achievement of these skills by students and workers themselves.

- As alluded to earlier, there is an increased competition in the ODL landscape with many conventional universities moving into the ODL marketplace. This scenario has been exacerbated by the development of MOOCs, Webinars, open educational resources, online courses, inter alia, by conventional universities. These are no longer the prerogative of ODL institutions.

2.5 Leadership that Confronts Head-on the Existing Institutional Cultures

The difficulty often experienced by large bureaucratic organisations such as universities or ODL institutions is the slowness with which changes are affected, exacerbated in some cases, causing resistance to arise from the fear of change. People are afraid of change and new things. There is often a challenge to shift quickly to new models of delivery and throw away the old technologies on a massive scale when large student numbers are involved. There are sometimes challenges of a technical skills gap which is at times difficult to fill among others.

To achieve critical goals in the twenty-first century, ODL leadership at every level needs to:

- Set up SMART objectives together with all stakeholders in the organisation, including the implementers. For the goals to be achieved, there must be a buy-in from those that implement them. There is a need for the product offering to be of high quality and different in many ways from those of others for a competitive edge.

- Faculty and all stakeholders such as technical support staff need to be involved in designing courses around the new web–based multi-media instructional technologies of the 21st century e.g My Vista at ZOU.

- Involve the implementers in the faculties in operational decision-making and train both staff and students in the new instructional technologies and how to use them.

- Manage the costs of developing new course designs and delivery models from a business perspective.

ODL/DE continues to play a pivotal role in the education of many people in Africa and developing countries globally. With the development of the paradigm shift from ODL to ODeL and the exigencies of the global COVID-19 pandemic situation that has affected the delivery of education in many countries across the globe, it has become pertinent for serious providers of educational services across the globe to move and move quickly to ODeL modes of instruction. Institutions of education at every level have suddenly been thrown into the deep end of education provision with a difference. The shift to ODeL is inevitable and innovations in educational provision have become a necessity. Such a shift comes along with several changes in staff training and conditions of service.

In this chapter I consider the Zimbabwe Open University's imminent transition from ODL to open distance e-learning (ODeL). There are several issues at stake, with respect to the Zimbabwean context, concerning e-learning/ teaching skills required for both students and lecturers for such a radical move. There is poverty that is rampant across the country; the poor salaries, the unemployment of youths and adult learners, the accessibility of e-learning gadgets, the availability of internet facilities in remote areas of Zimbabwe, the availability of electricity and recently, the COVID-19 restrictions to people's movement, among others. A transitional shift by Zimbabwe Open University to ODeL requires staff training if it is to be smooth sailing.

The ODeL framework is premised upon the assumption that student learning can be optimally supported using modern electronic technologies and other digital tools. The assumption is that students would be able to use modern electronic technologies to access their study materials and interact with lecturers at a distance. That way, the distance between the student and lecturer is reduced to zero, as these modern electronic technologies lead to the utilisation of e-learning, online or digital learning, using distant electronic communication. In ODeL, it is assumed that learner-centred educational theories will play a bigger part. Moreover, conversational interaction between the student and lecturer is supposed to play a bigger role in ODeL. This can be achieved using, for example, videoconferencing for discussions between lecturers and students as well as between students placed in different locations. Such an approach to teaching and learning leads to many training needs required for both lecturers and students. For example, there is the need for these groups to be skilled in the use of the internet as well as electronic gadgets. They need to be digital natives, ie. they must be equipped with ICT skills. Digital literacy is called for. New learning design approaches are called for as well as methods of e-tutoring. There is no doubt that the introduction of new teaching approaches will be met with resistance by the less technologically competent lecturers. There is a view that modern technologies force traditionally inclined lecturers out of the comfort zone of their usual/customary and familiar techniques and pedagogies. They may become apprehensive and dead set against any envisaged change in the mode of operation. This is because they must change the way they teach, and they are not prepared for it. Furthermore, as alluded to earlier, they will need to learn new ways of designing their learning programmes and respond to changing learning environments. Learning materials will have to be easily accessible to a diverse student population online. Assessment procedures will need to change, and lecturers need to be trained for that.

2.6 Training of Staff and Students in an ODeL Institutional Set Up

Scholars have defined training in several ways. For example, it has been defined as a process of acquiring specific skills to do a job in a better way. Others have argued that training helps people to become proficient and better qualified in doing their jobs (Jucious, 1963; Dahama, 1979). Training has been attributed to the organisation's efforts in facilitating the learning of its employees through training. That way, their modified behavoiur because of the training leads to the achievement or organisational goals and objectives. In the views of others, training is a process of teaching, informing, or educating workers so that they become qualified enough to do their jobs. Alternatively, training helps employees to perform in positions of greater difficulty and responsibility.

According to Flippo (1961), the difference between education and training, pointing out that education is general as opposed to specific training. In this view, while training is concerned with those activities which are designed to improve human performance on the job that employees are at present doing or are being hired to do, education is concerned with increasing general knowledge and understanding of the total environment. Education is the development of the human mind, and it increases the powers of observation, analysis, integration, understanding, decision making, and adjustment to new situations.

In any situation that an institution encounters, particularly a shift from one mode of instruction to another, in the case of ZOU from ODL to ODeL, the first step to take would have been to identify training needs for both staff and students. This would have been followed up by the identification of skilled trainers and the development of a training plan/ programme for the various groups of staff and students. For a while now, ZOU has striven to move from ODL to the ODeL mode of instruction. The question is whether the culture of the use of the various modern modes of instruction through electronic technologies to communicate and share information between lecturers and students is feasible and compatible with the existing situation and learning environment at ZOU. Particularly so given the deficit of skills and experience in an ODeL mode of instruction concern that a clear and unambiguous distinction between, on the one hand, distance education, and on the other hand, 'e-learning', is necessary given that the two are "not the same thing" (Guri-Rosenblit, 2005).

2.6.1 Identification of Training Needs

Needs identification was done through interviews with workers through the aid of the Microsoft Teams App as well as stakeholders raising their training needs through various groups and media such as WhatsApp portals, among others. The training needs identified were as follows:

The academic staff, while trained intermittently on the use of the ZOU e-learning platform, MyVista, still needed further training and mastering the use of the platform. For example, it turned out that a lot of staff members in this category required training in the use of the platform like uploading learning materials, uploading videos, and so forth. Moreover, members needed training in the handling of assignments and research projects as well as student feedback on the platform. Moreover, ZOU, being heavily reliant on part-time staff and part-time tutors, needed training on the use of MyVista. There is therefore the need for ongoing training of academics on the use of the ODeL learning/teaching platform. This has become even more important to do in the COVID-19 era. ODeL institutions of learning must continuously train lecturers on the use of the teaching platform. Such training should be accompanied by making the internet available in the form of WiFi, connection terminals, and correct bandwidth to both academics and students in the form of data bundles, smartphones, computers such as laptops and desktops among others.

Another training need identified was the making of teaching aids such as videos, written materials, modules, as well as sourcing them and culling them from other sources for the teaching platform. Such a need would have been accompanied by the general training on the use of the internet to source for teaching recourses.

The other training need identified and required as a prerequisite to teaching in ODeL institutions is the digital skills. In other words, this critical skill as alluded to earlier is required for all academics/ lecturers in ODeL institutions. The biggest challenge is that some lecturers are on the old side and may find it hard to switch to digital teaching and learn the required skills. Some may even resist the training and may need to be laid off. Briefly, every academic/lecturer would need training in ICT skills of communication, ie. use of computers, internet, and other relevant skills required for ODeL teaching.

Furthermore, the following training needs were identified for nonacademic technical support staff: While some of the staff in this category claimed to know what they were doing, it was glaring that they needed the requisite training skills. In the world of training, there is the theory that the training of adult staff/andragogy in addition to the relevant training skills that are required and are lacking in the trainers. Some even lack the knowledge to impart and are not as knowledgeable in the ICT skill to impart to academics.

Moreover, the following training needs were identified for students, among others. By their nature, ODL/ODeL institutions provide learning opportunities to mature working students and of late inexperienced young school leavers have come aboard as they fail to access campus-based higher education institutions due to cost, poverty, unemployment, and inter alia.

Moreover, it can be argued that for ODeL to succeed, there must be a functional and optimal student support system. With the shift from ODL to ODeL, most students in the former ODL institutions find themselves with many challenges with training needs. Most students have struggled to hand in their assignments online. There is therefore the need to train students to upload their assignments onto the teaching-learning platform. They also need training in document formatting skills so that they can upload user-friendly documents onto the platform. Some students have struggled to do online registrations, and some have struggled with ICT skills. In other words, some students are not literate in the critical skills alluded to earlier and need training. As a result, they are not able to access learning materials on the ODeL teaching platform. The learning situation has changed. As such, student training needs, just like those of the institutional staff, will have to be identified as well concerning the teaching mode so that they are able to access the learning materials and communicate on the learning platforms with success and effectiveness. That way, students can learn in this era of increasing proliferation of modern technologies such as the internet, computers linked to the internet, wi-fi, videos, smartphones, satellite technologies, webinars, MOOCs, and tablets.

Moreover, in the identification of training needs, an ODeL institution needs to take into consideration the diversity of stakeholders it serves. For example, the training needs of the disabled such as hearing and impairment, the blind, the poor, women, and children. For example, in ODeL, what are the needs of the blind stakeholders? In the past, it was the machines. How about their needs now as we move to ODeL? In needs identification, the needs of these individuals must not be forgotten. There is also training required that is geared towards stakeholder attitude change.

2.7 Theories and Types of Training

In all educational and training activities, there are basic learning theories that are usually applied. A trainer should be someone who understands learning theories for them to make decisions and apply them to achieve the objectives at stake. Different oriented trainers emphasise different aspects of the teaching-learning process depending on what they intend to achieve. That is are they behaviourist, cognitivist, or humanist in their approach towards training. All the same, the purpose is to train individuals to a level of skill and a knowledgeable trainer will get the trainee there despite the different schools of approach to training.

Moreover, there are several approaches to training that a trainer may engage in such as the traditional, experiential, and performance-based approach (Rama, Etling, & Bowen, 1993). If a trainer is not knowledgeable in training approaches, then their training of academics will hardly train them to operate efficiently as ODeL practitioners.

Two types of training for ODeL staff both academic and non-academic can be discerned/identified. For example, new academics can be sent for pre-service training if they are new to the ODeL mode of teaching. They could be sent to institutions that specialise in training ODel teaching skills for a certain period, for example, a six-month diploma in online teaching. Such seasoned ODeL institutions like Athabasca in Canada or Phoenix in Arizona, US, could be used as an advantage for this type of training by organising for staff training and attachment. On the other hand, those who are already in the institution at the time of the shift to ODeL could be given in-service training by the organisation for the development of the required ODeL skill. This is where the in-house trainers should be skilled enough to handle such training. In-service training comes in several forms. For example, new staff needs to be inducted or oriented through training into the ODeL institution. Foundation training is in-service training which is also appropriate for newly recruited personnel. Besides technical competence and routine instruction about the organisation, every staff member needs some professional knowledge about various rules and regulations of the government, financial transactions, administrative capability, communication skills, leadership ability, coordination and cooperation among institutions and their linkage mechanism, report writing, and so on. Foundation training is made available to employees to strengthen the foundation of their service career. This training is usually provided at an early stage of service life. Secondly, staff who are already employed can be given refresher courses occasionally to update their knowledge and skills on ODeL. For example, with the advent of COVID-19, new ways of teaching and materials production become necessary, hence refresher courses for ODeL practitioners are needed. Innovative ways of teaching and training in ODeL institutions are called for. Moreover, in-service training may involve what is termed "on-the-job training," which involves a specialist helping to train subordinates or staff on new skills required for the job. Such training is ongoing in ODeL institutions as new technological innovations may dictate the use of new teaching methods and the use of new technological gadgets or tools.

Furthermore, training can be termed as career development and involves the upgrading of knowledge, skills, and ability of staff to help them assume bigger responsibility in senior organisational positions. Training is circular in nature, starting with needs identification, followed by several steps, and ends with an evaluation of the training activity. There are generally three phases of the training cycle i.e., planning which involves needs identification among others, implementation, and evaluation. The evaluation may be formative or summative. Formative evaluation can be used to identify setbacks and unintended outcomes from the training and can be used to revise the training plan and structure of the training programmes to satisfy the needs or goals of training. Summative evaluation happens at the end of the training programme and gives the overall assessment of the training programme's effectiveness in relation to objectives and goals achievement. Evaluation has, however, been classified into four major types such as evaluation for planning, process evaluation, terminal evaluation, and impact evaluation (Raab et al., 1987).

2.8 Summary

To sufficiently prepare lectures for the change from ODL to ODeL, it is imperative that lecturers/academic staff, support staff, and students must be given appropriate and enough training, retraining, and continuous support. Moreover, ICT infrastructure needs to be put on a stronghold by strengthening it. Issues of poor bandwidth need to be resolved to avoid slow uptake when logging into the system. There is also there need to avail and train enough ICT support staff at every station who are available 24/7. Such a move will ensure fast and reliable internet connectivity. The biggest challenge is to reach most students in often poor, remote, rural peripheries of developing countries. The digital divide sometimes excludes such students who may struggle for accessibility of modern electronic technologies such as gadgets and internet reach. Moreover, training of staff in ODeL institutions should strive to mong the following: train all faculty in online teaching, produce graduates that are critical, innovative, and collaborative. Create academic programmes that are built around the 21st Century digital technologies.

2.9 References

Bargh, C., Scott, P., & Smith, D. (1996). *Governing Universities: Changing the Culture?* Buckingham: SRHE/OU.

Bozkurt, A. (2019). From Distance Education to Open and Distance Learning: A Holistic Evaluation of History, Definitions, and Theories. https//www.research gate.net/publication/332652740

Brown, B. F., & Brown, Y. (1994*). Distance Education around the World*. In B. Willis (Ed.). Educational Technology (1994). Englewood Cliffs, New Jersey.

Burns, M. (2011). Distance education for teacher training: Modes, models and methods. http://go.edc.org/07xd.

Dahama, O. P. (1979). *Extension and rural welfare*. New Delhi: Ram Parsad and Sons.

Flippo, E. B. (1961). *Principles of personnel management*. New York: McGraw Hill.

Gaidzanwa, R. B. (2007). Alienation, gender and institutional culture at the University of Zimbabwe. *Feminist Africa 8*, 60-82.

Gonzales, L. D., & Terosky, A. L. (2016). Colleagueship in different types of post-secondary institutions: a lever for faculty vitality. *Studies in Higher Education*, 43(8), 1378-1391.

Guri-Rosenblit, S. (2005). Distance Education and e-learning: Not the same thing. *Higher Education, 49*, 467-493.

Jucious, M. J. (1963). *Personnel management (5th ed.)*. Homewood, IL: Richard D. Irwin.

Kogan, M., & Teichler, U. (eds.). (2007). Key Challenges to the Academic Profession.

Kouzes, J. M., & Posner, B. Z. (2007). *The leadership challenge (4th ed.)*. San Francisco, CA: Jossey-Bass.

Mama, A. (2003). Restore, reform but do not transform: The gender politics of Higher Education in Africa. *Journal of Higher Education in Africa, 1*(1), 101-125.

Mama, A. (2005). *Gender studies for Africa's transformation*. In T. Mkandawire (Ed.), African intellectuals: Rethinking politics, language, gender and development, pp. 94-116. London: CODESRIA in association with Zed Books.

Maunde, R. (2003). *Higher Education in Zimbabwe, history and background*. In D. Teferra & P. Altbach (Eds.), An international reference handbook. *Bloomington and Indianapolis*: Indiana University Press.

Morgan, J. (2020). What is leadership and who is a leader? https://www.chieflearningofficer.com/2020/01/06/what-is-leadership-and-who-is-a-leader/

Noui, R. (2020). Higher education between massification and quality. https://www.emerald.com/insight/2514-5789.htm

Organisation for Economic Cooperation and Development (OECD). (2001). Education Policy Analysis 2001. Centre for Education Research and Innovation. Paris: OECD.

Perkin, H. (2007). *Higher Education of women in USA. 1820-1920*. In H. S. Wechsler, L. F. Goodchild, & L. Eisenmann (Eds.), The History of Higher Education. Boston: Pearson.

Raab, R. T. Swanson, B. E., Wentling, T. L. & dark, C. D. (Eds.). (1987). *A trainer's guide to evaluation*. Rome: FAO.

Rai, L. (2019). The shifting landscape of open and distance learning. *Open Learning: The Journal of Open, Distance and e-Learning, 35*(1), 1-3.

Rama, B. R., Etling, A. W. W., & Bowen, B. E. (1993). *Training of farmers and extension personnel*. In R. K. Samanta (Ed.), Extension strategy for agricultural development in 21st century. New Delhi: Mittal Publications.

Robinson, B. (1997). Distance education for primary teacher training in developing countries. In J. Lynch, C. Modgil, & S. Modgil (Eds.), *Education and Development: Tradition and Innovation, Volume 3: Innovations in Delivering Primary Education*. London: Cassell Educational Press.

Rowley, J. (1997). Academic leaders: Made or born? *Industrial and Commercial Training, 29*(3), 78-84.

Shahmandi, E., Silong, A. D., Ismail, I.A., Samah, B. B. A., & Othman, J. (2011). Competencies, Roles and Effective Academic Leadership in World Class University. *International Journal of Business Administration, 2*(1), 44-53.

Tlali, N., Mukurunge, T., & Bhila, T. (2019). Examining the Implications of Education on Quality Assurance and Assessment in Higher Institutions in Lesotho. *Journal of Scientific Research and Development 3*(3), 102-109.

UNESCO. (1998). *World Education Report: Teachers and Teaching in a Changing World*. Paris: UNESCO.

UNESCO. (2000). *The Dakar Framework for Action. Education for All: Meeting our Collective Commitments*. Paris: UNESCO.

UNESCO. (2001). *Guidelines for Teacher Education at a Distance*. Paris: UNESCO.

Van Schalkwyk, R. D. (2011). The impact of leadership practices on service quality in private higher education in South Africa [Dissertation]. University of South Africa.

Yang, X. (2005). Institutional Challenges and Leadership Competencies in Chinese Ministry of Education Directed Universities in Implementing the 1999 Chinese Action Scheme for Invigorating Education Towards the 21st Century [Doctoral Dissertation]. Texas A&M University.

Chapter 3

Leading Open, Distance and E-Learning Organisations in a Virtual Environment: Leader mindset

Chrispen Chiome

Zimbabwe Open University

Abstract

In virtual learning environments, leadership is a key process that is needed for motivating people to work together and cooperate in person or virtually. Leadership helps inspire online learning abilities and capabilities. It motivates online facilitators so that they are responsible, better committed, inspired, and innovative in pursuit of excellence. Online learning is undertaken 24 hours a day and each time of leading is a challenge. Leaders then embrace the hurdles they encounter rather than avoiding or ignoring these obstacles. Because leadership is a key concern in online learning environments where everything begins and ends with leadership, this chapter examines, exposes, and shares the leader mindset for leading successful open, distance and e-learning organisations in an increasingly virtual environment. The chapter seeks to further share experiences from institutions of higher education involved in open, distance and e-learning so that the reader is:

1. acquainted with the mindset of a leader in an increasingly virtual environment and
2. acquainted with the characteristics that make for a good and bad leader in the context of online and blended modalities.

In sync with these two objectives, this chapter will define leadership and then define mindset. Since mindset is one way of telling the story of who we are, the chapter goes on to explore leadership as a lifestyle, the leader mindset for successful organisations, and characteristics that distinguish a good leader from a bad one.

Keywords: Leadership; mindset, leadership mindset, virtual learning environments, blended learning, visionary, reflective learning, self-directed learning

***

3.0 Introduction

Blended learning, virtual learning spaces, technologically extended classroom teaching, and net-based distance education have made universities virtual environments. In an increasingly virtual environment, institutions of learning scramble for opportunities to use online teaching tools, best practices in online teaching, acquisition of online teaching capabilities, and the best practices of delivering online teaching strategies among others. Open, distance and e-learning is a form of education that requires facilitators who can competently teach online to reach many learners. The philosophy behind open, distance, and e-learning is that of equality of opportunity in the provision of education. In this regard, leadership is key to the success of open, distance and e-learning in all parts of the world. Leaders have the capacity to influence others towards the vision of providing inclusive education to all learners from anywhere at any time. Without conscious leadership mindset, this will hold you, your organisation, and your team back (Ostergaard, Block and Ostergaard, 2019). This chapter will examine, expose, and share the leader mindset for leading open, distance and e-learning organisations in an increasingly virtual environment. This chapter will share experiences from institutions of higher education involved in open, distance and e-learning so that the reader is:

- acquainted with the mindset of a leader in an increasingly virtual environment and
- acquainted with the characteristics that make for a good and bad leader in the context of online and blended modalities.

In sync with these two objectives, this chapter will define leadership and then define mindset. Since mindset is one way of telling the story of who we are, we are going to explore leadership as a lifestyle. We then move onto leader mindset for successful organisations before rounding off with characteristics that distinguish a good leader from a bad one.

3.1 Definition of Key Terms

We need to be on the same page as to the meaning of mindset and the meaning of a leader. In this section, we attempt to define these two terms.

3.2 Leadership

Fiedler, cited by Chiome (2011), noted that there are as many definitions of leadership as there are leadership theories, adding that there are almost as many theories of leadership as there are psychologists working in the field (p. 1). Nevertheless, even in this absence of universal agreement, a broad definition of leadership is necessary before introducing leadership as a domain of scholarly inquiry.

Leadership is the "ability of an individual to influence, motivate, and enable others to contribute towards the effectiveness and success of the organisations of which they are members" (House, 2004). Chiome (2011) defines leader as a person who is driven by the right motivation in the process of influencing and rallying organisational members towards a shared vision. In an increasingly virtual environment, leaders are those that make a positive impact on people anytime anywhere.

Bass (1990) is of the view that leadership is, "the principal dynamic force that motivates and coordinates the organisation in the accomplishment of its objectives." We can come up with a working definition from these two. What is needed is to ensure that definition encompasses issues of influence, motivation, positive impact, others, dynamic force, and the accomplishment of goals as indicated by House (2004) and Bass (1990).

3.3 Mindset

Korn Ferry Institute (2021) is of the view that leadership mindset is defined by how we see ourselves in our professional roles. It is also defined by the stories we tell others about who we are (Wilson, 2015). Leadership mindset is important for organisational success, but it is the least understood. In some instances, mindset is one of the most neglected elements in the evolution of a leader (Korn Ferry Institute, 2021). Korn Ferry Institute (2021) posits that mindset manifests in countless ways. However, it exists in the private space within a person's psyche, and it is neither tangible nor accessible.

According to Ostergaard, Block and Ostergaard (2019, p.2), the "mindset is the omnipresent set of thoughts, paradigms, and philosophical approaches that we, the conscious leaders, base every action on." They then went on to clarify that the "mindset is nothing without actions, and the actions are nothing without the mindset" (Ostergaard, Block & Ostergaard, 2019, p.2). For this definition of the mindset to make sense, it is also important to broaden the meaning of leadership and view it as "a complex, and multidimensional thing, covering philosophy, approach, daily governance, and interpersonal activities" (p.2). We will explore many of these important areas that are associated with the leadership mindset in this chapter.

3.4 Leadership as a Lifestyle

In virtual learning environments, leaders must be able to integrate emerging technologies in online education, collaborate virtually with colleagues, make available remote learning-enabling resources, and be immersed in virtual spaces to meet their stakeholder demands. They must monitor that all staff are adequately utilising available online learning resources, especially in African environments, where many faculties lack the experience of being an online student themselves. For this to happen, leadership must be exercised as a lifestyle. This is because the virtual environment is operational 24 hours a day and 7 days a week. Ostergaard, Block and Ostergaard (2019) share with us useful information on the kind of leadership with the mindset to influence transformation and succeed in the global and complex work environment. They point out that the mindset of that leader should be exercised as a lifestyle. Ostergaard, Block and Ostergaard (2019, pp. 5-6) agree and offer the following to suit that kind of leadership for this lifestyle:

- **Leadership is not only for your 9-5 job; it is a lifestyle:** What this means is that leadership is a part of an approach to everyone for example family, parents, friends, peers, colleagues, children, teammates, spouse, and even subordinates. This is also done in all the situations encountered, for example funerals, meetings, leisure, sports, business, politics, in the shop, offline, online, and other virtual spaces.

- **Leadership is about people:** In this sense, leadership is about trust, respect, safety, and well-being. Leadership should enable people to thrive even when facing more complex challenges created by differing cultures, geographic spaces, time zones, and others in virtual environments. When associating with other people, wherever you meet them, physical or virtual, leadership comes in as a means of releasing the power in yourself, the individual follower, and the team. This is best done by acknowledging each other's existence, approach, and opinion.

- **Leadership is about believing in each other:** The belief comes in the fact that one can only be his/her best, when he or she is at his or her best. It then follows that we must strive to make each other exceed our dreams. Leadership in a virtual environment must copy online social activities that are flourishing in a virtual environment, nurture collaboration and build alliances across geographic distances.

- **Leadership is about authenticity:** This implies that a leader should always be herself/himself, not to leave one's personal life at the doorstep when one goes to work. Being the same in all situations, physical or virtual, at work, at the hospital, in traffic, and other places is very important to gain the trust of the people around you. "If you change your leadership style from situation to situation, you lose people's trust in you" (Ostergaard, Block & Ostergaard, 2019, p. 5).

- **Leadership is about emotions:** What this means is that the leadership culture embraces emotions, beliefs, and opinions. Leaders in virtual environments, should strive to be empathetic and sympathetic all the time. They must build trust and foster bonding through connectivity.

- **Leadership is visionary and ambitious:** this implies that a leader should be able to come up with long-term strategies anchored on visions and dreams for individuals in his/her staff, for him/herself, for his/her team and for the organisation. Ambition, vision, and dreaming are done personally and on behalf of others.

- **Leadership is about profit:** Business organisations are about making money. Leadership must then focus "on results, revenue, and profit, on deadlines and great products, and on great and long-lasting customer experiences and relations" (Ostergaard, Block & Ostergaard, 2019, p. 6). Even if many open, distance and e-learning organisations are non-profit, still they must focus on a positive return on investment.

- **Leadership is about purpose:** A leader in a virtual learning environment must establish and maintain trust in a diverse environment by rallying for the cause with great energy and determination. It is important to rally people for a purpose and influence them to own the vision as this is the strongest catalyst for commitment. It is also a great catalyst for excellent results, efficiency, productivity, and effectiveness in multiple cultures.

- **Leadership is also about joy and freedom at work:** 21st century leaders should have the mindset to build organisations that are based on freedom, not fear and control, especially when teams work remotely. Virtual workplaces should be about joy and happiness at work through excellent teams, relations, and results. Such interactions brought about by shifts in workplace dynamics that promote freedom over fear lead to greater engagement and higher productivity.

- **Leadership is a habit:** Workers experience loneliness that comes from working remotely unless leadership is exercised as a habit. "The more you practice it, the more it becomes a habit, to the extent where your intuitive actions are all based on the leadership style" (Ostergaard, Block & Ostergaard, 2019, p. 6)

- **Leadership should be fun:** As a leader, you need to be there for your team to succeed. You need to be virtually visible. You need to be ambitious and enthusiastic. However, it must not be a yoke, working too much and becoming a martyr.

3.5 Leadership Mindsets Necessary for Successful Teaching in Virtual Environments

In a virtual learning and teaching environment, leaders must depict a mindset that promotes transformative yet authentic learning experiences. They must nurture team-based learning experiences, using immersive technologies such as virtual worlds in lieu of simple web-based tools like wikis, blogs, or Google applications (Han, & Resta, 2020). Leaders operating in virtual environments should create learning communities, immersive learning platforms, off-campus learning experiences, and knowledge construction processes. They must enforce students' reflective learning processes through using avatar interactions to overcome real-world barriers so that success in virtual environments is assured. Several authors argued that there are leadership mindsets that are key to successful organisations (Bennis, 1989; Avolio, 2011; Chiome, 2011; Armstrong, 2012; Yukl, 2013). Other authors such as Ostergaard et al. (2019) and Korn Ferry Institute (2021) pointed out that it is important for current or emerging leaders to be willing and ready to improve because leadership development is a force that drives profitability, ROI, productivity, and growth. Han & Resta (2020) agree and add that social interaction in a virtual world is the most influential factor contributing to students' learning success. Leaders must demonstrate mindsets that nurture transformation, change, interactivity, development, and growth. Leaders must understand that people are their most precious resource in increasingly virtual environments. These mindsets will be discussed in this section. It is important to note that this list of leadership mindsets necessary for successful teaching in virtual environments is a pointer to leadership mindset in such environments.

3.5.1 Ambition

Self-directed learning is a concept that helps students to learn in all environments. It requires learners to be ambitious. Ambition as a leader mindset has been seen to influence success in organisations. This is because leaders with ambition are open to improvement. They are always driven by career advancement opportunities because they are ambitious. When a leader with ambition reaches the apex of the organisation, ambition is then focused on organisational growth, profitability, growing market share, increasing shareholder value, and meeting the challenges of accelerated business disruption and global change. Ambitious leaders invest in the growth of their students. The students, through self-directed learning, can be their own facilitators in many facets of technology such as Word, Google,

Moodle, PowerPoint, Zoom, Microsoft Teams, and others. This influences team members so that they reach their ambitions

3.5.2 Belief in Robustness with Agility

Robust and resilience is key to success in leading remote learning that could be improvised upon in the face of an uncertain future. However, this robustness is based on flexibility and ability to help others with issues such as Learning Management System (LMS), assignment submission online, and online facilitation among others. It is now known that leaders with a strong, yet agile mindset see themselves as the dominant force in their own story (Korn Ferry Institute, 2021). It is important to continually create rich stories of leaders' lives based on organisational agility that leads to higher business performance. It is also important to identify and work towards their core purpose which is online facilitation. Robustness, agility, flexibility, and resilience prepare leaders for changes (planned or not), and they are fast to respond to them. This is because the agile mindset goes together with this leadership mindset especially in environments where services and future scenarios are unknown, contested, or unpredictable.

3.7 Nursing Collaboration, Trust, and Lasting Relations

Leadership is a social process. Relationships and collaborations are key to this social process. Relations are the key to collaboration, especially in virtual spaces. Organisations thrive when led by teams that are established based on their internal relations. Teams established based on skill are not as cohesive as teams that are rooted in relationships. Collaboration and relationships will increase trust. Teams established on collaboration and relationships perform better than teams that are established based on skills. Open, distance and online learning organisations must ensure their teams spend time together for them to build strong relationships in virtual environments. They do this by showing trust and respect by being personal and by paying attention to the views of others through listening.

3.8 Fearing Consequences of Inaction

Open, distance and online learning organisations must live with the consequences of their actions and decisions, especially the atrocious cost of the status quo. At the same time, they must also face the repercussions of their inactions and indecisions. Leaders with the motivation, drive, ability, zeal, skills, and willingness to grow the organisation also have the mindset of fearing the consequences of what might happen if they fail to act. They fear damaging the reputation and integrity of the organisation. They fear damaging the trust with those they are leading. They fear damaging the trust of the organisational shareholders. Fearing consequences of inaction is a leadership mindset that force leaders to become exceedingly proactive and not to be reactive like a dog that barks after the fact. This happens in the background of the choices that leaders have not made or shied away from that have far more shaped their organisational future. In an increasingly virtual environment, it is highly dangerous to play it safe and stick to the status quo when the world is fast-changing.

3.9 Confidence

Confidence is a sign of a mindset of a great leader who is a model to others. Confidence is a sign of a great leader who anticipates the needs of students facing a technology-driven future. This is because confident leaders are accountable for their own actions and behaviours. Confidence strengthens the mindset and at the same time reduces worry and doubt in leadership. Confident leaders are not into the blame game. They have the confidence to admit when they are wrong. Confident leaders stand up when they are right. Admitting when you are wrong, suffocating the blame game and standing up when one is right, are clear signs that shows a leader has the mindset of a great leader. Confidence is indispensable in online learning and blended learning environments because of its flexibility and increased opportunity for students. Technology-based learning is easier to impart when a leader can orchestrate a culture of support, trust, open communication, and collaboration. The changing roles of blended learning leadership in a technological world consists of confidence, shared responsibility, flexibility, and drive. In online and blended learning environments, faculty and students are inspired by boldness and courage. They are motivated when their leader has the capacity to fulfill multiple roles and is open to new experiences.

3.10 Leading by Example

Leading by example is a sign of great leadership that is indispensable in the 21st century. The 21st-century leader will always step down and show others how it is done and show others that he/she cares for staff and contribute to team efforts. A leader leads by example, both when it concerns interpersonal care and concrete actions. Ostergaard, Block and Ostergaard (2019) sum it up by saying that leaders will not get due respect from sitting in the Ivory Tower, thinking big thoughts, and laying five-year plans. They humbly step down, write some code, open PowerPoint or Photoshop, and give feedback where necessary. They also listen to ideas and concerns from the shop floor and show respect to others below them.

3.11 Leadership Belief in the Power of the Networked Organisation

In open, distance and online learning institutions, networking is very important to professional growth. Through networking, online and blended learning leaders foster relationship-building where they open doors to possible career opportunities. They also find trusted mentors and meet individuals who challenge and broaden their worldview. They are exposed to like-minded colleagues who come from diverse backgrounds. Leaders can use video conferencing tools, Zoom, Skype, or Google Hangouts and other tools to facilitate meetings and share real-time feedback with peers. A well-built and maintained professional network can be used to expand career opportunities, build teams, gain a competitive edge in the market, source talent, and create partnerships.

A networked organisation can tackle current challenges as a collective unit. In a networked organisation, the power is distributed in and to the team. The team has the power to make a valuable difference to each other and the networked society. They are able to meet their objectives because the power is greatest when distributed in and to the team. The mindset in which leadership relies on power from the position is shallow, fake, and short-lived. It cannot be compared to the collective intelligence and power of the networked organisation. A networked organisation's power is the strongest force. Powerful leaders matter through people and because of people.

3.12 Conviction

An increasingly rare trait that is a prerequisite for effective leadership in online learning environments is conviction. Conviction enables leaders to overcome obstacles through a strong belief in what they are doing. We may have seen that many organisations have a vision, mission, and values. They single out values because these values and convictions matter in leadership. A leader with conviction is aware of who she is. She is aware of what she/he believes in. She is aware of the importance of integrity. With conviction, it means you are fully aware of your values. With conviction in all what you do, you show total commitment to these values. That commitment will inspire the people around you. Networked organisations are inspired by commitment and passion from great leadership. Remember leadership is about inspiring others. To capture hearts and minds, solve problems nurture creativity, promote innovation, and influence virtual learning requires conviction in leadership.

3.13 Transparency

Great leadership requires transparency. Great leaders are at home explaining any reasoning behind decisions that they make, the figures that they present, and the communiques they communicate. It is important to be transparent in terms of decisions that are made. It is important to be transparent regarding sharing of scarce resources in the organisation. Great leaders are transparent regarding direction, prioritisations, status, results, and opinions among many aspects that require transparency in organisations.

3.14 Communication and Dialogue

Fostering original, out-of-the-box ideas, enhancing MOOC learners' self-management skills, leveraging technology to support student learning and designing intuitive interfaces in open, distance and e-learning requires transparent communication (Dembo & Seli, 2013). The issue of transparency is one way that is teaching us the importance of communication and dialogue. This communication must be timely. This communication must be transparent. In undertaking transparent communication, leaders must be reminded of the basic requirements of listening skills and dialogue. The involvement of a networked team is done through transparent dialogue. The organisation and the team should be involved in decision-making. They are given opportunities for solutions, inputs, opinions, suggestions, and feedback. They do this to a listening leader who employs what is called active listening. It is most likely that a leader cannot see all solutions, problems, or opportunities from his/her chair. The team might even be smarter than the leader. A leader understands that he or she does not know it all and therfore needs input and support from the team. *If you want to go fast, go alone. If you want to go far, go together* (African proverb).

3.15 Accountability

Great institutions involved in virtual learning are accountable to their stakeholders scattered around the world. They know that they must not disclaim accountability by acting as if there is no ultimate responsible person, leaving it all up to the employees. They can spread accountability through shared leadership so that the shared purpose and direction will not fade. They cement the collaboration through being ultimately accountable so that collective and shared purpose will not erode. They are answerable to the actions and decisions made by them and made by those under them. Accountable leaders deliver on their commitments and can be trusted because they take responsibility for the outcomes. They transform effort into results that will benefit everyone anywhere anytime. The quality of their work and the quality of their decisions is emulated by others.

3.16 Nourishing a "No Blame"-Culture

Open, distance and e-learning institutions operate in a complex connectivity environment, are involved in critical thinking and problem solving and their lives revolve around a digital world (Kipp, 2019). Innovative and creative people working largely in a virtual environment are prone to making mistakes. Creative, innovative, productive, and problem solvers are prone to mistakes. It is part of innovation to make mistakes and, at times, to fail. However, a leader with the right mindset that nurtures creativity and innovation and creates a culture where the networked community does not hide their mistakes. They share their mistakes and failures with other people so that they can also learn from their experiences.

3.17 Nursing Cross-Cultural Collaboration and Diversity

The world has become a global village. In such circumstances, diversity is an asset. Diversity in terms of religion, age, background, skillset, and nationality, among others. Diversity in terms of "diverse cultural, ethnical, social, political, economic and religious backgrounds of the contemporary globalised world that we live in today" (Chiome, 2019), should be encouraged in organizations. All employees must feel respected in their diversity. Cultural differences must be respected. Religious tolerance must be upheld. Approaches to feedback must take these cultural, religious, skillsets, social, ethical, and other differences into consideration. Education Scotland, cited by Chiome (2019), maintains that diversity is a way of recognising, celebrating, and valuing differences, and adding that diversity is a sure way of creating a fairer society in which all citizens can freely contribute and have the opportunity to be all they can be.

3.18 Change and Transformation Mindset

Change and transformation mindset enables leaders to inspire innovation and culture change in the face of unprecedented disruption. Many organisations face high levels of change and leaders must be prepared and willing to embrace change and transformation. When organisations fail to transform in the face of unprecedented change, they face the possibility of extinction. What is known now is that what worked well in the past is no longer working as well now in the face of unprecedented disruption. What worked well in the past, may not work at all in the future due to unprecedented disruption.

Great leaders foster a good relationship with change and transformation because they know that change is inevitable. The pace of change places enormous demands on leaders. Their organisations, their staff, and the leaders themselves are ready for anything that the future may bring, and they never waste time trying to uphold the status quo. Great leadership means embracing the concept of change and transformation and not upholding the status quo.

3.19 Communication

A great leader is a great listener. Many of us who know the importance of communication focus on speaking and writing well but forget about the critical skill of listening. Great leadership means making yourself into a great listener and encouraging others to share their thoughts. Related to communication is listening. Many people concentrate too much on reacting and forget to listen to others. Great leaders are open to new opportunities, new ideas for the networked community. The people around them will always come with new ideas and opportunities because they know they will get a listening ear. A leader who allows others to come to him/her with new ideas, new opportunities and visions have the right mindset for organisational growth, development, and profitability.

3.20 Commitment to Self-Improvement

Leaders with a mindset for self-improvement are lifelong learners. Open and distance e-learning seeks to develop lifelong learners. The limit is the sky because they are always ripe for growth. Continuous quality improvement is a constant journey as opposed to a destination. Such leaders will always find ways of making improvements on what they do. They are never satisfied with the status quo.

3.21 Empathy

Empathy is among the most important leadership skills that are important in a virtual environment where participants are from diverse cultural and educational backgrounds (Zhu, 2021). Empathy allows leaders to connect and quickly tune in to how others are feeling. Through empathy, leaders show care and compassion to others. In virtual environments where leaders work to nurture cross-national team-based collaborative learning, empathy is seen as a component of great leadership.

3.22 Summary

To conclude this chapter, we learn from successful open, flexible, and distance learning institutions that successful leaders are results-oriented, hardworking, inspirational, people-oriented, engaging, motivational, and empathetic leaders. They enrich student learning experiences where they produce communicators, creators, collaborators, and critical thinkers. They provide access to learning resources. They increase the automation of functions in line with global changing trends. What it means is that is for staff who work in these institutions, going to work is a nice, great, and rewarding experience. Leadership in these open, flexible, and online institutions is about creating stimulating opportunities, developing online teaching competencies, guiding students for them to reach their best, giving direction, making conscious efforts to inspire, and enabling others to spread their wings through empowerment. It is also nurturing high self-regulation and self-management skills in online learners so that they can take responsibility for their learning. It is important for leaders in contemporary educational space to reinvent not only themselves but also their organisations and their teams simultaneously in the face of unprecedented change and transformation. This requires nurturing a new leadership mindset that allows leaders and their organisations to keep pace with and stay ahead of the changes that are swirling around them.

3.23 References

Armstrong, M. (2012). *Armstrong's Handbook of Human Resource Management Practice*, 12th edition. London: Kogan Page.

Bass, B. (1990). *Bass and Stogdill's handbook on leadership: Theory, research, & managerial applications*, 3rd edition. New York: Simon and Schuster.

Bennis, W. (1989). *On becoming a leader*. New York: Perseus Books Group.

Capowsky, G. (1994). Anatomy of a leader: Where are the leaders of tomorrow? *Management Review, 83*(3), 10-14.

Centre for Creative Leadership (2021). *What are the characteristics of a good leader?* Retrieved from: https://www.ccl.org/blog/characteristics-good-leader/. On 27 February 2021.

Chiome, C. (2011). Preparing school leaders for a changing world: Lessons from Zimbabwe. In Townsend, T. & MacBeath, J. (Eds.) *International Handbook of Leadership for Learning* (pp. 445-465). London: Springer Science & Business Media.

Chiome, C. (2019). Diversity and School Leadership in rapidly transitioning schools in Zimbabwe: Towards school cultures that are inclusive in their diversity. In Chikoko, V. (Ed.) *African Handbook on School Leadership*. Durban.

Chiome, C., & Mupa, P. (2014). *Organizational development in education*. Harare, Zimbabwe: Zimbabwe Open University.

Day, D. V. (2014). *The Oxford Handbook of Leadership and Organizations*. Oxford: Oxford University Press.

Dembo, M. H., & Seli, H. (2013). *Motivation and learning strategies for college success*. London: Routledge.

Han, S., & Resta, P. E. (2020). Virtually authentic: Graduate students' perspective changes toward authentic learning while collaborating in a virtual world. *Online Learning, 24*(4), 5-27.

House, R. J. (2004). *Culture, Leadership and Organizations: The GLOBE study of sixty-two societies*. Thousand Oaks, CA: Sage.

Kipp, K. (2018). Exploring the future of the learning management system. *International Journal of Innovations in Online Education, 2*(2).

Korn Ferry Institute (2021). *Leadership mindset: Why leaders struggle to change*. Dublin: Korn Ferry Institute.

Leary, H., Dopp, C., Turley, C., Cheney, M., Simmons, Z., Graham, C. R., & Hatch, R. (2020). Professional development for online teaching: A literature review. *Online Learning, 24*(4), 254-275.

Ostergaard, E. K. (2019). *The mindset of a leader: A guide to conscious leadership.* Block & Ostergaard. Available at: http://blochoestergaard.dk/. Accessed on 24 February 2021.

Wilson, T. D. (2015). *Redirect: Changing the Stories We Live By.* Boston: Little, Brown and Company.

Yukl, G. (2013). *Leadership in organizations.* Boston: Pearson.

Zhu, M. (2021). Enhancing MOOC learners' skills for self-directed learning. *Distance Education, 42*(3), 441-460.

Chapter 4

Effective marketing in ODeL

Felix Chikosha

Zimbabwe Open University

Abstract

The Internet comes to the forefront as a very important medium in marketing ODeL programmes in the present day. Effective marketing requires ODeL institutions to identify their target audience, and understand and communicate with them as directly and interactively as possible. ODeL institutions are recommended to use, in an online enhanced manner, a set of seven marketing-mix tools in planning their market relationships: programme, price, place, promotion, processes, physical facilities, and people. For ODeL institutions, there are numerous methods of recruiting and engaging with students, including institutional websites, mobile marketing, and social media, among others. ODeL institutions should strive to automate all of their marketing processes.

Keywords: website, marketing strategy, marketing process, online marketing, social media marketing, mobile marketing

***

4.0 Introduction

Competition between higher education organisations has dramatically increased and currently, the market has become saturated. Additional to the high level of competition, Zimbabwean universities are facing operational problems stemming from a lag in technological advancement, greatly affecting service. The diverse changes in the global environment have also had a direct impact over higher education institutions and are forcing them to tailor their marketing efforts to better suit their stakeholder needs. Online environment offers universities various marketing instruments designed to fulfill their needs to provide accurate and up-to-date information to their target groups, whether they are current or prospective students. This chapter deals with the role of marketing in ODeL institutions, marketing strategy of ODeL institutions. The marketing process comprising the processes of Segmentation, Targeting and Positioning is also dealt with. Regarding educational services nature, ODeL institutions are recommended to use, in an online enhanced manner, a set of seven marketing-mix tools in planning their market relationships: programme, price, place, promotion, processes, physical facilities, and people.

4.1 Role of Marketing in ODeL Institutions

In terms of higher education, Kotler and Fox (1995, p. 6) defines marketing "as the analysis, planning, implementation and control of carefully formulated programs designed to bring about voluntary exchanges of values with target markets to achieve institutional objectives. Marketing involves designing the institution's offerings to meet the target markets' needs and desires, and using effective pricing, communication, and distribution to inform, motivate, and service these markets."

Marketing adoption in higher education favors the fulfillment of organisational social responsibility. ODeL institutions should be able to identify which are the real needs of the community and labour force market regarding educational programmes. Before defining academic products, they should consider the requirements of stakeholders. This will increase institutional performances and students' success in finding the desired jobs.

Another role of educational marketing can be pinpointed from a services marketing perspective. The key role of marketing in ODeL is stakeholder satisfaction, with the student being the principal stakeholder. Cognisant of the fact that ODeL services subscribe to services characteristics of intangibility, inseparability, heterogeneity and perishability, there is need for unique marketing strategy implementation. A main determinant of student satisfaction in ODeL institutions is the effectiveness of online marketing strategies by the institutions.

4.2 Marketing Strategy

Effective marketing requires higher education institutions to identify their target audience and understand and communicate with them as directly and interactively as possible. This is achieved through the marketing process of segmentation, targeting, and positioning (STP). Following STP, marketing strategy is formulated in terms of the marketing mix. For ODEL institutions, this step involves determining the programme, price (tuition), communications (promotion), distribution (place), people, process, and physical evidence strategies that will provide the customer with superior value. Thus, marketing strategy formulation for organisations takes place via the process of integrating segmentation, targeting, positioning, and the services marketing mix.

4.3 Segmentation, Targeting and Positioning

Taking into discussion segmentation of markets in ODeL, it is highly accepted that the sector has multi-clients, as students, employers, and society are seen to be the main beneficiaries of higher education services. Students are the direct and immediate customers of ODeL services. While students are principal consumers, employers can be seen as secondary or indirect consumers of ODeL services; employers, as they use the skills and abilities that graduates acquired during their studies. Finally, society benefits from the results of ODeL services.

Other stakeholders that have an interest in higher education besides students, employers, and society, are the government and other funding bodies, quality assurance agencies, other regulating authorities, and professional bodies. It is important to focus on segmentation for students who are the primary clients. All other stakeholders are more difficult to segment as they have varying interests. Soutar and Turner (2002) identified for three major student market segments: international students, mature students, and high school leavers, segments with different motivations when making their higher education choice and different needs and wants from educational services.

Online programme designers must consider several cost and demand factors in segmenting their markets and positioning their offerings. Some design the entire programme online and there is very limited or no face-to-face interaction with the target population. Others, on the other hand, combine the benefits of online education and traditional education to create their hybrid programs.

The design of online distance learning must overcome major obstacles such as reach, cost of creating courses/programs, the need for technical support, opposition from senior faculty who are less technically-oriented, and consumer perceptions regarding the equivalency of online education with the traditional form.

The identified market segments can be described in terms of demographics, disciplines, and geographic location. One or more of these segments are then selected as target market based on the institution's capabilities relative to those of its competition, considering current economic and technological conditions.

The very essence of institutional positioning is to differentiate itself from competitors. This is rather difficult to do in the ODeL as academic products are seen to be rather similar. Despite the similarity of products in higher education, there are suggested key dimensions that can be used by ODeL institutions to occupy positions of distinctiveness: teaching-led vs. research-led; science-based vs. arts-based; basic teaching vs. higher level teaching. But even these factors cannot ensure totally differentiated positions of higher educational institutions in the marketplace. Consequently, positioning in the ODeL sector involves effectively presenting institutional image rather than differentiation.

After the STP (segmentation, targeting and positioning) process, ODeL institutions must blend the services marketing mix elements into a marketing strategy that reflect the institution's desired position to their target market. Thus, ODeL institutions, through its programmes, may be a science, art, engineering, or multi-programme institution.

4.4 The Marketing-Mix Tools for ODeL Institutions

Considering the specific nature of the educational service, Kotler and Fox (1995) adapted the marketing-mix model by McCarthy (product, price, place, and promotion) in an educational context by including additional elements, proposing a set of seven marketing tools: programme, price, place, promotion, processes, physical facilities, and people.

4.4.1 Programme

ODeL marketing strategies usually start with the identification of student needs regarding programmes type and structure. An institution's identity is formed based on the nature and quality of its educational programmes and their degree of differentiation in relation with competing academic offers. An effective marketing strategy should result in programmes being cooperatively designed, developed, and refined. ODL programmes must not be historically developed. Rather, a needs assessment should be done prior to the development of a programme. This will ensure the programme so developed meets the specific needs of students and employers.

One strategy is to have superior programmes that serve to attracting students to the institution. These are called flagship programmes and include highly rated degree programmes like law, medicine, and recently, information technology degrees. Institutions of higher education may also promote alumni engagement by offering lifelong learning or continuing education benefits, or by offering online resources. For example, ODeL institutions can offer free or reduced-price classes to alumni, while alumni-focused online resources may include webinars, podcasts, and recorded lectures, classes, and courses.

4.4.2 Price/Tuition

Price for ODeL institutions is basically the tuition fees, which is the main revenue source for the institutions. The price policy must consider the specific target profile and the impact on overall university image. In other cases, discounts and scholarship offers may also attract potential students. Another concern of educational price strategy is to attract sponsorship and funding from the private sector.

Most educational institutions depend heavily on tuition fees to keep operating, and pricing, therefore, becomes very important. Price plays a role in determining who will apply, who will attend, who the institutions will serve, what the institutions will be able to offer, and whether the institutions will meet its enrolment objectives and revenue needs.

ODeL institutions should be cognisant that tuition fees represent only a fraction of the total cost of attending a higher education institution as living costs and other education-related expenses must also be considered. ODeL institutions should consider three factors when setting prices for their educational programmes:

- Firstly, cost, by determining the amount of revenue needed to cover expected operating expenses.

- Secondly, customer demand, which emphasises that the final price decision is always made by the customer; and

- Thirdly, competition, as institutions must weigh their "value" and establish their price relative to their competitors.

Institutions should always consider the effects of a given pricing policy on enrolment, the nature and mission of the institution, the prices charged by competition, and the effect of their prices and price changes on actions of competition (Kotler & Fox, 1995).

ODeL institutions need to establish some flexibility in terms of the price set. The institutions need to have some discounts incentives or flexible payment schemes. For example, students who pay in advance may be accorded some form of price discount. Students may also be allowed to commence their studies once they pay a fixed minimum deposit with the rest of the fees being paid gradually as the semester wears out.

An institution's price policy should take into consideration the facilities needed quality of education and competitiveness as students often use the price of a product or service as an indicator of quality. For example, more expensive institutions may be viewed as providing better education. Some institutions make use of their price/quality relationship by trying to raise the prestige and attractiveness of their institution by raising the tuition fees.

ODeL institutions must carefully consider the role of price in the marketing mix, as price can be used as a quality indicator and thereby influence the perception of the institution's position. Students are often looking for the best overall deal in terms of educational quality and prices. Higher tuition fees will enable institutions to improve the quality of education.

However, institutions should be aware that charging top fees may cause institutions to lose students. Universities worldwide have resorted to increasing fees as government funding for education is decreasing.

4.4.3 Promotion

Promotion is used to maintain a continuous dialog with students, employers, professors, and other relevant stakeholders. To reach a specific target audience, ODeL institutions can appeal to different communication techniques, which are usually classified into four major categories: advertising, sales promotion, public relations and personal selling. The institutions can use various tools belonging to each category, from educational show exhibits, open days or academic conferences to direct-mail, web pages, and social networks.

To ensure an effective, integrated marketing communications strategy, ODeL institutions must consider the following: students' perception of the institution, students' reasons for attending the institution, students' perception of other higher education institutions, benefits the students will receive by attending the higher education institution, making the benefits the institution offers believable to students, distinguishing themselves from other higher education institutions, and determining the actions that the institutions wants students to take as a result of communication efforts (Jones, 2002).

ODeL institutions should have stand-alone communication departments with the sole purpose to enhance effective communication with students and other stakeholders. More funds should be allocated to marketing, and this should be coupled with the appointment of marketing managers or external communication experts to help with promotional activities. Besides the traditional media forms like radio, television, newspapers, and open days ODeL institutions should make use of online media platforms. Digital promotions should be at the core of ODeL institutional promotion strategy since the mode of delivery is largely online.

The most popular communication/promotion objectives are general image enhancement and awareness of the institutions. ODeL institutions need to select a medium that will attract attention, arouse interest, and present the message clearly. The institutions need knowledge about the language of the prospective students, knowledge of forms of communication and general background information about the prospective students to encode successfully.

The promotional mix that an institution uses is determined by the student market's expectations and requirements of the service products, together with the other elements of institutions' marketing decisions. ODeL institutions have at their disposal a huge array of online promotional elements such as internet advertising, direct marketing, sales promotions, public relations and personal selling. The promotional mix elements are used by ODeL institutions to communicate to their current and prospective students as well as other stakeholders.

4.4.4 Internet Advertising

Internet comes to the forefront as a very important medium in advertising the distance education programs in the present day. Internet allows for the individuals to have immense information. In this context, individuals may receive information about a distance education program by pressing a key and enrol in an education programme which suits them best. There are some types used in the internet advertising. The basic ones of such types are as follows: web sites, banners, buttons, skyscrapers, pop-ups, advertorials, interstitials, superstitials, minisites, and search engine advertisements. The common forms are discussed below.

4.4.5 Web Sites

Institutions that provide ODeL services may use as an advertising medium either their own websites or those of their subsidiaries. The website may constitute a large-scale booklet concerning their programmes in the site and adorning the site with a variety of graphics, thus trying to attract the attention of the target group and to lead them to frequently visit their sites. Detailed information and benefits about an educational program provided may be placed in a website.

4.4.6 Banner Advertisements

Banner advertising or banner ads are a form of Internet advertising. The ad can be constructed in a variety of shapes and sizes. The purpose of banner ads is to direct potential customers to the advertiser's website and generate a sale. Banner ads can be targeted to selected groups of online customers and evaluated using web advertisement metrics such as click-thru and page-view rates.

Designs of the banner advertisements of the ODeL programs must be attractive. The basic objective is to cause the target group to click on the banner and direct them to the site and ensure them to obtain information about the contents, benefits, and properties of the program. In this context, banner advertisements of ODeL programmes must have eye-catching copies and graphics.

4.4.7 Buttons

Button advertisements are a type of banner advertisement. They cover less space compared to banners but serve the same function. This advertisement type which is cheaper than banners, as they cover less space, may go ahead of the banners in the media selection due to their price.

Button advertisements provide very successful access and direction to the sites of the ODeL programs when they are used in the promotion of such programs. Button advertisements are effective in ensuring the memorability of the logo of the education program and establishing its awareness as well.

4.4.8 Skyscrapers

Skyscraper advertisements differ from the banner advertisements in that they do not take place on the top of the page but on the right or left side and cover almost the whole page. Skyscrapers attract the attention of the target group by regularly flashing and changing graphics. Skyscraper advertisements ensure that the advertisements of ODeL institutions are more visible to the target group.

4.4.9 Pop-up and Pop-Under Advertisements

Pop-up advertisements are an advertisement type which suddenly appears in the screen when a site is entered and tries to influence the target group by staying there for a long time or by re-appearing in the screen at regular intervals. Pop-Up and Pop-Under ads are similar to banner ads except a pop-up ad opens above the current window and pop-under opens under the current window.

4.4.10 Search Engine Advertisements (GoogleAds)

Search engine advertisements are "small" advertisements appearing upon the entry of certain keywords in the search engine page. Pricing is made by the number of the clicks of the visitors on the advertisement. Adwords is based upon the overlapping of the words as searched by the web user who seeks information about a product or service with the keywords targeted in the advertisement. For ODeL institutions, Adwords would provide extra information about the programme related with the words entered in the Google search box. Adwords is located on the right side of the Google page. Google Adwords is based on the principle of making payment only when the person in the site clicks on the firm advertisement with the per-click-cost practice.

4.4.11 Sales Promotions

ODeL institutions' sales promotions could take the form of special events to encourage students to enrol for specific courses. Promotional material such as t-shirts, folders and pens can be manufactured to promote the ODeL institution' brand image. During open days and exhibitions, promotional materials can be used to enlighten prospective students on open, distance and e-learning. ODeL institutions can also make use of school visits, competitions, or discounts as possible sales promotional tools.

4.4.12 Public Relations

Public relations) are the marketing communication function that evaluates public attitude, identify areas of the institution that the public may be interested in and execute a programme of action to earn public understanding and acceptance. ODeL institutions can make use of public relations and publicity, not only to maintain a positive image but also to educate the public about the institutions' goals, objectives, introduce new programmes, or to help support the sales effort. Employees within the institution should be kept informed about the institution's practices and other matters that affect their work and welfare.

The following public relations tools can be represented on an institution's website:

- E-newspaper
- Online-Radio
- Online-TV
- Programme Catalogues
- Reports
- Corporate Publications (bulletin, e-journal, newsletters)
- Brochures
- Movies
- Online prospectus
- Publications: Annual Review
- Campaigns
- News releases
- Media Affairs media contacts, executives' speeches, media releases, contact directory

ODeL institutions should make use of faculty newsletters, in-house journals, and annual reports to keep staff informed. The intranet can used to disseminate information and as a medium for discussion and debate. The public relations department must research the available media, identify media contacts, brief the contact, and provide background material on the institution. The public relations department must also design the logo of the institution and monitor all publications sent to external publics to make sure the image of the institution is not compromised. Webpages and brochures must be user-friendly and reflect the image of the institution. ODeL institutions must make use of press releases or articles that will be highly visible on search engines like Google. Nowadays most prospective students are making use of search engines as a tool for finding higher education institutions.

Conferences, career exhibitions, and open days can also be used to create awareness of the institution and the programmes it offers, to create a positive attitude towards the institution, to create demand for certain programmes, enhance the image of the institution, and to convert interested students into enroled students.

4.4.13 Personal Selling

In ODeL, various departments within the institution perform the personal selling function. It is the responsibility of the industrial liaison officer to maintain good relationships with the heads of various governmental and non-governmental organisations because they are role-players that can influence the institution's ranking against competitors.

Open days and social events can be used by ODeL institutions to improve and maintain the relationship. ODeL institutions must strive to build relationships with their students from admission through graduation and even beyond. Institutions must treat each student as a valued partner who has not only joined them for the period of enrolment but also as a satisfied alumnus (positive word-of-mouth), donating to, and supporting the institutions after graduation and later in life. Attempts ensure retention have seen ODeL looking into and putting more emphasis on systems such as admissions, financial aid, academic assistance, and career development and placement.

ODeL institutions must plan which schools to visit, which exhibitions to attend, and when and how to have open days. Planning is vital to ensure effectiveness, as these activities are costly and time consuming.

4.5 Direct Marketing

ODeL institutions can also use direct marketing tools as the telephone, e-mail, and other non-personal tools to communicate directly with specific consumers to obtain a direct response. The major form directing marketing in ODeL institutions is through social media.

Social media comprises of activities that involve socializing and networking online through words, pictures, and videos. Social media is redefining how we relate to each other as humans and how we as humans relate to the organisations that serve us. It is about dialogue - two-way discussions bringing people together to discover and share information (Solis, 2008). The most used social media instruments within ODeL institutions are publication tools such as blogs and wikis, sharing tools for videos and slideshows, discussion tools like forums, social networks, and micro publication tools such as twitter.

ODeL institutions can use social media for different activities, including gathering and sharing information, showcasing student and faculty work, broadcasting special events, emergency notifications, and creating a dialogue in addition to communicating with their students or prospective students. The most important aspect of this instrument is that the accent is put on the idea of two-way communication. Unlike the website, social media instruments offer ODeL institutions the possibility to engage the public and to receive feedback because in the end, it is all about the conversation.

4.5.1 Place/Distribution

The place element relates to the educational delivery system and should be designed to create service availability and accessibility, in terms of time and geographical distribution of teaching and learning. The distribution decision faced by ODeL institutions is to decide how they can use distance learning and new technology. Distance education refers to instruction that occurs while there is a separation in time and/or distance between the learner and the instructor. Technological developments have helped higher education organisations to increase service accessibility, through electronic platforms use.

E-learning programs have been adopted by many international universities to gain market share and target those consumers who perceive geographic or time difficulties in physically attending university courses. ODeL institutions need to ask themselves three questions before using technology:

- Is the new technology likely to be more effective than the technology it replaces?

- Is the alternative channel appropriate for the intended market?

- What will the additional resource cost and added benefits be of adopting the new channels?

In recent years, marketing in higher education has significantly changed in the online space, with an increased focus on new platforms for external engagement and communication. ODeL institutions have wholesomely turned to the website, mobile marketing, and social media channel to ensure service availability and accessibility.

Institutional Websites

The presentation website is a vital communication instrument for a higher education institution because it is designed to offer a vast amount of information that can be easily brought today. At the same time, the cost of dissemination is clearly lower than the one imposed by printed materials, and it can be distributed virtually to an unlimited number of persons.

The interactive features of the website allow students to have a glimpse not only the academic program but also the location, facilities, and resources of the university, as the site can have pictures, movies, virtual tours of the institution, and information about the academic staff.

Social Media Channels

ODeL institutions should adopt effective social media marketing practices. Below is a list of social media platforms and the exemplary features of each platform can provide.

Table 4.1: Social Media Usage in ODeL

Platform	Standout Features
Facebook	Effective use of photos, video, and user polls
Twitter	Connects directly with potential students
Google+	Effective use of hashtags; content is interesting and relevant to target audience
Instagram	Multiple Instagram accounts; photo contests
YouTube	Weekly institutional newscast; admissions videos; featured lectures

Source: http://circaedu.com/hemj/social-media-and-higher-education/

4.5.2 Mobile Marketing

With this rise of mobile technology and connected devices, ODeL institutions can make greater investments in having a mobile presence. This includes not only mobile versions of websites and other content, but also making a greater amount of course content mobile friendly. Mobile marketing in ODeL is particularly important noting that most consumers, including students, use mobile devices as their primary mechanism for surfing the Internet.

However, mobile optimisation is "not just about making information fit on a smaller screen." Instead, mobile marketing strategies must ensure that information is quickly accessible, rewarding, and easy-to-navigate. In terms of accessibility, students should be able to find exactly the information they want and the actions they want to perform (e.g., "Schedule a campus visit"). The mobile session should reward the student by producing a desired result (e.g., "download a program brochure"). Lastly, the institution should make the design and functionality as error-free as possible to ensure students can accomplish tasks on their phones.

4.5.3 People

People refer to all the teaching and administrative staff through which the service is delivered, and customer relations built (Kotler and Fox, 1995). Because of educational services inseparability, teachers' skills and professionalism have a decisive influence on student's satisfaction with existing programmes. Current and former students are also included in this category. Communication and dialogue with students, professional skills, and the ability to explain are basic qualities of a good teacher in students' opinions.

A student's first impression of a higher education institution is often based on his/her interaction with the people of the institution. The people strategy of an organisation thus impacts the needs satisfaction of the customers. Employees are an essential ingredient to any service provider. Both support personnel and customer contact personnel need to have an external customer orientation. Organisations should emphasise hiring, training, supporting, evaluating, and rewarding service personnel.

It is important for higher education institutions to pay attention to the quality of employees and to monitor their performance. If employees tend to vary in their performance, it can lead to variable quality. Management must work in close harmony with the faculty and administrative personnel, as this makes a substantial contribution to student perceptions of good quality services.

4.5.4 Processes

Processes refers to the way things happen in an institution, such as the process of management, enrolment, teaching, learning, social, and sports activities. They are of critical concern to high-contact services, such as education. Many higher education institutions adopt quality management systems to ensure consistency in teaching and other educational processes.

ODeL institutions need to ensure that students understand the process of acquiring a service. They must further ensure that delivery times are acceptable to their customers, the students. Policies and procedures provide students with a tangible source of assurance of consistency in the service provided. The institution should set quality standards for processes and related variables such as registration, records, rules, and procedures. ODeL institutions should have stand-alone quality assurance departments to oversee conformance to quality standards in all institutional activities.

The institutions must also implement retention and recovery processes to retain customers after complaints have been received. They suggest that organisations re-evaluate their personnel training, customer complaint processes, and service recovery procedures to accommodate the different types of complaints.

Perhaps of most importance, ODeL institutions may have to rely more heavily on marketing automation to establish and maintain meaningful relationships with students. Marketing automation refers to software platforms and technologies designed for marketing departments and organisations to market on multiple channels online more effectively (e.g., email, social media, websites, etc.) and to automate repetitive tasks. Through marketing automation, the institutions can capture and leverage a wide range of student data to develop more personalised, multichannel messages, and marketing communications. Automation tools can integrate email, content marketing, social media marketing, landing pages, and comprehensive analytics to perform a wide range of functions, including:

- Definition, segmentation, scheduling, and tracking of marketing campaigns.
- Build automated workflows to reduce repetitive tasks associated with the marketing process.
- Nurture students to enrol and advance in their lifecycle.
- Provide development, testing, and integration of website calls to action, forms, and landing pages for lead generation.
- Scoring to identify lead quality of students and follow-up priorities; and
- Provide campaign analytics

4.6 Physical facilities vs Virtual Campus Model

Physical facilities help an educational institution to increase the tangibility of its offering and include every aspect related to the built environment, equipment, technical infrastructure, course books, etc. Often, these are the most visible issues perceived by students in their intention to differentiate between various universities. They are also useful in supporting teaching and learning processes. Investments in infrastructure should be paramount in the strategic plans of higher education organizations.

ODeL institutions should offer the online versions of several traditional campus-based programs by creating a virtual campus such as ZOU Virtual Region Campus, e-Cornell, and NYU Online. The products and services of ODeL institutions can be given a name, sign, symbol, design, or some combination that identifies them with the institution and differentiate them from competitor offerings. Branding adds value and increases customer satisfaction. ODeL institutions must work to raise their profiles. By strengthening and building their brand name and brand equity, institutions are maximising their competitive position.

Thus, an ODeL institution's online environment serves as the packaging of the academic programmes. Therefore, special attention should be given to the layout of the website encompassing utilities such as the e-learning portal, e-library, staff information, programme information, calendar, and events.

Physical evidence, as represented by the services provided through an institution's website, plays an important factor in service quality evaluation by students. Given that services are intangible, in an ODeL institution, the nature and quality of the relationship developed during the service encounter are, to a large extent, influenced by the online environment.

4.7 Summary

Due to the opportunities and threats in the ever-changing higher education landscape, globally and locally, ODeL institutions need to adopt effective marketing strategies to survive and grow. The institutions should deliver consumer satisfaction by adopting marketing strategy formulation which encompasses the segmentation, targeting, and positioning process and marketing mix elements using social and digital technologies.

ODeL institutions need to identify possible market segments and then choose an attractive segment(s) to target. Institutions need to determine the image or position they want students to have of their service products, brand, or institution. Based on the desired position, higher education institutions then must develop a marketing strategy by implementing and coordinating the services marketing mix elements to achieve the chosen position. It is the combination of the services marketing mix that meets students' needs and provides satisfaction.

For ODeL institutions, there are numerous methods of recruiting and engaging with students, including institutional websites, mobile marketing, and social media, among others. It is important that the channels work in harmony to attract and convert new students. This underscores the importance of marketing automation software that incorporates a multichannel strategy to engage prospective students, build relationships with current students, and continue to engage alumni.

4.8 References

Jones, M. (2002). The effectiveness of marketing communication strategies employed by universities and technikons in the Cape Peninsula with specific reference to career exhibitions and open days in attracting first year students. http://hdl.handle.net/20.500.11838/1706

Kotler, P., & Fox, K. (1995). *Strategic Marketing for Educational Institutions* (2nd ed.). Englewood Cliffs, N.J.: Prentice-Hall.

Sohail, M. S., & Shaikh, N. M. (2004). Quest for Excellence in Organisation Education: A Study of Student Impressions of Service Quality. *The International Journal of Educational Management, 18*(1), 58-65.

Soutar, G. N., & Turner, J. P. (2002). Students' Preferences for University: A Conjoint Analysis. *The International Journal of Educational Management, 16*(1), 40-4.

Chapter 5

Managing Student Affairs in Distance Education

Cuthbert Majoni

Zimbabwe Open University

Abstract

This chapter gives an outline of the origins of Student Affairs and the functions of the Student Affairs Department in higher education. The functions of student affairs in distance education are discussed and the related theories of student development as they apply in distance education. The theory and practice that the Student Affairs staff need to be equipped with to advise students and promote their social and academic development and the roles they need to play in the light of the ever-changing student body and its needs are presented. In the digital age, online student services need to be developed and applied to assist the virtual student.

Keywords: Student Affairs, Student Services, Student Development

***

5.0 Introduction

Distance Education has transformed dramatically due to advancements in information technology. The growth in the use of computers and the internet has influenced the expansion of distance learning via the World Wide Web and has created virtual institutions. The number of students studying at a distance has increased since the outbreak of the COVID-19 pandemic. The student affairs in distance education (DE) need to evolve and expand due to the growing complexity of new demands associated with the contemporary distance education (DE) student (McClellan & Stringer, 2009). In light of globalisation and the increase in students studying through distance education, there is a need for the evolution of student support services to incorporate technology and successfully support students to complete their studies. This chapter defines the term "student affairs" and gives a brief history of student affairs. The main functions of Student Affairs are discussed, as well as the virtual student services that can be provided online by distance education institutions. This chapter discusses the challenges related to the application of Information Technology in Distance Education in the ever-changing student body.

5.1 Meaning of Student Affairs

Student Affairs is a concept used to describe units that provide student support services in higher education institutions (Ciobanu, 2013). The other terms used for this sector are student services, student success, and student personnel. Student services include all activities and services for a student in educational institutions for the achievement of their personal goals and objectives (Akpan, 2016). According to Akinnubi and Kayode (2012), student services include, among others, welfare services provided in educational institutions to prevent an unnecessary increase in the rate of anti-social activities among students. It also involves encouraging positive thinking and actions that would promote the attainment of the pursuit and choices of future careers by students. Student services cater for students' cognitive, emotional, and social needs. Student Affairs serves as the interface between the institution and the student (Krishnan, 2012). It is there to assist the isolated and decentralised student, ensuring they get support, physically, emotionally, and socially, online. In distance education, student support services include counselling, career guidance, and financial assistance online (Pulist, 2001). Student Affairs also assists students to perform well in their studies and integration into the institutional community. Research has confirmed that student success in distance education is to a large extent related to the support services availed by the institution (Mannan, 2008). High dropout rates and low pass rates have been linked to inadequate student support services (Perraton, 2000). Student support services are important in ensuring the academic success of the student. Interaction with the Student Affairs staff is done through various electronic media as Student Affairs embraces technology in their delivery.

5.2 History of Student Affairs

Student Affairs can be traced to the founding colleges in the USA between 1636 to 1850 (Nuss, 2003). The founding entities were religiously-centered residential institutions. The main objectives included the acquisition of training and knowledge of the development of the ability to govern. The enactment of Student Affairs was mainly paternalistic with discipline, guidance, and supervision as the prime foci. In the 19th century, the strict philosophy began to wane and there was the incorporation of extra-curricular activities such as athletics and sports (Nuss, 2003). Diversification of the field of student affairs occurred between 1850 and 1900. The personnel included Deans of Men and Deans of Women. The 20th century began what is referred to as the modern student affairs movement, which includes systems of student personnel functions. During the 1960s and 1970s, students in universities started engaging in political activities and more freedom was extended to female students and the relationship between students and institutions changed. The 1980s and 1990s saw the creation of new departments in student affairs. These included students with disabilities, minority students, first-year students (freshmen), students with mental issues, as well as students with different sexual orientations (Rhatigan, 2009). The expansion of students' needs calls for Student Affairs to deal more with areas such as admissions, financial aid, registration, personal and academic counselling, orientation, as well as student support services (Garland & Grace, 1993).

5.3 The Functions of Student Affairs in Distance Education

Distance education has evolved considerably over the last decades and has embraced information communication technology in its delivery. The growing number of students studying at a distance has forced student affairs to integrate technology into many of the services they provide to students. It is important for student affairs to provide opportunities for students to connect with the distance education university. (Kretovics, 2003). The DE academic institutions have been forced to develop online student services. The new roles of student affairs in the digital age and the possibilities of engagement with students through digital and social technologies are now a reality. As institutions and students diversify, Student Affairs has adopted online tools to meet the needs of DE students (McClellan & Stringer, 2009). Student Affairs must use digital and social technologies to engage students and teach the students how to navigate the ICT tools. Student Affairs professionals need to be equipped with knowledge and skills to meet the needs of the student using technology and social media. The functions of Student Affairs are many and varied and they include organising, orientation, registration, guidance, and counselling, disciplining matters, promoting, and supporting learning, safety, and health of students and co-curricular activities alumni, and organising exchange programs. The array of Student Affairs activities provided by an institution depends on the financial status of the institution, the demand for the activity by students as well as the vision, mission, and goals of the institution. The student affairs services and activities should blend with the instructional process of the institution to enhance students learning outcomes (Nsama & Makoe, 2017; Krishnan, 2012; Pulist, 2001). A few roles of Student Affairs will be discussed below among many functions.

5.3.1 Admission Services

According to Long (2012), online application and admission have become the latest development in distance education. ODeL institutions have admission systems that enable students to apply online. Students can apply from different locations in the world. Online application and admission enable students to take responsibility for their enrolment. The disadvantage is that students located in rural areas have poor connectivity, lack of electricity, and lack of ICT skills to navigate the registration and application platforms. An effective and user-friendly admission system will go a long way in attracting potential students.

5.3.2 Registration Services

When the admission of a student is confirmed on the institution's portal, the student needs to be guided, directed, and advised on how to go about the registration process; this is the work of Student Affairs. Registration involves filling in registration information, paying the acceptance fee, and registering with the department or faculty. These activities can be done online, and students need to be guided and trained on how to use the institutional registration portal. It is the responsibility of Student Affairs staff to ensure students are admitted and properly registered. The system can screen the academic qualifications. Students pay fees online and register for their courses online. The challenges online, such as connectivity and power supply, need to be taken into consideration.

5.3.3 Orientation

Orientation is a systematic effort made by an educational institution to minimise the problems faced by students to ensure they settle well for effective study. It is the means through which new students are assisted in meeting their heads for security, sense of belonging information, and directions in the new institution. New students need to familiarise themselves with institutional, policies, rules, and regulations as well as the cyber layout of the institution. New students need guidance and information to enable them to familiarise themselves with the new environment. The main objectives of orientation include welcoming students and making them feel important as members of the institution. It enables students to familiarise themselves with institutional administrative structures and virtual functions. New students are made aware of the services and programs available in the institution. Orientation also helps students understand their academic responsibilities as students. Students will get information on their personal, social, and health rights in the institution and facilitate the interaction of new students online. An online orientation program will assist students who are geographically separated from the institution.

These are students in different locations; these might be regions, provinces, or countries, both continental and international. A well-designed online orientation programme will ensure new students are integrated into the student body of the university.

5.3.4 Academic Advising

Academic advising is the function of the student affairs department, and it is an essential service new students need throughout their study period. Academic advising is a function that should be embedded in the online student services system. The academic adviser can engage with the students on WhatsApp, Twitter, or Facebook where possible, and social media platforms can be used effectively in academic advisement. Academic advising is a very important support service needed by students throughout their study period. The academic adviser should be well equipped with the knowledge to work with students. The student affairs professional should be humble, emotionally stable, withstand stress, and be able to manage time effectively. The academic adviser should be able to help students in decision-making and career guidance. The online adviser will assist students on what programme to study, course registration, payment of fees, as well as accurate information concerning the choice of courses of study. The advisers should be equipped with information on academic regulations such as a repeat of or carryover of courses, deregistration courses, or change of program (Suleiman, 2018). For example, guidance on courses to register or how to deregister courses on the system and help the students understand the academic and administrative processes of the institution. Students are expected to know the set standards of achievement and level of success by the institution. Students need to discuss their educational and career objectives which is one of the main functions of the academic adviser. The advisor can help the students understand the relationship among the courses, programs, undergraduate research opportunities, internships and other academic experiences provided by the institution (Long, 2012).

5.3.5 Guidance and Counselling Services

According to Long (2012) students come from a variety of socio-cultural backgrounds with various problems ranging from psychological, emotional, and physical to spiritual and academic deficiencies. Guidance and counselling services for students can ameliorate their academic and psycho-social problems. Online guidance and counselling services require the students to be advised to behave even if they are off campus this includes social media and other social media platforms. Students who are geographically separated from the institution need to be provided with information on good study habits and learning strategies. This involves assisting the students to make good career and personal decisions. The distance education institution needs to develop online guidance and counselling services for students. Lines of communication should always be open for students to access counselors to ensure students have an equal opportunity for counselling services (Suleiman, 2018; Long, 2012). Students need to know that counselling services exist within the institution and the people or offices responsible. The institutions need to ensure students are interviewed to determine students' behavior for personal social and educational programs (Rhatigan, 2009). For face-to-face contact institutions counselling on an individual can be achieved virtually through teleconferencing hence the need for suitable technology and gadgets. Administration of guidance and counselling programmes in distance institutions need to be designed and done well to ensure the successful completion of the study.

5.3.6 Student Sports and Recreational Services

UNESO (2012) identified the main functions of Student Affairs personnel concerning sports. These include developing sports recreation and intramural programs based on student-centered philosophy, as well as providing extracurricular educational opportunities through participation in recreational sports. The other function is promoting learning and development in students by encouraging activities such as physical fitness and skills development, productive use of leisure time, and achievement of personal and recreational goals.

The importance of sports and recreation activities to students includes productive use of leisure time and an improved association of participants with other students. Sports also enable students to develop ideas and habits about culture, fair play, courtesy, and teamwork, as well as provide opportunities for citizenship. This also involves character training, getting rid of anti-social acts and the neglect of others, and promoting the physical, mental, and health of students (Garland & Grace, 1993). Generally, sports can promote good habits, skills, honesty, integrity, and ambition for self-improvement and achievement. Students physically separated need can have online programmmes to enable them to participate in institutional games. Online games and sports can be promoted. Students can do online games and sporting activities from different locations, for example, debate and chess while geographically separated. Online instructions can enable students to train physically on their own.

5.3.7 Special Needs Support Services

Students with special needs need to participate fully in the life of the university and derive the greatest benefit possible from their educational experience (Long, 2012). Student affairs professionals assess students' unique needs and plan ways in which students can be assisted to succeed wherever they are. Despite the physical impediments student affairs should facilitate services needed by the student living with a disability. For example, blind students might need transcription services or audio services or converting print tutorials to audio tutorials. Student affairs professionals need to assist students with special needs access to e-resources, legal rights, rules, and laws that they are entitled to under the laws of the respective country or institution (Long, 2012; Rhatigan, 2009).

5.4 Technology and Student Affairs

The explosion of online technology has opened access to education through distance education. Distance education institutions have embraced online education to teach their students. Distance education online learners are a combination of working adults, individuals with access challenges as well as young people from High School (Italsene, 2002). Online students are full-time workers, professionals, and the unemployed and all these students have unique qualities and needs that need to be attended to. Examination of the literature shows that little research has been done on the use of technology and student affairs (Langhorst, 1997). Research also shows that online students struggle to complete their degree programmes and there is high drop out and failure rates among distance learners (Nash, 2005). Online successful students have been found to have limited access to the required software, technological services, and ICT skills. Student Affairs professionals may not be well equipped with skills of integrating technology and online learners in their work of student advisement. However, Student Affairs has gone on to incorporate internet use and speech task software in their daily operations (DLTF, 2000, NACADA Tech missions 2003) Student affairs graduate preparations programmes in distance education tend to lag behind in addressing the needs of learners through online support services. (Engstrom, 1997; Kretovics, 2003).

There is a realisation in the education system that student advisement that happens on campus can be translated to a virtual cyber campus. Student Affairs need to integrate technology in their daily operations and provision of student services. Student Affairs professionals need to be equipped with skills to use technology in the workplace; hence, computer skills are a necessity. Distance education (DE) universities are challenged to innovate new ways of providing high-quality online student support services (Floyd & Case-Powell, 2004). DE Student Affairs has been forced to examine all areas of student services from admissions, registration, orientation, and library services to determine the best online support services they can provide virtually. Western higher education institutions have developed a wide range of technologies transferring traditional student services to the online environment. For example, admission and registration processes can be done online student affairs has the capacity to answer questions and address student needs online and through email and other media. Students can confirm their academic study online and online chat sessions and respond to student questions (Vail, 2006). Library systems can offer online collections as well as link the library to Facebook to connect with distance students (Charnigo & Barnett- Ellis, 2007). Online financial systems have been developed to allow students to apply, accept, and utilise funds online. Online student services can be developed in basic communications through email, online chatrooms (in real-time), and video conferencing. Students can be provided with self-service systems, and these are tools students can use to find answers to areas they may need support, e.g, checking results, applications for financial aid, or check-status of an application. (Carlson, 2002). Other ICT tools allow students independent online services where the student can complete processes on their own for example, ordering a transcript and enrolment verification (Dahl, 2005). The online student support services benefit both the student and the institution. However, distance education institutions need to invest large sums of money to establish and maintain these social service technologies and software, as well as train staff (Meyer, 2005).

5.5 Summary

The digital age of Student Affairs has extensive opportunities to improve student experiences online. The digital and social technologies have provided Student Affairs professionals with an opportunity to unlock new and innovative ways to engage the distance education student. Online services and tools can be useful to DE universities in gathering student background data for meaningful engagement and assistance. As technology continues to develop, Student Affairs needs to evolve to keep pace with technological advancement to ensure the provision of effective online student support services and ensure successful completion of the study.

5.6 References

Akinnubi, O. P & Kayode, D. J. (2012). Influence of student personnel services on students' behaviours in University of Ilorin, Ilorin: Management implications. *Global Journal of Applied Sciences, Management and Social Sciences*, 4(1), 279-284.

Akpan, C. P. (2016). Student Personnel Services. Accessed August 16 2020.

Carlson, S. (2002). Virtual counseling. *The Chronicle of Higher Education*, 49*(12)*, 35-6.

Charnigo, L., & Barnett-Ellis, P. (2007). Checking out facebook.com: The impact of a digital trend on academic libraries. *Information Technology and Libraries*, 26*(1)*, 23-34.

Ciobanu, A. (2013). The Role of Student Services in Improving Student Experience in Higher Education. *Procedia - Social and Behavioural Sciences*, 92, 169-173.

Dahl, J. (2005). Online services keep Syracuse students satisfied. *Distance Education Report, 9*(21), 6-8.

Distance Learning Task Force. (2000). *Distance learning and student affairs: Defining the issues. Report of the Distance Learning Task Force.* Washington, DC: NASPA.

Engstrom, C. M. (1997). Integrating information technology into student affairs graduate programs. In C. M. Engstrom & K. W. Kruger (Eds.), *Using technology to promote student learning: Opportunities for today and tomorrow* (pp. 59-70). San Francisco: Jossey-Bass.

Floyd, D. L., & Casey-Powell, D. (2004). New roles for student support services in distance learning. *New Directions for Community Colleges, 1*(128), 55-64.

Garland, P. H., & Grace, T. W. (1993). *New perspectives for student affairs professionals: Evolving realities, responsibilities, and roles. ASHE-ERIC Higher Education Report No. 7.* Washington, DC: The George Washington University, School of Education and Human Development.

Kretovics, M. (2003). The role of student affairs in distance education: Cyber-services or virtual communities. *Online Journal of Distance Learning Administration, 6*(3).

Krishnan, C. (2012). Student Support Services in Distance Higher Education in India: A Critical Appraisal. *International Journal of Research in Economics & Social Sciences, 2*(2), 459-472.

Langhorst, S. A. (1997). Changing the channel: Community colleges in the information age. *Community College Review, 25*, 55-72.

Long, D. (2012). The foundations of student affairs: A guide to the profession. In L. J. Hinchliffe & M. A. Wong (Eds.), *Environments for student growth and development: Librarians and student affairs in collaboration* (pp. 1-39). Chicago: Association of College & Research Libraries.

McClellan, G.S. & Stringer, J. (2009) *The Handbook of Student Affairs Administration,* San Francisco, CA: Jossey-Bass.

Meyer, K. A. (2005). Planning for cost-efficiencies in online learning. *Planning for Higher Education, 33(3)*, 19-30.

NACADA Tech Commission. (2003). National Academic Advising Association Technology in Advising Commission.

Nuss, E. M. (2003). The development of student affairs. In S.R. Komives & D.B. Woodard, Jr. (Eds.), *Student Services: A Handbook for the Profession* (4th ed., pp. 65-88). San Francisco, CA: Jossey-Bass.

Nsama, A., & Makoe, M. (2017). Evaluating Quality of Student Support Services, *Turkish Online Journal of Distance Education 8*(4), 91-103.

Perraton, H. (2000). *Open and distance learning in the developing world* (2nd ed). London: Routledge.

Pulist, S. K. (2001). Student Support Services in Correspondence Distance Education in India: A Historical Perspective. *Journal of Distance Education, 8*(1), 66-82.

Robinson, B. 1995. The management of Quality in Open and Distance Learning. In Indira Gandhi National Open University, Structure and Management of Open Learning Systems, *Proceedings of the Eighth Annual Conference of the Asian Association of Open Universities.* New Delhi, India.

Rhatigan, J. J. (2009). A brief history of student affairs administration. In G. S. McClellan, J. Stringer, M. J. Barr, & National Association of Student Personnel Administrators (US) (Eds.), *The handbook of student affairs administration* (3rd ed., pp. 36-216). San Francisco, CA: Jossey-Bass.

Suleiman, M. M. (2018). The Role of Student Support Affairs Services in Managing Tertiary Institutions. A paper presented at the first National Conference by the academic and Research Development Committee: Kano State University.

UNESCO (2012). The role of student affairs and services in higher education. Paris: UNESCO.

Vail, K. (2006). Back to basics: How to run a first-rate program. *Distance Education Report, 10*(3), 5-7.

Chapter 6

Effective Library Services in ODL Institutions

Kudzayi Chiwanza
Zimbabwe Open University

Abstract

This chapter deals with how distance education (DE) has revolutionised and democratised the delivery and accessibility of education, and how it has revisited critical support services, such as library and information services. It goes on to demonstrate how distance libraries and librarians are as important to distance learning as they are to conventional education. Access to information has been identified in this chapter to produce quality students. The goal of every ODL university library in Africa, as highlighted in this chapter, is to facilitate the realisation of the tripartite functions of the university, which include teaching, research, and community service. No tertiary institution can exist without adequate library services.

Keywords: Library services, Distance librarianship

***

6.1 Introduction

As the cornerstone of higher education, academic libraries have long supported the instructional endeavours on college and university campuses across Africa. Open and Distance Learning (ODL) has revolutionised and democratised the delivery and accessibility of education, and has also changed how critical support services, such as library and information services, are provided. This chapter examines how library services contribute to open and distance learning and will look at ways librarians can deliver effective distance library services as well, as the issues affecting the service delivery. Academic libraries carry a philosophical mission to provide access to educational resources and services, as well as instruction on locating, accessing, evaluating, and using resources successfully to all its users. Libraries exist because they add value to teaching, learning, and the production and dissemination of knowledge (Munde & Marks, 2009).

6.2 Open and Distance Library Services in Africa

Historically, libraries in developing countries have been under-resourced, under-staffed, and remote from the distance learner. Generally, these libraries were unable to provide the range of services and materials needed, especially to support post-secondary education, and do not have hours of operation that are convenient to the distance learner. These factors remain significant challenges for the developing world, and for the institutions that provide DL services.

The following methods helped overcome some of these challenges:

- Rotating book boxes and other temporary "libraries" between pre-determined locations, such as community centres.
- Collaborative and reciprocal borrowing arrangements between local and regional institutions and public libraries, such as partnerships with British Council Libraries.
- Developing pre-packaged primary, secondary, and tertiary library resources for circulation.
- Establishing "distance library corners" in other libraries.
- Establishing sub-regional groupings of libraries to support distance learning.
- Establishing information delivery partnerships with a broad range of institutions.
- Using mobile libraries, including buses, book-boxes, and donkey libraries.
- Using commercial delivery services, such as courier services.

It is imperative to delve into the current trends in ODL from the African library viewpoint, which is the core aspect of this chapter. This is because the African continent is not left out in the scheme of things as far as current trends in open-distance learning libraries are concerned. Open and distance e-library services will be an important element of future education and training systems. The emergence of new forms of library services based on new Information and Communication Technologies (ICTs), especially those supported by the Internet and using the World Wide Web (WWW), has significant economic, pedagogical, and organisational implications. Furthermore, there is a significant trend towards intensifying globalisation. According to Oladejo and Gesinde (2014), most of the discernible current trends in ODL are linked to the ever-increasing growth in information and communication technology. Considering the challenges of education and development, both in developing and developed countries, it is not surprising that open and distance learning libraries are often seen as an important strategy that could make a significant contribution towards resolving problems of access, quality, and equity. In Sub-Saharan Africa, where the knowledge gap between the North and the South takes on its most dramatic character, the current trends indicate that ODL libraries are being mainly used to widen access to information. ODL has also been used in non-formal education and community development by national and international organisations. However, there are strong indications that ODL is becoming more central to the education policy of many African countries. This assertion is attested to in a report submitted by Hanover Research (2011) on current trends in global distance learning. In the report, it was found that Africa and India represent two of the growing markets for distance learning programmes. Libraries exist in these institutions to serve as the backbone of the academic work.

A remarkable phenomenon in South Africa according to the UNESCO (2001) is the shift on the part of learners from single mode to dual mode institutions. This has significantly increased the population of students for ODL programmes. Unisa has more than 400,000 students in some 130 countries.

In 1993, the Zimbabwean Government established the Centre for Distance Education (CDE) at the University of Zimbabwe. The CDE, however, became the University College of Distance Education (UCDE) in 1996 and transformed into a fully-fledged University known as the Zimbabwe Open University (ZOU), which has a student population of around 20 000. The Distance Education Association of Tanzania (DEATA) is responsible for organising Distance Education and enroling over 18,000 students. It was not until 1990 that the University of Abuja established the Centre for Distance Learning (CDL), and in the year 2001, the Federal Government of Nigeria re-established the National Open University of Nigeria (NOUN) to run some courses. Today, NOUN admits over 30,000 students annually (Adekanmbi, 1993). The large number of enroled students in distance education institutions need effective library support services.

Libraries are indispensable institutions in tertiary education. University libraries play an important role in contributing to student and faculty members' academic achievement throughout ODL institutions in Africa. Jagannathan (2006) also asserts that libraries have always been a major focus for all kinds of learning, formal and informal. The library is at the heart of the traditional university or college, providing access to collections, specialist help support, use of technology, and a place to study alone or with fellow students (Watson, 2006). In this modern world, the rapid development of science and technology has entered a new era. Information technologies, especially the Internet, have brought about great changes in the working and learning environments. The advent of ICT has brought about a dramatic transformation in all aspects of education, including library and information services. Four key trends influencing the shape of the library services in Africa are: globalisation, the information explosion, electronic access of information, and a growing need for lifelong learning and retraining. In the changing academic library settings, demands for high-quality library resources and services from the students' communities are consistently increasing.

Across Africa, current trends in ODL libraries revolve around regional collaboration policy. In ODL libraries, there is much to be gained from enhanced regional collaboration on policy issues, development of delivery systems, and sharing of materials. There are now many initiatives, such as establishing networking through national and regional library associations, to strengthen and improve capacities for ODL libraries in the region.

6.3 Open and Distance Learning and Distance Librarianship

Open and Distance Learning (ODL) is a method of study that is pursued by students who are physically separated from their tutors and institution of instruction for the greater part of their study (Watson, 1992). The distinguishing characteristic of distance education from other forms of education is the physical separation that exists between the students, their tutors, and the institution of instruction. This separation has been termed the 'tyranny of distance' within the literature of distance education. It is the factor of distance that redefines the role of libraries in distance education and leads to the specialisation of distance librarianship. In traditional library services, students go to the library to access the range of information services that they need to satisfy their learning needs. In distance education, a cocktail of modalities must be used to take library services to distance learners. Thus, the tyranny of distance applies not only to education but also to the ability of those who study at distance to access library services. Librarians, distance educators, and administrators must therefore adopt new strategies to ensure that quality library and information services are available to those who learn at a distance. These new strategies or paradigms must be applied to every aspect of library and information services. Thus, distance librarianship has brought a change in what is "common" in librarianship through the introduction of several qualitative changes in library and information services. Libraries and librarians are as important to distance learning as they are to face-to-face education. Librarians need to understand the mechanics and concepts of DE to provide effective distance library services. In DE, learning takes place at the location of the student and not at the institution of instruction. Traditionally, distance learners were rural-based, middle-aged, and female. Today's distance learner is located anywhere, of any age and gender. There are many terms used for DE, including asynchronous learning, external studies, and individualised learning. Regardless of the terminology used, remoteness between learner, tutor, and institution of instruction is constant.

According to the Information Resource Centre, in Distance Education, librarians need to:

- ensure that library and information services conform with accreditation requirements
- develop and maintain quality DE information resources, such as reading lists for students, course developers, and tutors
- help distance learners acquire library skills, critical thinking, study, and information literacy skills
- advise distance tutors on new and appropriate course materials
- support the research and scholarship activities of DE students
- identify other institutions that can assist with delivering distance library services to students.

Librarians must be included in DE course teams to ensure that timely distance library services and professional advice are available to students and tutors as well as to ensure library collections effectively support student and faculty information needs.

6.4 Establishing and Managing Distance Librarianship

Library and information services for distance education are often an extension of the institution's existing traditional library services. When establishing distance librarianship (DL) procedure, traditional library standards and procedures can be applied as a guide. DL is used to provide most traditional library services such as consultation, reference and bibliographic searches, and course reading material. Generally, providing post-secondary level DL service is the most challenging, as the information and consultation needs of students and faculty cannot be satisfied just with pre-packaged reading and information.

When starting as a distance education library, one of the first things to do is stop and listen. Listen to what is going on in the institution, in the library, and consult your peers. Having done thorough research, learn from others and identify successes and failures. Be familiar with the Association of College and Research Libraries (ACRL) standards for Distance Learning Library Services. Upon listening to what is happening around, focus on what is happening in the university. Do not underestimate the power of casual conversations with people across campus. Conversations inside the library are also imperative as you tap on the knowledge of other people. Conversing with many stakeholders (and do not forget students are stakeholders too) will give you a greater perspective and build a strong relay team on your campus.

In addition to building relationships, consider essential components for a distance education librarian include taking risks, trying new ideas, and trying new tools and techniques. Another important area is collaboration. Collaborate with faculty members or other departments in the library. Serving distance and online learners should not be a singular endeavour. Consider the needs of distance/online patrons. Listen to them through surveys, conversations, or focus groups, and use the information in planning. Also, consider plans in the context of the library's missions and goals; make this constituency part of library wide strategic planning and decision making.

After learning the importance of building a team, proceed to plan for distance education support. Check the time to launch off the diving board and keep stride with the currents of technology. Developing a portal or website for distance students creates a personalised space for discovery, access, and help while letting students realise that the library understands their distance situation. Campus policies, branding, and restrictions might limit what can be done, but creating a winning campus relay team may assist to overcome these challenges. Orientation is rare for distance learners, so creating a personal welcome video will help ease their anxiety and build links with their online library. Meeting students at their point of need is critical. Consider embedding a library chat widget on major library webpages, in databases, or in failed searches in the library catalogue.

It is a challenge to reach distance learners for instruction. For synchronous instruction, acquire a web conferencing room to offer online workshops, such as Tools for Research or using EndNote Web or create your own informal online monthly chats with a few other librarians in your area.

6.4.1 The Basic Library and Information Services Distance Learners Need Are:

- Access to information resources, such as texts, supplementary reading, and reference services.
- Learning how to find the information they need from the information that is available.
- Developing ways to apply the information gleaned and to make sound, information-based decisions.

6.4.2 Some Guidelines for Establishing Distance Librarianship

- Produce a mission statement that defines clear goals and guiding principles for providing library services tailored to the institution's DE programming.

- Assess the library and information service needs of the institution's DE programme, in consultation with DE course teams, faculty, and possibly a student survey.

- Determine the best media and delivery methods for DL services, such as audio or video tape, print or online material, to be distributed through traditional mail, courier, e-mail, or for download from a website.

- Determine additional costs for the DL component, such as new or additional materials, equipment and staff, and any staff training that may be needed.

- Establish the level of funding available for DL from the institution and explore ways to minimise and share costs through funding grants, collaboration with other institutions, or by forming corporate partnerships.

- Establish a review and continuing education process, to ensure that DE student and faculty needs continue to be met.

- Initiate a public relations programme to promote awareness of DL services targeted to students and faculty.

6.5 Standards for Distance Library Services

Institutional guidelines or standards for DL service, such as mission statements, help librarians to:

- Meet international, professionally accepted, and established standards.
- Maintain consistent services between institutions.
- Gauge the relative standard of their existing services.

6.6.1 The Duties of a DL Services Librarian According to ACRL Guidelines Committee (2008) Can Include:

- Staffing out-of-hours services.
- Staffing remote library points.
- Fielding inquiries, mailing, and receiving materials.
- Administering intellectual property clearances.
- Offering input to DE course teams. ACRL Guidelines Committee (2008)

i) Public Relations

DL service needs an ongoing, aggressive public relations (PR) programme to awaken and educate students, administrators, educators, and others to the benefits of DL and to any new services or issues. PR activities can either be a direct library initiative or part of the institution's broader information and advertising package.

ii) Effective PR Methods Include:

- Posting DL services information on the institution's website.
- Short general flyers on DL services.
- Circulars about timely, specific issues in DL.
- Sending personalised information mail-outs to target groups of students or faculty.
- Conducting personal visits to remote library sites.
- Networking with faculty.

The library seeks to win and retain the understanding, sympathy, and support of those who are or maybe concerned. Library public relations is a deliberate, planned, and sustained effort to establish and maintain mutual understanding between the library and the publics (users) public relation activities help to provide a coordinated effort to communicate a positive image of the library and promote the availability of the library's materials, programmes, and services www.topnz.ac.nz/library/students.html. The importance of public relations activities cannot be over-looked in any library, especially in academic libraries. The significance of academic libraries, especially university libraries, cannot be over-emphasised. University libraries assist the universities in the discharge of their functions by acquiring all relevant information resources necessary for sustaining the teaching, learning, research, and public services functions of their universities. Hence, the objectives of any academic institution cannot be achieved without the presence of public relations. Any library activity, directly or indirectly, is an act of public relations, in as much as it is done to promote the library image and use.

The reference librarian plays the role of public relations officer for the library. They go outside the confines of the library to carve a good image of the library in the minds of the potential users. A good number of libraries especially academic libraries offer so many commercial services unknown to users; it is the duty of the reference librarian to inform the public about these services. The reference librarian may use handbills to pass on information to people and advertise library services. The reference librarian is part of the overall professionals working to bring the required desire to fulfilment and therefore has a lot to contribute to make the services of the library a success. Reference librarians can be referred to as the public relations officer of any library. Thet should be the image booster to the library since their main duties include working directly with the users. They become the intermediary between the users and the library and identify the needs of users. Therefore, the role of the reference librarian in academic libraries and its relationship with public relations activities cannot be overstated. Having services that no one knows about is as good as having no service at all. Watson and Jagannathan (1996) say Academic libraries are very important in education institutions. However, they are not achieving their full potential because of a lack of or failure of public relations. No matter how libraries respond to the needs of their users, their values will not be appreciated without an aggressive, systematic, and determined programme of publicity to stimulate, inform, and attract the information seeker/library users. Academic libraries have to covey signals and projected images to their users through public relations that accurately reflect what they are and what they do. It is true that all library professionals should be involved in public relations activities, but those professionals whose work is directly related to the users perform more of a public relations activity than the others.

6.7 Issues in Providing Distance Library Service

6.7.1 Access to Materials and Document Delivery

In addition to distance and time-difference barriers, national censorship, and religious beliefs in receiving countries affect document and information delivery. In some countries, Zimbabwe, for example (for prominent/political people), all e-mails and internet sites are monitored before individuals can access or download them, or access may be blocked altogether. Electronic information sources (e-mail, e-books, databases, virtual libraries, webpages) are heavily used in developed countries but are not readily available or in widespread use in many developing countries. DL services must be sensitive to these realities and establish non-electronic ways to field enquiries and to deliver services. For example, mail, fax, or phone can be used for enquiries. Print copies or audio and videotapes of materials can be sent through regular mail or by courier. Borrowing and service arrangements can also be made with libraries in other locations. Simon Fraser University Library (www.lib.sfu.ca) in British Columbia, Canada provides library services for distance learners of several other institutions. Librarians must identify libraries with collections and services appropriate to their students' needs before finding out if the libraries are interested in collaboration. A pilot assessment period with student feedback can help determine if the proposed service is accessible to them and appropriate to their needs. Fees for these "loaned services" can be either charged to the student user or paid through an arrangement between the contracting institution and the library providing the service. The library should assess and inform students of any overlap in services provided by the commercial vendor and the DE institution to avoid students having to pay for services already covered by their tuition fees.

6.7.2 Consultation Services

Consultation can be conducted through e-mail, toll-free telephone services, pre-packaged mail-out information, or scheduled remote site visits. Institutions that have a toll-free telephone service should, if possible, also use it for library consultation. The frequency and duration of remote library site visits depend on the institution's DL budget, as well as how far the sites are from the parent institution. Institutions with large numbers of overseas students may not have the funds for site visits, whereas those with students within a reasonable distance can schedule frequent visits.

6.7.3 Reference Services

In the DE environment, students can use forms to make research queries, either in print or electronically. In the form, "trigger" or "prompt" questions replace face-to-face assistance in helping the student properly complete a request. Institutions that already have dedicated library telephone services can use them for DL reference inquiries. Some institutions with Web-based services purchase online versions of major reference works to provide students with a convenient access point, such as Athabasca University's Digital Reference Centre (library.athabascau.ca/drc).

6.7.4 Bibliographic Searches

In some cases, and where staff is available, librarians execute full searches for distance learners. Another way is to provide a student manual on conducting bibliographic searches which explains search methods, such as moving from general to specific questions, and lists basic texts, journals, and reference sources in various disciplines. More detailed "help "manuals can also be developed on a discipline-by-discipline basis.

6.8 Bibliographic Instruction (BI) and Information Literacy (IL)

i) Instruction

Librarians must help learners access, evaluate, and use information effectively and efficiently. For delivering BI and IL instruction at a distance, librarians take on a more active teaching, rather than a facilitative role. Centra e-Meeting (www.centranow.com) is an electronic communication utility that has been used successfully to deliver BI at a distance. Deakin University, Australia's Smart Searcher Tutorial service (www.deakin.edu.au/library/findout/learn) uses interactive, web-based IL tutorial software from UNILINC Ltd. (www.unilinc.edu.au). Alternative BI and IL delivery methods include radio, which has been used at the University of South Africa (UNISA, www.unisa.ac.za/library), and computer and video conferencing, which have been used by the Central Queensland University, Australia (www.library.cqu.edu.au).

ii) Information Literacy

Libraries must provide information literacy programs such as user education and IT skills to the user learning community as stated by ACRL Information Literacy Competency Standards for Higher Education. According to the information literacy standard for high education (2000), information literacy is a set of abilities requiring individuals to "recognise when information is needed and can locate, evaluate and effectively use the needed information." Boylston (2015) restates that information literacy is the set of integrated abilities encompassing the reflective discovery of information, the understanding of how information is produced and valued, and the use of information in creating new knowledge and participating ethically in communities of learning. This implies that distance learners should be given adequate information literacy skills to be able to locate, evaluate, and use information effectively.

iii) Information Literacy and Active Learning

According to ACRL, information literacy is the set of skills needed to find, retrieve, analyse, and use information, and to guide instruction librarians interested in promoting information literacy skills (ACRL, 2000). Building upon this, ACRL's Distance Learning Section developed a SPEC Kit for the Association of Research Libraries entitled Collaboration for Distance Learning Information Literacy Instruction (ACRL, 2005), and in its study, the committee observed that the ability to utilise a variety of tools and technologies, from face-to-face instruction to synchronous and asynchronous online assistance, appears to be a trend for libraries that are taking the lead in distance information literacy instruction. Many of those libraries that are engaged in distance information literacy instruction appear to be approaching the unique challenges of the distance learning environment dynamically and creatively (ACRL, 2005). Orr and Wallin (2001) also recognised the need for creativity that the individualistic information literacy needs and learning styles of off-campus students require a realignment of traditional services and flexible delivery of instruction. The Off-Campus Library Services Conference and several journals have produced a good deal of scholarship concerning the creative development of information literacy programs for distance education students (Lockerby et al., 2004).

6.9 Copyright in Distance Librarianship

As libraries need to distribute multiple copies of the same information to distance learners, librarians must be very familiar with all the current copyright issues affecting distance library provision and need to be aware of local and international laws governing intellectual property. For example, present international agreements on broadcasting require an institution to obtain broadcast rights for any video and related formats used in DE. Libraries providing distance services should have a "rights clearance librarian" or "copyright librarian" to acquire on the library's behalf the legal right to make multiple copies of an information source. Usually, these rights are given for a prescribed period, for an agreed fee. When a license expires, the officer is responsible for either renewing the license, or for removing and disposing of the relevant documents/duplicates. Establishing Copyright Procedure in Distance Education, a Commonwealth of Learning (COL) Knowledge Series title for 2003 (www.col.org/knowledge), has more detailed information on dealing with copyright issues.

6.10 Role of Librarians

Nothing in the Teaching Act mentions duties of librarians, but the growth and complexity of distance education throughout the country have escalated the need for innovative library services. Fundamentally, librarians have a mission centered on the management and dissemination of information resources. Distance education is simply another form of exactly that pursuit. More pragmatically, distance education has stirred greater need for reserve services and interlibrary loans to deliver information to students in scattered locations. Librarians are also often the principal negotiators of licenses for databases and other materials; those licenses may grant or deny the opportunity to permit access to students located across campus or around the world.

6.11 Technology Use in Distance Libraries

The rapid spread of ICT, recent reductions in technology costs and connection services due to economies of scale, and a rise in personal ownership of ICTs are making ICT use for DL seem more attractive. Many libraries in developed countries already use ICT as their main method of delivering information services and resources, through online chat rooms, e-mail services, listservs, fee-based or free online databases and reference services, teleconferencing, and toll-free numbers. Nevertheless, an estimated 95% of the world's population does not have ready and immediate access to ICT. Often, the cost of the technology is prohibitive. If an institution relies primarily on ICT to deliver DL services, a potentially large number of learners, many of them from developing countries, will be unable to participate or benefit fully. Grants are available to help bridge the technology divide, such as a project by the Bill and Melinda Gates Foundation (www.gatesfoundation.org) to place computers in libraries in developing countries. However, perhaps a longer-term, sustainable way to begin and maintain a start in ICT is to partner with other education institutions or an Internet Service Provider (ISP) on infrastructure costs. In the latter relationship, the ISP often offers reduced information technology (IT) connection rates for students at the partner educational institution.

ICT may be used effectively for DL if:

- The institution is committed to providing a high level of library services to distance learners.

- The initial and ongoing cost of hardware, software and connectivity charges are within the institution's financial means.

- End users (students and faculty) have access to the ICT at their location.

Using Telecentres in Support of Distance Education, one of COL's Knowledge Series titles published in 2001 (www.col.org/knowledge), provides some useful information on the role of technology in distance learning and how telecentres can be used to deliver distance library services.

6.12 The Expanded Use of Technology to Provide Distance Library Services

Distance education is the kind of education in which students may not always be physically present at a school. In other words, you learn, study, and qualify in your chosen subject online without having to attend an exam centre, a college building, or university campus. According to Ryan (1997), most of the distance education today takes place using the Internet, now readily accessible for most students whether in their own homes or at facilities such as local libraries. These electronic means are used to distribute the learning material, keep students in touch with teachers, and provide access to communication between students. Of course, distance learning can use other technological formats as well, including television, DVDs, teleconferencing, and printable material, but the immediacy and functionality of Web learning has made it a first choice for many distance learners. Online programs often take advantage of several emerging technologies to make keeping in touch and effectively communicating ideas easier and more efficient than ever before and students may find themselves using interactive videos, e-mail, and discussion boards to complete their lessons (Vlasenko & Bozhok, 2014).

The convergence of technology and communications offers distance education institutions an array of options to delivery library and information services. The expanded use and role of technology in the delivery of library and information services has served to reduce the barriers to library and information services that are occasioned by distance for these students. To take library services to distance learners, many libraries in these institutions have placed most of their services on-line. The digitalisation of information makes it possible to take library and information services to distance students regardless of their location. In addition to on-line catalogues (OPACs), students can search databases, examine abstracts, and in some instances, read full-text documents. Some of these networked services also include non-print resources in their information databases. Another use of technology in library and information services in distance learning is the delivery of information literacy, bibliographic instruction, and reference skills as online courses. Thus, distance students are able to enjoy training in information-related skills using technology. Many libraries use electronic communication as the medium of choice to maintain contact with students, making it possible for students to use e-mail as a means of sending and receiving communication related to their need for information. While technology has reduced the distance between library services and students, distance services librarians are charged to remember that not all countries or all distance students are able to access technology with the same degree of ease. Thus, while technology is an important modality to reduce the tyranny of distance, it is important for librarians and others to include other modalities in their delivery of information strategies. This is important because access to technology is not universal, neither all technological systems are equal, therefore total reliance on technology will cause some distance students to experience information disenfranchisement (Watson & Jagannathan, 1996; Cavanagh & Store, 1998). The differential between countries regarding levels of technology caused the following comment: "one concern that I have personally for the future of off-campus library services involves the drift towards increasing disparity between the technology-rich and poor." The inclusion of technology depends on services demands of those institutions, "say, the technology course," in terms of upgrading hardware, software, and having access to technical services for maintenance and training. Thus, while technology can be used as a means of linking the world, it can also act as a very harsh divider between the "have" and the "have not". Therefore, librarians and others are charged to integrate other modalities of communication and service delivery to ensure that all distance students have access to information services for their studies. This is particularly important in developing countries where distance education is a channel to expand educational opportunities but where access to technology is extremely limited to large urban areas and to those who have the economic ability to purchase technological and communication services.

6.13 Service Delivery

The delivery of library and information services to those who learn at a distance is undisputedly the most pressing challenge that distance education librarian will encounter. Distance librarianship demands that libraries and librarians recognise that their roles have transformed from being custodial in orientation to become cutting edge in nature, particularly with respect to the delivery of information services. Distance education and librarianship demands that students are placed at the centre of the educational paradigm. There must be a shift from institutional-centred programmes and activities to a focus that centres on strategies to help the student overcome the array of challenges caused by distance and temporal factors. Flexibility must be a cardinal parameter. Distance students must have the ability to access library and information students when, where and how they choose. In response to meeting these requirements, the library at James Cook University sees that it must be "responsive and innovative" to meet the library and information needs of its students. It sees distance education as introducing a new marketplace into the profession. To keep and expand its share of demand for distance education services, a university sees that a flexible approach is a critical and necessary factor. In addition to traditional delivery mechanisms libraries must introduce bold and innovative strategies into their delivery process. The strategies must be deployed to deliver the gamut of services that distance learners require, including document delivery; bibliographic instruction; information literacy instruction; reference services; interlibrary loans and access to electronic resources. In traditional librarianship, information seekers go to an information service point to access the information they need. In distance services, the information must be sent to the student. Allied to this factor is the need to have an expeditious document delivery service. Time and distance are real foes when distance students try to access information. The institutional of procedures and channels to get information to students quickly must be an important aspect of distance librarianship. Another new feature of distance library service is the creation of research assistants and others who act as intermediaries between the information seeker and the information source. The existence of intermediaries who link the information source and the information seeker represents a new professional paradigm in librarianship. To bridge the gap between the information source and the information seeker it is necessary to use a variety of delivery strategies to take the information to the student. The use of technology features heavily in this regard, particularly in developed countries. According to Magusin and Johnson (2004), the use of OPACs, online systems and services, networked databases, and other information providers, as well as other technologically dependant information services, are found in many distance education library and information services in these countries. The low cost of technology, cheap communications charges, and widespread access to these facilities makes the deployment of technological-based information services an important modality to provide access to information in distance learning. Once these systems of information transfer are available for distance learners, it makes it possible to extend their use to on-campus teaching and learning, thereby introducing new paradigms in information delivery in library services.

6.14 Continuing Education for Distance Librarianship

Librarians need continuing education to keep current with developments in DE and DL. Whilst there are no formal DL courses, many stand-alone conferences, seminars, and workshops have a DL component. Watson (2006) opined that distance librarians should attend DE conferences as well as library conferences to network with distance educators, keep up to date on trends, developments, and issues in DE, and to sensitise distance educators to the benefits of DE library support services. There is also professional literature on DL, online librarianship, and DE-oriented sites.

6.15 Distance Library Services in Developing Countries

Historically, libraries in developing countries have been under-resourced, under-staffed, and remote from the distance learner. Generally, these libraries were unable to provide the range of services and materials needed, especially to support post-secondary education, and did not have hours of operation that were convenient for the distance learner. These factors remain significant challenges in the developing world, and for the institutions that provide DL services in such locations.

The following methods will help overcome some of these challenges:

- Rotating book boxes and other temporary "libraries" between pre-determined locations, such as community centres.

- Collaborative and reciprocal borrowing arrangements between local and regional institutions and public libraries, such as partnerships with British Council Libraries.

- Developing pre-packaged primary, secondary, and tertiary library resources for circulation.

- Establishing "distance library corners" in other libraries, e.g., "IGNOU library corners" throughout India.

- Establishing sub-regional groupings of libraries to support distance learning.

- Establishing information delivery partnerships with a broad range of institutions.

- Using mobile libraries, including buses, book-boats, and donkey libraries.
- Using commercial delivery services, such as courier services.

6.16 Summary

Distance educators and administrators must appreciate the critical role that libraries play in providing support services for DE, and institutions must provide financial backing for staff, facilities, and resources. Librarians, in turn, need to stay in touch with the changing needs of DE students and faculty. As Mark G. R. McManus puts it, "libraries must be active, political and effective builders of learning knowledge structures" if they are to provide effective, quality library and information services for DE.

6.17 References

Adekanmbi, G. (1993). Transformation in distance education: In search of a paradigm. In Scriven, B., Lunden, R., & Ryan, Y. (Eds.), *Distance Education in the Twenty-First Century* (pp. 336-340).

Association of College and Research Libraries (ACRL). (2008). Guidelines for distance learning library services.

Boylston, Massachussetts. (2016). Boylston's 2015 Annual Town Report. http://archives.lib.state.ma.us/handle/2452/428804

Hanover Research (2011). Trends in global distance learning. Retrieved from http://www.hanoverresearch.com/wp-content/uploads/2011/12/Trends-in-Global-Distance-Learning-Membership.pdf

Jagannathan, N. (2006). Library without walls for distance learners of South Asian region: A dream far-fetched. The Fourth Pan-Commonwealth Forum on Open Learning, Jamaica.

Lockerby, R., Lynch, D., Sherman, J., & Nelson, E. (2004). Collaboration and Information Literacy. *Journal of Library Administration, 41*(1-2).

Magusin, E., & Johnson, K. (2004). Collaborating on Electronic Course Reserves to Support Student Success. In Mahoney, P. (Ed.), *The Eleventh Off-Campus Library Services Conference Proceedings: Scottsdale, Arizona, May 5-7, 2004.* Mount Pleasant, MI: Central Michigan University (pp. 189-195).

Munde, G. & Marks, K. (2009). *Surviving the future: Academic libraries, quality, and assessment.* London, England: Chandos Publishing.

Oladejo, A. M. & Gesinde, M. A. (2014). Trends and Future Directions in Open and Distance Learning Practice in Africa. *Journal of Education and Practice (Online), 5*(18), 132.

Orr, D. & Wallin, M. (2001). Information literacy and flexible delivery: Creating a conceptual framework and model. *The Journal of Academic Librarianship, 27*(6), 457-463.

Ryan, M. (1997). Education Casts Wide Net. *Tech Web News.*

UNESCO. (2001). Distance education in the E-9 countries: the development and future of distance education programmes in the nine high-population countries. Paris: UNESCO.

Vlasenko, L. & Bozhok, N. (2014). *Advantages and disadvantages of distance learning*. Ukraine: National University of Food Technologies, Ukraine.

Watson, E. (2006). "Panel Description: Libraries Without Walls." The Fourth Pan Commonwealth forum on Open Learning, Jamaica.

Watson, E.F. (1992). *Library services to distance learners: A report*. Vancouver: Commonwealth of Learning.

Watson, E. F., Jagannathan, N., & Carnegie, J. (1996). *Library services to distance learners in the Commonwealth: A reader*. Vancouver: Commonwealth of Learning.

Watson, T. (2006). *Organising and Managing Work*. London: Pearson Education.

Chapter 7

Performance Management in an ODeL Institution

Rittah Kasowe

Zimbabwe Open University

Abstract

This chapter provides a valuable opportunity to explore the status of performance management systems to be used in ODeL higher education institutions since it is a complex and difficulty reality if procedures are not well followed. Introduction and development of a performance management system highlight the tensions between collegiality and managerialism, which often lead to knee-jerk debates about academic freedom among academics in ODeL institutions. The chapter highlights the need for staff development initiatives to improve management capacity and change management skills in ODeL institutions considering the goal system and expectancy theories. "It will explain through various models that clear performance management needs to be an integrated collaborative effort that draws on the experiences and expertise of both academic and support staff and transcends traditional distinctions between academic and support staff in higher education.

Keywords: Performance; Management; Open and Distance E-learning

***

7.0 Introduction

This chapter explores the importance of Performance management, its strength, and its weaknesses in ODeL institutions. It further discusses monitoring of ODeL academic staff performance to improve performance management. Furthermore, the chapter elaborates on how e-learning can be embraced in the performance of academics in ODeL institutions. Finally, the chapter discusses the link between organisationl culture and performance management system and the model and leadership roles to be practiced in order to improve the performance management system in ODeL institutions.

7.1 The concept of Performance Management

A performance management system has been variously described by authors as a combination of several functions and processes that have been carefully planned and carried out with the intention of achieving predetermined organisational objectives through employees' work performance (Aguinis, 2013; Armstrong, 2009; Sousa, De Nijs & Hendriks, 2010; Taticchi, Balachandran & Tonelli, 2012). Performance management is the integration of performance appraisal systems with broader human resource systems as a means of aligning employees' work behavior with the organisation's goals. Performance management should be an ongoing, interactive process designed to enhance employee capability and facilitate productivity. It is true that universities can respond to the challenges of the changing higher education environment and the effective management of performance at organisational, institutional, and individual level are therefore critical to success.

Therefore, performance management is considered as an integral and inalienable managerial function in any organisational setting (Islam & Rasad, 2006). This is moreso true as organisational managers attempt to devise an objective criterion that measures the performance of employees, both as individuals and group, and to determine the extent to which such performances have contributed to the overall achievement of business effectiveness (Stanton & Navenkis, 2011). It provides a mechanism through which organisational rewards are objectively matched with individual employee's contribution to the achievement of organisational goals. The complexity involved in the design and implementation of this performance measurement criterion has, over the years, posed a challenging operational consideration for HR managers (Saeed & Shahbaz, 2011). Notwithstanding the complexity and challenges that are associated with this performance management activity, it remains the responsibility of management to provide a link between organisational effectiveness and employee performance.

Performance Measurement is a cycle of never-ending improvement. It plays an important role in identifying and tracking progress against organisational goals, identifying opportunities for improvement, and comparing performance against both internal and external standards. In an ODeL university, performance management highlights some of the influences and barriers amongst the organisations, stakeholders, and academic staff, administrative staff, and students. Performance management includes activities that ensure goals are consistently being met in an effective and efficient manner. It can focus on the performance of an organisation, a department, an employee, or even the processes to build a product or service, as well as many other areas. Performance management is the systematic process that compels an ODeL university to involve its employees, as individuals and members of a group, in improving organisational effectiveness in the accomplishment of its vision, mission and goals (Islam & Rasad, 2006).

Employee Performance Management includes:

- Planning work and setting expectations
- Continuously monitoring performance
- Developing the capacity to perform
- Periodically rating performance

Performance management is the current buzzword and is the need in the current times of cutthroat competition and organisational battle for leadership. It involves the integration of performance appraisal systems with broader human resource systems as a means of aligning employees and work behavior with the organisation's goals. In an ODeL university, performance management should be an ongoing, interactive process designed to enhance employee capability and facilitate productivity. It is a goal-oriented process directed towards ensuring that organisational processes are in place to maximise the productivity of employees, teams, and ultimately, the organisation. It is a major player in accomplishing organisational strategy in that it involves measuring and improving the value of the workforce. PM includes incentive goals and the corresponding incentive values so that the relationship can be clearly understood and communicated. There is a close relationship between incentives and performance.

7.2 Changing Nature in the ODeL Educational Sector

An academic revolution has taken place in higher education and in ODeL institutions, particularly in the past half century marked by a paradigm shift in scope and opportunity. Over the years, the higher education system has become an enterprise having much of business orientation with all its exposure to fierce competition at different levels of stakeholders. With unprecedented growth of knowledge typically in information and communication followed by globalisation shrinking the world into a global village, competitiveness has become a decisive force of growth. As a part of ODeL institutions' integration into the world economy, the role played by potential foreign participants needs a special mention. The impact of potential entrants on higher education systems can be felt in most of the functional areas like access, equity, and quality. Moreover, in view of the inherent lapses in the regulatory structure of the system, unregulated foreign participation may lead to unfair and exploitative practices; to mention a few high capitation fees, misrepresentation of courses and corruption in admission process which may further accentuate the functional and ideological differences. Quality and Accreditation, Public-Private Partnerships, Governance Knowledge are the factors by which employees in the higher e-learning educational institutions are evaluated.

7.3 Theories Underpinning Performance Management

Performance management is broadly conceptualised within the framework of motivational theories as Kandula (2006) argued that unless the motivational composition of individuals is correctly understood and managed effectively, no performance could ever be successful. Therefore, performance excellence comes from people who are well motivated. This treatise is underpinned by the goal-setting theory and expectancy theories (Atkinson & Shaw, 2006) respectively.

7.3.1 Goal-Setting Theory

Goal-setting theory is essentially premised on the understanding that some individuals perform better when specific goals are set, as there is the tendency for them to remain focused and expend additional efforts to achieve set goals (Locke & Latham, 1990). The theory is predicated on the argument that (1) individuals have different goals, (2) act to achieve such goals if there is a chance of succeeding and (3) the value of the goal affects the level of motivation (Locke & Latham, 1990). The theory further postulates that not only does assigning specific goals to individuals or teams result in enhancement of performance but also enhances goal acceptance through employee involvement and increases the challenges of goals, leading to increased motivation and improved performance. Apart from being challenging, goals should also be clearly stipulated and have a feedback mechanism installed. Involving employees in the goal-setting process is crucial for performance management to be effective and successful.

7.3.2 Expectancy Theory

Vroom (1964) posited the expectancy theory on three basic factors: valence, instrumentality, and expectancy. Valence refers to the value, that is, the attractiveness of the task outcomes (e.g., rewards); instrumentality is the degree of expectation that improved job performance will lead to the desired task outcomes and the expectation that increased effort is perceived to lead to increased job performance (outcomes). Therefore, the greater the value of a set of rewards and higher the probability that receiving each of these rewards depends upon effort, the greater the effort that will be expended in achieving the set outcome. The applicability of the expectancy theory found empirical support in a study conducted by Aguinis (2013), which demonstrated that PMSs are more effective when results (performance) are directly tied to the reward system (valence).

7.4 The Growth of Performance Management in ODeL University Education

The use of indicators of performance as a way of managing and improving performance in education is now so widespread across universities that it is difficult to imagine educational life without them. Yet, they are relatively recent in their current form and differ in significant ways from previous practice, for example, providing data on examination and success rates.

Policymakers have always collected data on the functioning of education systems, and have drawn on these data to monitor systems, identify trends and promote change. There has been a related policy goal of shifting teaching staff from a perceived overemphasis on the teaching process to a stronger focus on attainment outcomes, together with a desire to increase the accountability of the teaching profession.

7.5 Performance Management of an ODeL University Education Process

The production metaphor for an ODeL university needs to be taken literally. The product and the production process are inspected and moulded into comparable terms, and the results are presented to the potential buyers who are the students and stakeholders. The motive for the transformations is the same when expressed in market terms: to raise the quality of the production process and thereby to improve the product and develop a "competitive edge" vis-á-vis the competitors within and outside the higher education organisation field. It is difficult if not impossible to assess the quality of the production process and its results in an ODeL university. This does not mean, of course, that attempts should not constantly be made. Although it's known that teaching evaluations establish only the popularity of the lecturers/ teachers and the quantitative indicators measure what can be measured, but not what it is important to measure, the activity still flourishes. This is because the market requires detailed information about both production and product. Knowledge about the product or its technology is not enough to win over the competition. All universities obviously claim that their knowledge production is superior to that of others, in terms of the process itself and its results. Thus, if an ODeL institution is to enter the competition for resources, attention, or legitimacy, it must be possible to compare with conventional higher education institutions. The ODeL university is itself a powerful standardiser as it sets the criteria for higher education certificates. What the university is not accustomed to, however, is to think about itself as an object of standardisation. ODeL universities have been subject to various institutional pressures which have led to the introduction of new accounting practices and new performance measurement systems. Research performance is usually measured by the number of publications in well-accredited academic journals, with the international rankings of these journals being used as an indicator of quality.

Like other conventional universities, teaching performance in ODeL universities also relate to the number of students, the degrees awarded, and the "quality" of the education provided. Hence in assessing teaching quality, students' experiences, and perceptions play an important role (Bogt & Scapens, 2011). Performance indicators and external quality evaluations are an integral aspect of the new model of distant steering, and several countries have introduced some degree of performance-based funding. There has been a growing appetite for performance and quality measures from both higher education public and private stakeholders, as well as from the HEIs themselves. Of particular concern to policy makers is the magnitude of non-completion, often perceived as a waste of financial and human resources. Despite the adoption and development of sophisticated quality assurance systems in most ODeL universities, recently, failures and inefficiencies in the learning process have not been eradicated (OECD, 2012). In the framework of performance management, ODeL higher education is seen as a process for transforming inputs (notably students' time, academics' time, consumables, and the services of equipment) into outputs, which can be broadly classified as relating to teaching, research, community and university service, innovation, and industrialisation. Outcomes are the products of a university in the long run and include, for instance, building a well-educated society. All these processes need to be monitored and controlled. At the end, the output and the outcome are measured against pre-established goals and, if there is a difference between these and the actual outputs/outcomes, corrective action occurs. If working well, a PMS should provide information on important matters, promote appropriate behaviour, provide mechanisms for accountability and control, and create a mechanism for intervention and learning. Indicators drawn from all five sub-domains are important for policy purposes. The increasingly popular alternative of examining outcomes alone ignores important differences in ODeL institutional context, including both invested resources and differences in practice that may be largely responsible for variation in outcomes.

7.6 Importance of Performance Management in ODeL Higher Educational Institutions

Today, there is a constant need to measure and quantify activities and performance in universities. Higher education institutions, including ODeL institutions, need to comply with government mandates and compete globally for researchers and students, review programmes, substantiate accreditation, and make strategic decisions about whether to build on existing strengths or develop new areas.

Business performance management is not a very new concept in the field of management. A performance management system can serve many important purposes within an organisation by motivating employees, strengthening organisational goals, and facilitating discussion of ideas and areas for improvement. This is designed to promote interaction and feedback between management and employees, establish expectations for individual work performance, and serve as a foundation for rewarding higher performer top employees. Performance Management can help the institution to identify ways in which to improve its performance and provides the opportunity to discuss career direction and prospects. It presents the opportunity to plan for and set objectives to further develop employees' careers. In ODeL universities, performance management will help staff to gain any additional training or mentoring which can act as a basis for developing future succession plans. ODeL institutions must be prepared to operate in a competitive education market, assuming greater managerial autonomy for each of them, a flexible regulatory framework and adequate financing. Today, being competitive as institutions of higher education, ODeL institutions require more openness and transparency, review of services, and a digital marketing culture.

7.7 Strength of Performance Management in an ODel Institution

Performance management seems to enjoy the support of top management and a high participation rate of staff in the annual performance appraisal in the institutions that have already implemented formal systems and the development of a more formalised system. The current formalised systems indicate that academic staff and managers value the opportunity to have a discussion on performance since it provides an important structural moment to reflect on performance. Employees in ODeL institutions appreciate efforts to increase the flexibility in performance management systems since there is creation of a more balanced perspective on academic workloads. The computerised system in ODeL focus on strategic alignment and help to enhance management capacity and strategic thinking, since the system provides managers with easily accessible detailed information about staff.

7.8 Weakness of Performance Management

Format and Procedures

In ODeL institutions the computerisation of performance management systems provides a way of getting around the debates since formats and procedures can be manipulated more easily. If management lacks capacity, it will complicate the functioning of the systems. Differing levels of knowledge and understanding of performance management by different levels of management might lead to unrealistic expectations, which view performance management as a product instead of a process. The lack of capacity might relate to the subjectivity of the more informal collegial operating system that lacks transparency of criteria and rating practices. Most ODeL public universities struggle to give staff remuneration increases that are big enough to make a difference in performance. If diverse rewards, including development opportunities and promotion systems, are not availed, this might affect the performance management system.

7.9 Monitoring of ODeL Academic Staff Performance: A New Trend

Managers of higher education institutions now expect employees in the sector (particularly academics) to embrace organisational innovation practice that is typical of the private sector organisations (Hill, 2010; Parsons & Slabbert, 2004; T rk, 2007). Ironically, such practice conflicts directly with the age-long established tradition of a self-defining work mechanism expressed within the context of autonomy and academic freedom (Pityana, 2004). However, the implementation of PMS in ODeL institutions of higher learning suggests that the work roles of academics are being defined by managers based on values and purposes that are dictated by the market economy rather than the academic enterprise (Pityana, 2004). This management tendency has been described as the 'new public management,' which is oriented towards outcomes and efficiency through better management of public budget (Shishkina, 2008). The introduction of this managerial approach in ODeL higher education sector could be problematic as managing a university is quite different from that of a conventional university. Therefore, the introduction of this newfound management practice in the ODeL university system should be carefully considered as this could severely compromise the principle of work autonomy and academic freedom.

Management of ODeL higher education institutions has been under pressure by the higher education authority to increase student enrolment and research productivity without a corresponding increase in budgetary allocation (Parsons & Slabbert, 2004). A possible way of achieving the government's demand by management is the implementation of PMS which measures work outputs in quantitative terms. However, available studies indicate that the operationalisation of the PMS in ODeL higher education institutions around the world is challenging (Mapesela & Strydom, 2004; Osei-Owusu, 2013; Tam, 2008). Further literature resists any attempt to commercialise academic institutions whose social objective is the production and dissemination of knowledge through research and teaching (Shishkina, 2008).

The outcome of a study conducted by (Mapesela & Strydom, 2004) in three higher education institutions in South Africa regarding the introduction and development of a performance management system in ODeL institutions could bring the tension between collegiality and managerialism as it affects academic freedom. This tension reflects the outcome in the business sector, and such an outcome is difficult to manage in an ODeL university system that is complex and diverse (Tam, 2008). The most controversial issues associated with designing a workable PMS for academics in ODeL institutions is to first determine the content of the scholarly activities that would be incorporated into it (e.g., teaching, research, community engagement, academic citizenship innovation, and industrialisation) (Martz, McKenna & Siegall, 2001). Therefore, for PMS to be effective in the ODeL higher education environment, a typical business performance management model and approach needs to be adapted to the peculiarities of higher education institutions.

Academics have contested the validity of PMS arguing that it fails to measure all the activities it is supposed to measure (Pienaar & Bester, 2007). Therefore, PMS should be designed to incorporate a full range of academic activities performed by academic staff for it to be accepted and trusted. An effective PMS should account for the complex linkages between task performance and time factor. Based on a comparative study of some universities in the United States, United Kingdom, Nigeria, Australia, and South Africa, Molefe (2010) concluded that the introduction of PMS will likely be resisted by academics if its performance assessment criteria do not consider the following broad issues:

- Teaching workload or distribution of workload between members of the departments
- Results of student evaluation based on an acceptable format used by the faculty
- Student numbers per course research output with emphasis on accredited output
- Corporate citizenship which encompasses service to the community without compensation.

The debate around the implementation of the PMS in academic institutions is a balanced one. While some academics argue that the approach is unethical to the academic culture, others submit that PMS can improve performance in the higher education system. For example, Tam (2008) emphasises that the introduction of performance indicators in an academic institution can motivate its members to work harder, especially academics who are inclined and motivated by extrinsic rewards such as money and other financial rewards. However, people who are intrinsically motivated would be disinclined to support the PMS (Ryan & Deci, 2000). Instead, they would be motivated by factors such as recognition or quality of life, including factors such as leisure and holiday with family and friends.

7.10 Workload Model in Open Distance E-Learning Institutions

An ODeL system of education is an approach that seeks to remove all unnecessary physical barriers to learning to provide more people with a meaningful platform to acquire higher education (Saide, 2009). The teaching methodology in an ODeL university does have implications for the workload model of academics. Performance of their primary responsibility of teaching involves substantial administrative engagement, unlike their contemporaries in conventional universities. These cumbersome administrative duties impact significantly the time available to conduct research by ODeL academics, yet research productivity accounts for a substantial amount of subsidy accruable to the university from the Department of Higher Education.

The administrative bottleneck in the ODeL course delivery is embedded in the design of the system, and this should not be compromised at the expense of research productivity. Tutors are employed in the ODeL system to provide academic support for learners (Maimela, 2016). These tutors are managed by the academic staff of the institution. This places additional responsibility on lecturers, and this has further implications on their research productivity. However, the impact of tutor management by lecturers in the ODeL system has been described as a negligible fraction of lecturers' workload as study and other learning resources are distributed to learners using internet facilities (Saide, 2009). This description may not be totally accurate as teaching and instructions through the distance education system involve the use of printed course materials and telecommunication devices such as Twitter, podcasts, and smartphones. All these processes are managed by academic staff. As a result, academics in ODeL institutions are office bound with fixed working hours, expending most of their productive time developing study materials and responding to student enquiries daily. This no doubt negatively impacts negatively the amount of time available for research, which is a critical component of the 'Key Performance' area in the PMS.

7.11 Embracing E-Learning and Performance of Academics in ODeL Institutions

ODeL practices are changing. New fields of study have emerged, policies have been revised, quality culture has emerged, student services have improved, new ICT-based delivery modes have been explored, and a variety of collaborative relationships have been developed. This section cannot provide a full picture of all the innovations and good practices of ODeL in progress. Instead, it reports a snapshot of innovative and good practices of e-learning in ODeL institutions based on the survey results and other available resources. Open education, open admission, innovative use of technologies, and promoting equality of higher education for both young and adult learners contribute to national development and lifelong learning society. The provision of quality education frequently appears in ODeL institutions' vision statements and mission. E-learning is increasingly being looked to by many ODeL institutions as an economical way of expanding their services, widening opportunities for students around the world, and making effective use of emerging technologies. In fact, quite a few ODeL institutions have integrated e-learning components in their ODeL services. Hence e-learning is not a supplementary mode of education but the main form of ODeL utilising digital materials produced by academics. This compels ODeL institutions to carry out e-learning course evaluations and monitor academic activities based on specific QA measures. Important QA measures include:

- Experts' evaluation of the appropriateness of e-learning development and objectives, accuracy of the contents, and structure of the contents before developing any e-learning course

- Experts' assessment of pedagogical strategies, multimedia components, user interface, and course management functions of each e-learning course during the course development

- Seeking comments from the public, including students during the course development, and

- Revising e-learning courses and services based on feedback from students and experts after the course delivery.

The new fields of e-learning identified in the cases above are all in fast-changing professional service areas and they require regular updates of the contents, continuous interactions with students, and multimedia supports. E-learning, compared with other modes of learning, can easily and rapidly adapt to the changing needs of students. Course contents of any e-learning programme can be updated upon needs without major cost increases, personalised interactions can be provided readily, and huge amounts of multimedia materials can be provided virtually. In this regard, the above-mentioned cases which focus on service industry sectors present good examples of selecting appropriate fields of study for an ODeL e-learning environment.

7.12 Performance Management System and Organisational Culture in an ODeL Institution

In an ODeL institution, the decision to introduce a PMS requires careful consideration by management of the compatibility of the intended change with the prevailing culture and tradition of the organisation. Previous literature stipulates that the introduction of a PMS is capable of transforming employee values, attitudes, and behaviour, thus leading to an eventual change in the overall culture of the organisation (Ogbonna, 2007). Culture evolves over a long period of time, and once established, becomes extremely difficult to change (Hatch & Cunliffe, 2006). An effective change in organisational culture involves changes in policies and procedures, and most important, managing the subconscious unaware assumptions and values which guide people's behaviour (Kandula, 2006; Ogbonna, 2007). This may imply that changes in ODeL institution's physical structures of the organisation are not capable of transforming established organisational culture and behaviour of academic staff. What is required for an effective change in behaviour is a reorientation of the thinking process from the old ways Open and Distance Learning (ODL), to embrace a new way of doing things, which is Open and Distance electronic Learning (ODeL). Therefore, changing existing organisational culture and employees' behaviour are crucial for the successful implementation of PMS (Robinson et al., 2005). The authors emphasised the traumatic experience that is associated with change, and this explains why employees' resistance to change should be expected by management as a natural phenomenon.

7.13 Employee Perception in the Performance Management System Process?

In an ODeL institution, the management needs to enlist the understanding and cooperation of the category of employees who would be affected by the operationalisation of the PMS. For this to happen, recipients of PMS must perceive the programme to be a fair, just and equitable one (Farndale et al., 2011; Islam & Rasad, 2005; Kavanagh, Benson & Brown, 2007; Luthra & Jain, 2012). It is only then that employees return the intended benefits of PMS to management. One can also reasonably assume that employees will not likely embrace a PMS that they perceived to be biased, unfair and lacking equity in the distribution of organisational outcomes (e.g., promotion, salary increment, research incentives). The whole essence of balancing employee input with reward output is located within the concept of organisational justice (Baldwin, 2006; Greenberg, 1990). Literature of organisational justice postulates an input–output ratio a comparison by an individual employee with those of his or her colleagues and reacts based on the outcome of the assessment. Employees who perceive injustice in the input–output ratio will likely embark on withdrawal activities that include reduced productivity, lateness, sabotage, or resignation from the organisation (Schultz et al., 2003).

7.14 PMS Model in ODeL Higher Educational Institution

One of the most important aspects of management is to monitor and assess the organisational performance. Performance management makes sure that the organisation has achieved its goals and highlight lack of performance wherever apparent. How could this be possible? Where should the starting point be? How should the performance be monitored? How should it be reported? How should the results be used for improving future activities? Answers to all these questions could only be provided by an institutional level performance management system specifically designed for respective organisational purposes. Performance management is usually linked with individuals, and this is not true at all. It should define how an organisation works rather than only individuals. Some people mistakenly assume that performance management is concerned only with appraising and rating a board, management, and staff's performance. This activity is only one part of the overall process.

Performance management is the systematic process of:

i) Planning work and setting expectations

ii) Continually monitoring performance

iii) Developing the capacity to perform

iv) Periodically rating and recording performance

Thus, following these processes will assist ODeL institutions to:

- help determine where an organisation is on its journey towards excellence.

- provide a common language to enable the exchange of ideas and information, both within and outside the organisation.

- integrate existing and planned activities, improving organisational efficiency, and providing a basic structure for the organisation's management system.

7.15 Leadership Roles, Styles, Delegation and Qualities in an ODeL Institution)

To be effective, ODeL institutions need to perform both transformation roles (leadership roles) and transactional roles (managerial). Some of these are:

- Articulating and communicating vision and values

- Formulating long-term policies and strategies

- Introducing and managing new technology and systems
- Inspiring, developing, and motivating juniors
- Managing juniors, colleagues, and seniors
- Culture building
- Internal customer management
- External customer management
- Managing unions and associations.

The management in ODeL institutions ought to:

- constantly guide staff and treat them with affection like how a parent treats his children; that is, applying a Benevolent or Paternalistic leadership style.

- closely and constantly supervise, direct, and remind employees of their duties and responsibilities; that is, applying the critical leadership style.

- develop the competencies of his staff and treats them as mature adults; that is, applying the developmental/empowering leadership style.

In an ODeL institution, employer satisfaction is the key indicator, and the institution's purpose is to identify who the key employer/stakeholders are and considering their wants and needs. Thus, an ODeL institution should focus on the strategy according to employer/stakeholders' demands. It should then focus on what processes are needed to deliver these strategies. An ODeL institution needs strategies because it wants to deliver value to employers/ stakeholders. Therefore, the starting point for any discussion of measurement must be the employers/stakeholders.

7.16 Evaluating the Effectiveness of Performance in ODeL Higher Education Institutions

Unless there are proper systems in place for collecting data and monitoring, analysing, and reporting on the information, then it will not be possible to evaluate performance with any confidence. There are several ways to evaluate performance, and even quality-related activities can be coasted using the P-A-F model that deals with 'prevention costs,' 'appraisal costs,' and 'failure costs.' It is assumed that expenditure on prevention and improvement activities should reap benefits, such as: a more productive workforce, reduced failure costs, lower appraisal costs, and an increased customer base. Prevention costs:

which are incurred before actual operation can therefore be planned, for example:

- Setting specifications for intended products, outcomes, or service requirements.

- Appraisal costs: which are associated with the stakeholders' evaluation of the organisation's products, outcomes, or services.

- Carrying out quality audits in relation to the maintenance of standards

- Failure costs: which are incurred either before the product or services reaches the students (internal) or are not detected until after transfer to the stakeholders (external); internal comprises of poor organisation, communication, or doing unnecessary work and reworking to rectify errors or mistakes; and external includes the costs involved in handling and resolving stakeholder complaints.

7.17 Summary

The concept of PM is present in the segment of ODeL Higher Education Institutions. However, it needs to be improved upon and tailored to the needs and vision of the institution. Universities need to implement PM procedures to improve the performance of individuals and align individual goals and objectives with the university strategic goals. This will improve the overall performance of the ODeL university to achieve its intended end. This chapter provided a valuable opportunity to explore the status of performance management systems to be used in ODeL higher education institutions since it is a complex and difficulty reality if procedures are not well followed. Introduction and development of a performance management system highlighted the tensions between collegiality and managerialism, which often lead to knee-jerk debates about academic freedom among academics in ODeL institutions. The chapter highlighted the need for staff development initiatives to improve management capacity and change management skills in ODeL institutions considering the Goal system and expectancy theories. It was eluded that performance management is the lightning conductor for poor people management and enhances the development of strategic staff development initiatives to help ODeL institutions deal with the demands of a fast-changing higher education environment and e-learning. It was explained that clear performance management needed to be an integrated collaborative effort that draws on the experiences and expertise of both academic and support staff and transcends traditional distinctions between academic and support staff in higher education. The development of this complex system needs to draw on the expertise of management, support, and academic staff for it to be successful. The chapter suggested that ODeL higher education institutions need to follow gradual introduction of hybrid approach that allows for a process of institutional transformation and systemic adjustment to incorporate e-learning. The chapter clearly spelt out that the outcomes of performance management in ODeL institutions should be employee satisfaction, motivation, and commitment, and to help the university to enhance accurate and constructive feedback.

7.18 References

Aguinis, H. (2013). *Performance management* (2nd ed.). Upper Saddle River, NJ: Pearson Prentice Hall.

Armstrong, M. (2009). *Human resource management practice* (10th ed.). Philadelphia: Kogan.

Atkinson, C., & Shaw, S. (2006). Managing performance. In R. Lucas, B. Lupton, & H. Mathieson (Eds.), *Human resource management in an international context*. London: CIPD.

Baldwin, S. (2006). *Organisational justice*. HR Network Paper MP73. Brighton: Institute for Employment Studies.

Bogt, H. J. & Scapens, R. W. (2011). *The management of performance in universities NPM and some of its effects*. Paper presented at the EGPA Conference, Bucharest.

Bowman, J. (1994). At last, an alternative to performance appraisal. Total quality management. *Public Administration Review, 54*(2), 129-136.

Farndale, E., Van Ruiten, J., Kelliher, C., & Hope-Hailey, V. (2011). The influence of perceived employee voice on organizational commitment: An exchange perspective. *Human Resource Management, 50*(1), 113-129.

Fox, C., & Shirkey, K. (1997). Employee performance appraisal: The keystone made of clay. In C. Ban, & N. Riccucci (Eds.), *Public personnel management* (pp. 189–204). New York: Longman.

Greenberg. (1990). Organisational Justice: Yesterday and tomorrow. *Journal of Management, 16*(2), 399-432.

Hatch, M. J., & Cunliffe, A. L. (2006). *Organisation theory: Modern, symbolic, and postmodern perspectives* (2nd ed.). Oxford: Oxford University Press.

Hill, C. (2010). *External pressures bring changes to higher education*. Retrieved October 31 2012. http://www.facultyfocus.com/articles/distance-learning/external-pressures-bringchanges-to-higher-education/

Islam, R., & Rasad, S. B. M. (2006). Employee performance evaluation by AHP: A case study. *Asia Pacific Management Review, 11*(3), 163-176.

Kandula, S. R. (2006). *Performance management strategies-interventions-drivers*. New Delhi: PHI Learning Pvt Ltd.

Kavanagh, P., Benson, J., & Brown, M. (2007). Understanding performance appraisal fairness. *Asian Pacific Journal of Human Resource Management, 45*(2), 132-150.

Locke, E. A., & Latham, G. P. (1990). *A theory of goal setting and task performance*. Upper Saddle River, NJ: Prentice Hall.

Luthra, P., & Jain, M. (2012). India's performance management problem. *Gallup Business Journal* (Online). Retrieved February 14 2012 from http://business

journal.gallup.com/content/153278/india-performancemanagement-problem.aspx

Maimela E. M. & Samuel M. O. (2016). Perception of performance management system by academic staff in an open distance learning higher education environment. *SA Journal of Human Resource Management, 14*(1).

Mapesela, M.L.E., & Strydom, F. (2004). November). *Performance management of academic staff in South African higher education system: A developmental project.* Paper presented at the OECD Conference on Trends in the Management of Human Resource in Higher Education, University of the Free State, Bloemfontein, South Africa.

Martz, B., McKenna, J., & Siegall, M. (2001). Applying a standard performance model to a university setting. *Business Process Management Journal, 7*(2), 100-112.

Molefe, G.N. (2010). Performance measurement dimensions for lecturers at selected universities: An international perspective. *South African Journal of Human Resource Management, 8*(1).

Molefe, G.N. (2012). Performance measurement model and academic staff: A survey at selected universities in South Africa and abroad. *African Journal of Business Management, 6*(15), 5249-5267.

OECD (2012). Assessment of Higher Education Learning Outcomes, Feasibility Study Report.

Ogbonna, E. (2007). Managing culture: Fantasy or reality? *Human Resource Journal, 3*(2), 42–54.

Osei-Owusu, M. (2013). *Performance management in Higher Education Institution – Review of experience.* Management in Higher Education Institution.

Parsons, P. G., & Slabbert, A. D. (2001). Performance management and academic workload in higher education. *South African Journal of Higher Education, 15*(3).

Pienaar, C., & Bester, C. L. (2007). The retention of academics in the early career phase. *South African Journal of Human Resource Management, 6*(2).

Pityana, N.B. (2004, April). *Higher education in South Africa: Future perspectives.* Keynote address delivered at Bill Venter/Altron Literacy Awards 2003, Johannesburg.

Robinson, H.S., Carrillo, P. M., Anumba, C. J., & A-Ghassani, A. M. (2005). Review and implementation of performance management models in construction engineering organizations. *Construction Innovation: Information, Process, Management, 5*(4).

Ryan, R. M., & Deci, E. L. (2000). Intrinsic and extrinsic motivations: Classic definitions and new directions. *Contemporary Educational Psychology, 25*(1), 54-67.

Saeed, M. K. & Shahbaz, N. (2011). Employees' perceptions about the effectiveness of performance appraisals: The case of Pakistan. *SIU Journal of Management, 1*(1).

Schultz, H., Bagraim, J., Potgieter, T., Viedge, C. & Werner, A. (2003). Page 4 of 11 *Original Research.* http://www.sajhrm.co.za

Shishkina, V. (2008). New public management strategies: Implications for universities in emerging economies [Unpublished master's thesis]. Blekinge Institute of Technology, Karlskrona, Sweden.

South African Institute for Distance Education (SAIDE). (2009). _SAIDE policy on open educational resources._ Retrieved November 23 2012, from https://www. google. com/search?sourceid=navclient&ie=UTF

Sousa, C. A. A., De Nijs, W. F., & Hendriks, P. H. J. (2010). Secrets of the beehive: Performance management in university research organisations. _Human Relations, 16_(9).

Stanton, P. & Nankervis, A. (2011). Linking HRM, performance management and organisational effectiveness: Perceptions of managers in Singapore. _Asia Pacific Review, 17_(1).

Tam, W. H. K. (2008). _Academics' perspectives of performance management in a British university context_ [Unpublished PhD thesis]. University of Leicester, Leicester, United Kingdom.

Taticchi, P., Balachandran, K., & Tonelli, F. (2012), Performance measurement and management systems: State of the art, guidelines for design and challenges. _Measuring Business Excellence, 16_(2).

Türk, K. (2007). Performance appraisal and the compensation of academic staff in the University of Tartu. _Baltic Journal of Management, 3_(1).

Vroom, V. H. (1964). _Work and motivation._ Wiley, New York, USA.

Willaert, P., & Willems, J. (2006). Process performance measurement: Identifying KPIs that link process performance to company strategy. _Emerging Trends and Challenges in Information Technology Management, 1_(2).

Chapter 8

ODeL and Inclusion of Vulnerable Students in Higher Education Institutions

Gilliet Chigunwe

Zimbabwe Open University

Abstract

The contributions of this chapter include challenges faced by Higher Education Institutions (HEIs) that the align ODeL model with the United Nations Conventions on the Rights of Persons with Disabilities (UNCRPD), to which most countries world over are signatories. ODeL is a salient model of inclusivity, thus, HEIs stakeholders are encouraged to maximize its usage for effective inclusion. This calls for proper planning of online activities and implementations. The chapter also informs stakeholders in tertiary institutions to observe inclusive policies as they adopt innovative strategies in this COVID-19 period as well as in the post-period. It finally challenges HEIs in Africa to develop digital transformation strategies that are holistic, inclusive, and sustainable for all students in spite of disability or vulnerability.

Keywords: Open and Distance Electronic Learning, Inclusivity, Vulnerable Students, Higher Education Institutions

***

8.0. Introduction

Around the globe, the lives of at least 1.5 billion students and their families have been significantly affected by the school closures caused by the COVID-19 outbreak (UNESCO, 2020). The virus in question has caused havoc and high death rates the world over, thus causing learning institutions to temporarily close and later shift to a home learning mode in most countries. In Africa, governments have recently responded by holding university classes remotely, largely online, to ensure that students continue to study. This chapter explores the high shift into virtual or digital transformation by most Higher Education Institutions (HEIs) that have been precipitated by the COVID-19 situation.

We explore how new technologies, in their various forms, can be utilised in redefining and revolutionising the HEIs mode of delivery. The discussion will be delimitated to HEIs in Zimbabwe and selected African countries. It will, however, explore experiences in some selected countries out of Africa. More so, it will emphasise the use of the ODeL model vis-a–vis inclusivity of vulnerable persons, such as persons with disabilities, girls, and students from rural areas, as well as those from low-income households.

8.1. Corona Virus and ODeL in Higher Education Institutions

Since 24 March 2020, when schools were officially closed in Zimbabwe, less than 40% of the 74% of households with school-aged children engaged in some educational activity (ZIMSTAT, 2020). The situation was worse in rural areas where only 20% did some form of learning (ibid). This implies the extent to which the COVID-19 epidemic has affected the education system, including tertiary activities, not only in Zimbabwe but in Africa and all over the world. In Zimbabwe, as of February 2021, cumulative cases and deaths had risen alarmingly. High accumulation of COVID-19 by nationalities and high death rates have seen educators and learners shift to distance education solutions which are more reliant on the virtual mode in most countries of the world. World Bank Education, Global Practice, and the Organisation Hundred presented the first set of online educational resources to support the continuity of teaching and learning during the 2019-20 COVID-19 pandemic with education leaders around the world. Additional online sources were included to enhance the list to support the continuity of learning for students who have access to the internet and digital devices (ibid). Around the globe, the lives of at least 1.5 billion students and their families have been significantly affected by the school closures caused by the COVID-19 outbreak (UNICEF, 2019). The virus in question has caused havoc and high death rates the world over, thus causing learning institutions to temporarily close and later shift to a home learning mode in most countries. In Africa, governments have recently responded by holding university classes remotely, largely online, to ensure that students continue to study. Like any other country in Africa, Zimbabwe is not exceptional. Most universities have shifted to Open and Distance Electronic Leaning (ODeL).

8.2. ODeL and Higher Education Institutions (HEIs)

ODeL is a different way of learning; there is a physical distance between the learner and the university. In open and distance e-learning, you are responsible for planning your studies and managing your time effectively. In other words, with this mode of learning, one does not attend face-to-face lectures but learn from a distance and connect to the university mostly via internet. This implies that the distance in open and distance e-learning is mostly interaction through a digital format. One wonders about the implications of this setup regarding persons with disabilities, students in rural areas, and low-income groups, as well as the girl child.

The United Nations Convention on the Rights of the Child recognises that state parties shall respect and ensure the rights set forth in the present Convention to each child within their jurisdiction without discrimination of any kind. Whilst this is so, the problem mitigating against the girl child education in most African countries, particularly in reference to Zimbabwe, is an age-long factor that revolves around cultural, social, and religious undertones. A study by Chigunwe and Mpande (2020) revealed that most communities in Zambia and Zimbabwe still perceive a girl child as inferior to the male and hence, most girls there are denied access to education and most of them get into early marriages, where their roles are relegated to that of home maker and child rearer and keeper. On the other hand, in this 21st century, a lot of programmes have been put in place to relegate the education of the girl child in Zimbabwe. In spite of these government and non-governmental efforts, research reveals that the girl child in Zimbabwe continues to be discriminated against from the earliest stages of life, from her childhood and into adulthood (Hegarty, 2018; Chigunwe, 2019). The reasons for the discrepancy include female genital mutilation, son preference, early marriage, violence against women, sexual exploitation, and gender-based educational processes. To counter the social aspect where families opted to educate the boy child when resources were few, the government of Zimbabwe put up a variety of educational facilities that funded both the girl child and boy child including the BEAM and STEM facilities. These programmes targeted vulnerable children such as orphans and those children who excelled in science subjects respectively.

Notable improvement has been made on a girl-child's access to education as a result of numerous intervention programmes of UNESCO, UNICEF, governmental, and non-governmental organisations all over the world, particularly in Africa and Asia (Bellamy, 2012). Moreover, the education aid facilities in Zimbabwe have seen a raise in the education of girl children in the country, from the primary level to the tertiary level. But one wonders how far these facilities continue to close the gap between the girl child and boy child considering the turn of fate in the education system in the country. There has been a shift in the way education is to be offered to all learners in face of the Covid-19 virus, which has seen the closure of schools and the introduction of e-learning to curb the spread of the virus through social distancing. Higher Education Institutions (HEIs) have not been spared by this shift of learning and teaching mode, as most institutions have shifted to an ODeL type of education.

In Open and Distance e-learning, one is responsible for planning his or her studies and managing time effectively. That is, one learns from a distance and is connected to the university mostly via the internet. The implication is that the "distance" in open distance e-learning means that most of the student's interactions with his or her institution will take place at a distance - mostly in digital format.

The concept of Distance Education is the process of providing instruction between a lecturer and students when they are separated by physical distance. In some institutes, a class may have several groups of students located at different places. A variety of technologies are used to deliver courses and programmes to students in a distance education programme, including online interactive videos. Students in Zimbabwe are learning from home, interacting with their lecturers through WhatsApp media, email, SMS, fax, and many other online modes of communication.

Results of a WhatsApp focus group discussion carried out among 10 girl students from two Zimbabwe tertiary institutions revealed that despite the provision of social distancing (COVID restriction requirements), online learning has also seen the safety of the girl child from sexual harassment and abuse (Chigunwe & Mpande, 2020) as they will be enjoying home learning. The results revealed that physical contact with lecturers had exposed most girl children to male lecturers who tended to take advantage of the girl students' vulnerability (ibid). Moreso, it was found that accommodation in most HEIs was limited, thus, most tended to accommodate beginners and final years, this meant that other groups had to seek accommodation in communities surrounding or near their institutions. Such arrangement had seen girl students exposed to serious sexual abuse or indulgence, especially students from low economic status or struggling backgrounds, as they wished to be supported to pay rent and buy food by older men whom they called 'blessers.' Thus, ODeL has been argued by some girls to be a vital 'girl protecting tool' and cost-effective in the sense that they are able to learn, research, write assignments, and submit in the comfort of their homes and home communities.

Review of literature on the education of a girl child brought out that, online learning for the girl child in most African countries is elusive. Mwangi (2014) wrote that a combination of poverty, disease, and backward cultural practices continue to deny the girl child's right to receive education. Even the introduction of free primary education, access to education is remaining a wide dream to many girl children in Africa (ibid). In Kenya, for example, despite the introduction of free primary education which accounted for an increase in enrolment, most girls found themselves out of school owing to several reasons. These included demands for their labour in the homes, such as assisting in after their young siblings, doing house chores, and looking after the sick member of family, just to name a few (Cramm, Lorenzo & Nieboer, 2017). Demands of doing too much house chores by the girl child are still very high in most African families. Such a scenario contradicts with the ODeL mode of learning in that it thwarts effective learning among girl children who will be learning online in their homes. Too much house chores and other demands compromise the girl child's high-grade performance as she will be tired by the time she goes to online learning. Factors influencing quality learning is at the heart of education, and what takes place in the environments of learning is fundamentally important to the future well-being of children, young people, and adults. According to Slade (2019), quality education is one that satisfies basic learning needs and enriches the lives of learners and their overall experience of living.

Thus, ODeL as a mode of teaching and learning in HEIs has its merits in that it provides quality education by connecting the learner and educator online where they can interact face to face despite distance through various online video calls. In Zimbabwe, the Zimbabwe Open University was the only state university that used online learning as its main mode of delivery. Most state universities were conventional, and their main mode of delivery was face-to-face teaching. However, the COVID-19 situation has changed the face of learning among most if not all institutions where mode of learning is shifting to online learning. The purpose of online learning is to protect the learner and educator from contracting the virus, as well as to minimise its spread and deaths. Thus, since institutions may wish to continue to meet students face-to-face, the COVID-19 situation has caused a lot of havoc in terms of deaths such that during the time of writing this manuscript, people in Zimbabwe are under lockdown and in a stay-home environment. Movement was restricted and students were encouraged to interact with their lecturers online as they prepared for their examinations. Thus, ODeL is becoming so significant in all HEIs in Zimbabwe and beyond as long as the Corona Virus persists beyond 2021. ODeL mode cuts off costs in terms of rentals and travel costs as students will be studying in their homes. However, other students argued that ODeL is an exclusive mode of a learning platform that is insensitive to students in the rural areas, where electricity and access to internet is not easy or even possible.

Figure 8.1: Students in the Rural Areas and Access to Internet

Plate 2: Secondary school background of some students enroled in universities.
Source: Author 2021

Zimbabwe's majority population is in a rural area, and some students who are enroled in universities and colleges reside there. Face-to-face interaction had seen most students from the rural area do their studies successfully as they will be using university resources, such as the internet, to research for their assignments and examinations. Moreover, face-to-face enabled them to get clarification of grey areas of their studies by their lecturers.

Students from local universities interviewed in Zimbabwe revealed that online learning is frustrating for students from disadvantaged families in rural areas. It was noted that most cannot access the internet, as they are in parts of the country where there is no electricity or internet facilities, which includes internet cafés. Futrell (2007) argues that ICT can be used to expand and enhance learning opportunities for students by allowing them access to courses not available in their schools and interact with students attending schools in other communities. The implication is that ICT enhances inclusive education in that it enables learners to reach out to knowledge from any corner of the world if a student is connected to internet or has a mobile phone. Gadgets like computers and laptops are not common among rural folks in most parts of Africa. The Zimbabwean government, however, made efforts in doing rural electrification that saw electricity in most part of rural areas, and some computers were donated in some rural schools so that students there would access online educative information. While this was so, a lot of electricity lines were vandalised in many areas of the country, thus drawing back government efforts. This vandalisation had a drawback on rural schools and homes, thus thwarting the students' connectivity to internet and the use of computers in those rural areas. During teaching practice assessments, the author of this chapter noted with concern that donated computers in schools were lying idle in schools due to a lack of electricity, and some computers had been vandalised as well as wrecked. Rural electrification and availability of computers in rural schools could have been viable to HE, as they would utilise the built-in infrastructure in rural schools for ODeL activities, especially in this period of COVID-19 where Higher Education has been made mandatory by the government of Zimbabwe to be mostly online.

Figure 8.2: Mobile Phones and Access to Tertiary Education

Source: Author 2021

Cell phones have been noted to be very reliable in terms of communication in most part of Africa, and are bringing parts of Africa into the digital age. New surveys from the Pew Research Centre show that the majority of adults in Uganda, Tanzania, Kenya, Ghana, Senegal, Nigeria, and South Africa owned cell phones in 2014. Though most people surveyed in the sub-Saharan countries still do not own smartphones, Pew says the widespread adoption of basic cell phones provides a "communication lifeline," connecting people like never before. According to Pew's research, which surveyed about 1000 people in each nation, 89% of adults now own a smartphone or basic cell phone in South Africa and Nigeria, 83% in Senegal and Ghana, 82% in Kenya, 73% in Tanzania, and 65% in Uganda. Research has also revealed that 95% of the Zimbabwean population have cell phones. These cell phones have cascaded to rural areas where even the old people are in possession of them and use them effectively; especially the small simple phones which the Zimbabweans call 'kambudzi.' Mobile phones can be utilised by Higher Education Institutions to connect rural students to the internet and therefore access ODeL facilities. Thus, an ODeL mode through cell phone infrastructure can reach out to those students who are in remote areas since communication providers in Zimbabwe have provided transmitters and boosters in most parts of the country. It was of interest to note that ODeL in HEIs are a very inclusive facility, as it can be accessed not only through computers but through cell phones. The implication of such a facility is that even persons with disabilities can be able to access education from home where there are no infrastructure barriers to access the lecture room.

A study by Chimedza (2010) brought out that most persons with disabilities were failing to access quality education due to social and physical barriers that they experience when trying to access education institutions from primary to tertiary level. Thus, with ODeL mode, students in a wheelchair, for instance, can enrol for a programme online and do his or her studies in the natural environment of their home, hence, no hustles of travelling and frustration of failing or difficulty to access buildings. Of interest to note is that most mobile phones have talking software, which is inclusive to persons with visual impairment, especially those suffering with blindness. Individuals who may face challenges in accessing ODeL mode of learning are those students with visual impairment, specifically students with deafness. Whilst they can see print, long-written English sentences are unintelligible and difficult to understand. Thus, there is a need for gadgets that translate learning mode to sign language. The latter scenario makes mobile phones unreliable to a certain group of students, implying that computers with sign language software may be called for. However, from the author's experience, such gadgets are rare in Zimbabwe or not found at all. But still, such challenges do not completely discredit ODeL as an inclusive facility in HEI, in that infrastructures used for online communication can always be adapted and modified to accommodate needs of learners with special needs. Videos in sign language, for instance, can be installed or placed on Whatsapp platforms by lecturers so that persons with deafness benefit from ODeL mode. Based on existing evidence, the Zimbabwe quality control board, called ZIMCHE, needs to be inclusive in its outlook by ensuring their staff have qualified persons who cater to the inclusion of persons with disabilities in HEIs, be it in the delivery of face-to-face lessons or online lessons.

WhatsApp platforms can be effectively utilised in reaching out to the unreached by HEIs in Zimbabwe because it is an affordable mode of communication. The study by UNESCO (2019) found that India is already into online learning starting from primary education to tertiary education (ibid) since the March 2020 COVID-19 lockdown. The education sector in India has devised online methods that are able to reach out to students who are able to access internet and those who cannot. A state-wide mobilisation by the government, political parties, business owners, private institutions, and citizens saw the contribution of smartphones, computers, and televisions to students from low-income families (UNESCO, 2019). This move by the Indian community, of mobilising resources by public and private sectors meant to assist students from low-income families, including those in the rural area, can be adopted by African countries with the same challenges as Zimbabwe. In this case, ODeL in HEIs as a mode of delivery can become more inclusive of vulnerable communities by diversifying its mode of delivery. WhatsApp platforms can be an online learning opportunity where universities or colleges can adopt to reach out to students in remote areas where internet network is a challenge. Lecturers can develop group forums for students partaking their courses and upload their lessons on this platform in the form of print, voice, or video. The same learning material can be uploaded on platforms that can be accessed through internet, for instance, the Myvista platform, module, etc. The COVID-19 situation that the world is in today demands countries, especially those with struggling resources, to think outside the box insofar as education of students, as well as inclusivity of all, is concerned.

Figure 8.3: ODeL through Radio Broadcasting of HEI Programmes and Courses

Source: Author 2021

African countries with mediocre resources can also consider introducing radio lessons in their Open and Distance Electronic Learning model so that it becomes more inclusive. Radios are an even more widely available medium than mobile phones in most countries in Africa. Thus, if the Corona Virus situation persists, the state-owned radio transmissions can be used by Higher Education Institutions to provide certain lecturers on air. Such a move can be a challenge to Zimbabwe, which has few radio stations. Since the country has many state universities, the media can fail to cope with the demand. However, countries like India have an advantage of utilising radios because they have many radio stations, including community radios, therefore making the organising of audio lessons feasible. All the same, universities can take it upon themselves to offer broadcasting alternatives, such as common content of certain courses. The Ministry of Higher Education and Tertiary Institution in Zimbabwe is introducing a common curriculum of similar programmes among all universities, hence making the radio broadcasting mode very viable. The Minimum Body of Knowledge (MBKs), which have recently been put in place in Zimbabwean universities, suggests that a student is able to transfer from one university to the other and be able to continue with the same programme if it is provided at that university. This implies that universities can collaborate and put on air certain courses for particular programmes so that those audio-taped courses are broadcast on the air at a stipulated time that will be known by students doing those programmes. The advantage of online learning using the radio is that a radio does not demand money to buy internet bundles; it only needs electricity or a battery to tune in. The latter would make ODeL mode cheaper to utilise, thus making it accessible to students from low-income communities, and in the process, make university education more affordable. The goal is to use every resource that can contribute to enable HEIs to be more inclusive and fulfil the rights of every person to education.

Figure 8.4: Digital Accessibility

Source: Author 2021

The challenge that most African countries may face is that digital access is yet to become a reality for the ordinary person. Most students are coming from homes where parents are not digitally literate, thus making it difficult for students to cope with the digital divides of today's universities or colleges. Whilst limited resources are contributory to a lack of computers in most Zimbabwean homes, a survey carried out in Zimbabwe brought out that there is also a correlation between computer literacy and the availability of computers in some homes. Such has seen students get enroled in HEIs without computer literacy skills, thus making it difficult to cope with ODeL or online learning. Interestingly, in spite of it being the world's second-largest internet user base and the biggest presence on social media sites, many of India's residents have no digital access either. India is one of the most important digital markets, but this is not a uniform trend across the subcontinent. The tech giant already has an ongoing programme in the country that aims to provide digital literacy to rural women and claims to have reached 26 million of them (Tabor, 2017). ODeL in HEIs can be inclusive to many if governments in Africa take the initiation of launching schemes that provide digital literacy workshops to community members, as well as provide scholarship packages and mobile phones to students from households below the poverty datum line, so that increased connectivity is realised. The COVID-19 pandemic has exacerbated inequalities and challenges that already existed for girls, rural folks, students from low-income backgrounds, and persons with disabilities in most developing countries, specifically Zimbabwe and Zambia. If governments hope to save these categories that are irretrievably behind, they must focus on foundational digital skills and literacy for students on the secondary school exit point to Higher Education Institutions. At the same time, they must provide basic digital resources, such as mobile phones, to special populations. The special population may consist of students from rural areas and low-income backgrounds as well as students with disabilities.

Figure 8.5: Students with Disabilities and Online Learning

Source: Author 2021

Inclusive education promotes the recognition of the need to work towards schools for all, and which include everybody celebrating the differences, supporting learning, and responding to individual needs. This is to say that inclusivity is not all about enroling all students, able bodied and disabled, girls and boys, in their home institutes; it is about developing education systems based upon a student-centred pedagogy capable of educating all students, including those who have adverse disadvantages and impairments. According to Chimedza (2000), the merits of such schools were not only that they can provide quality education to all children but that their establishments were also a crucial step in helping to change discriminatory attitudes in creating welcoming communities and in bringing about a society which is inclusive. Discriminatory situations that forced children with disabilities to withdraw are against the international and national laws on the education of children.

The United Nations Conventions on the Rights of Persons with Disabilities, (Article 24) and the African Charter on the Rights and Welfare of the Children (Article 11) emphasise the right of a child to education. Section 3e of Article 11 of the African Charter implores African governments to "take measures in respect of gifted and disadvantaged children, to ensure equal access to education for all sections of the community" (United Nation, 2016). Inaccessibility of buildings or infrastructure can be said to be an exclusionary practice that force students enroled in these schools to drop out of school or university. To address exclusive practices that persons with disabilities were exposed to the world over, the United Nations (UN) promulgated 22 standard rules on the equalization of opportunities for people with disabilities (USIS, 2016), Accessibility to buildings and other community infrastructures by persons with disabilities (PWD) were part of these standard rules. Most nations in the world have since adopted these UN standard rules on inclusivity. In Zimbabwe, some of the domestic inclusive policies include: The Disabled Persons Act (1992) and Policy Circular No.36 of 1996. Section 8 of the Disabled Persons Act (1992) makes it an offense to deny PWD access to any buildings and amenities (17:01; b). Whilst Policy No.36 mandates the enrolment of persons with disabilities in regular schools as opposed to institutionalisation. The latter entails that persons with disabilities can go up to tertiary education learning alongside their able-bodied peers. In fact, in response to the United Nations Declaration Charter on the Right of Persons with Disabilities to Education, Zimbabwean schools and tertiary institutions have seen the enrolment and education of persons with disabilities alongside able-bodied children in primary, secondary, and tertiary institutions. The inclusion of persons with disabilities to education includes the development of infrastructure that is accessible to all or a modification and adaptation to existing buildings so that they are accessible to all. The current Zimbabwe Constitution (Amendment No.20 of 2013) stipulates this explicitly.

The State must take appropriate measures to ensure that buildings and amenities to which the public has access are accessible to persons with disabilities (Chapter 2.22. 4, 2013).

The fundamental rights to Education for all are clearly articulated in the Zimbabwe Education Act (1987), revised in 1996 and 2006. The Education Act (2006) furthered the non-discriminatory policy by purporting that all students, regardless of race, religion, gender, and creed, have access to education. These non-discrimination provisions expanded the right to education in Zimbabwe for all students, including students with disabilities. Moreover, the revised Constitution of Zimbabwe (2013) emphasises the need to include persons with disabilities in all key areas of development, which includes recreation activities and employment. Chimedza (2000) argues that education is a means to ensure that people can enjoy and defend their rights in society and contribute to the process of democratisation and personalization, both in society and in education. Legislation has guaranteed persons with disabilities the rights to and opportunities for schooling, employment, and access to community facilities in various countries the world over.

Whilst various policies and legislation have been crafted to address the plight of person with disabilities, the challenges to access school buildings persists in most communities of Zimbabwe. Several buildings continue to be built in Zimbabwe, even after inclusive policies had been adopted, but still, they remain inaccessible or difficult to access. Limited access to social and environmental participation has continued to prevent persons with disabilities from responding to hazards and managing risks. ODeL comes at a time where environmental hazards such as COVID-19 need to be addressed in terms of accessing education in HEIs. This effort has seen challenges of persons with disabilities of accessibility of tertiary institutions' infrastructure being addressed, in the sense that they can now be able to access quality education in their homes. Home environments are more friendly in that people with disabilities, especially those with physical disabilities and blindness, would, in most cases, have adapted to their home environments. Thus, ODeL is likely to improve the lives of persons with disabilities who have been denied access to education time immemorial. It brings tertiary education right at their doorsteps and inside their homes.

Use of ODeL by persons with disabilities, however, demands consensus efforts by various governments in developing countries in partnership with private sectors as well as civil organizations to come up with a model that enables the latter to access electronic learning with minimum challenges. As elaborated in this chapter, most countries are signatories to the UNCRPD, which demands inclusion of persons with disabilities at all levels of society; it elaborates on the right to education for persons with disabilities (UNCRPD, article, 24). African governments, through the Social Welfare department, can assist students with disabilities who are enroled at tertiary institutions by providing them with smartphones or sourcing laptops. In Zimbabwe, for example, the Department of Social Welfare meets school fees demands of persons with disabilities enroled at tertiary institutions. The person is to close the gap that has existed for so long between able-bodied persons and persons with disabilities. Thus, it may be imperative for the same government to provide learning gadgets for students with disabilities so that they participate effectively in the online learning that most universities are switching to. Augmentative and alternative communication for persons with disabilities demands gadgets with software that are tailor-made to specific disabilities; for example, persons with visual impairment may demand talking phones and laptops. Most governments' fiscal budget are overburdened by social welfare allocation, and this can be largely reduced by equipping persons with disabilities who depend on social welfare with life skills by enabling them access to quality education.

Higher Education Institutions, on the other hand, can play a significant role by putting in place gadgets that are sensitive to persons whose disabilities are in various forms. The University of Zimbabwe has a disability resource center with various gadgets that cater to persons with disabilities. This center is manned by specialists in disabilities and special needs education. The writer of this chapter has seen persons with visual impairment and cerebral palsy benefitting much from this University of Zimbabwe resource center. Such efforts should be emulated by other universities in Zimbabwe and in other developing countries so that higher institutions become inclusive to all. Now that universities are shifting from face-to-face to ODeL mode of learning, Higher Education Institutions can domesticate inclusive policies by developing a virtual model that is sensitive to persons with disabilities and manned by specialists. I suggest a disability learning center at every university that is in a virtual mode and that is monitored by specialists in disability and special needs education. This Centre will be an online mode that registers all students with disability in the university and the courses they will be taking each semester. Specialists in this department can orient students with disabilities in the usage of electronic mode in registering, downloading assignments, uploading assignments, video conferencing, audio conferencing, etc. However, this virtual disability centre should augment online communication by designing or putting in place alternative communications that are sensitive to various communication modes demanded by persons with disabilities. Students with cerebral palsy, in most cases, need special computers that detect their speech and put it in print since typing is not feasible for most. They also need headbands that are sensitive to their thoughts and speech, just to mention some.

Digital transformation in HEIs can be argued to have been aptly chosen to stimulate dialogue on how African HEIs can digitally transform their various business processes – that is, teaching, learning, working spaces, events management, administrative operations (financial, student's records, health, accommodation, etc.), collaborations, knowledge services, research, community engagement, among several other functions of HEIs.

The World Bank (2015) defines digital transformation as "a series of deep and coordinated workforce, culture, and technology shifts that enable new educational and operating models and transform an institution's operations, strategic directions and value proportions." Thus, ODeL as a major platform for learning, teaching, and doing administrative and academic interactions is part of digital transformation, which, in the process, is going to equip and hone technological skills in both students and lecturers in tertiary institutions. Thus, the COVID-19 era can be noted to have fast-tracked HEI links to the African Union Commission's Digital Transformation Strategy (2020-2030), whose vision is "an integrated and inclusive digital society and economy in Africa that improves the quality of life of Africa's citizens, strengthens the existing economic sector, enables its diversification and development, and ensures continental ownership with Africa as a producer and not only a consumer in the global economy". The AU strategy identifies the digital infrastructure, digital skills and human capacity, and digital innovations as some of the key foundation pillars required to digitally transform the African continent. Thus, ODeL in HEIs can be singled out as a digital platform that is equipping the future generation. Thus, ODeL is one of the critical platforms to drive digital transformation, digital applications, as well as emerging technologies as key cross-cutting themes for realising a digitally transformed country in Africa. The fact that ODeL has the potential of taking on board people from different backgrounds, able-bodied and those with disabilities, suggests that the model is very inclusive in outlook; all that is demanded is for the tertiary institutions to work towards the ideal of that model.

Digital accessibility by all communities and sharing information and knowledge openly for the benefit of humanity is the way to go in this digital world, thus, as a panacea of knowledge, universities need to lead by example in leading communities into these digital explorations. ODeL gives individual students the opportunity of Open Access to online education and knowledge. Open Access, according to Olulube (2016) and Tubbs (2017), gives academics a worldwide audience and increases the visibility of their work; it gives consumers of knowledge barrier-free access to the literature they need for their research and other engagement. The implication is that universities in Zimbabwe and other African Universities practicing Open Access advance their mission to reach out to many students in various communities, and that they also increase the visibility of their researchers and their research.

8.3. Summary

When the coronavirus pandemic created a major global disruption to the operations of higher education, with most institutions moving to online instruction, the situation challenged African HEIs to adopt innovative strategies to continue to deliver their goals and objectives. These innovative strategies include creating a continental e-platform to share knowledge and experience among African HEIs. These institutions are also encouraged to develop digital transformation strategies to ensure a holistic, inclusive, and sustainable approach to digitalisation. Digital transformation should impact staff, students, institutional culture, as well as the know-how of the use of such technology. The success of a digital transformed project that is inclusive of people from vulnerable backgrounds, such as remote rural areas as well as persons with disabilities, depends on dynamic and supportive leadership and skilled staff in Higher Education Institutions. In the ideal sense, ODeL is a very inclusive model in HEIs. It just calls for proper planning, critical attention to information security, sustainable funding, digital integrations, and student-centric services that include a disability centre or hub.

8.4 References

Bellamy, C. (2012). *Accelerating Progress in Girls' Education---Towards Robust and Sustainable Outcomes.*

Chigunwe, G. (2019). The girl-child-education in Africa. A Presentation Made at the Women in Leadership in Higher Education Institutions. Abuja, Nigeria.

Chigunwe, G. & Mpande, F. (2020). Addressing Health Crisis Among Pregnant Women with Disabilities: From the Zimbabwean and Zambian Point of View. *Journal of Quality in Health and Economics, 3*(4), 1-10.

Chimedza, R. (2000). The Cultural Politics of Integrating Deaf Students in Regular Schools in Zimbabwe. *Disability in Society, 13*(4), 493-502.

Chimedza, R. (2010). *Special Education in African Perspectives: Different Voices.* Harare: College Press.

Cramm, J. M., Lorenzo T., & Nieboer A.P. (2013). *Applied Research in Quality of Life. 9*(3), 517–524.

Dakar World Education Forum. (2012). *Framework of Action Report.* Paris: UNESCO.

Futrell, M. (2007). *Working Session II: Reaching the Marginalized; Investing in Education for Rural People to Achieve EFA and MDG.* Paris: UNESCO

Hegarty, S. (2018). *Educating Pupils with Special Needs in the Ordinary School.* Oxford: Oxford NFER Nelson Publishing Company.

Jomtien World Declaration on Education for All Report (1990).

Mwangi, E. (2014). News and Vews from Africa. Retrieved June 2 2009, from http://www.newsfromafrica/indices/index_1707.html

Olulube, N. P. (2016). Appraising the Relationship Between ICT Usage and Integration and the Standard of Teacher Education Programmes in a Developing Economy. *International Journal of Education and Development, 2*(3), 70-85.

Tabor, S. W. (2017). Narrowing the Distance: Implementing a Hybrid Learning Model. *Quarterly Review of Distance Education, 8*(1), 48-49.

UNESCO Institute of Statistics. (2000). *EFA Global Monitoring Report 2015: Education for All 2000–2015 – Achievements and Challenges.* Paris: UNESCO.

UNICEF. (2019). *Children in Especially Difficult Circumstances.* Harare: Southern African Development Centre.

United Nations. (2011). *Millennium Development Goals Report.* http://www.un.org/millenniumgoals/pdf

United Nations. (2013). *Standard Rules on the Equalisation of Opportunities for Persons with Disabilities.* https://www.un.org/esa/socdev/enable/dissre00.htm

World Bank, (2015). *Poverty and Disability: A Survey of the Literature.* Washington DC: World Bank.

ZIMSTAT. (2020). Harare: Central Statistics Office.

Chapter 9

Innovation and Industrialisation in ODeL Institutions

Cuthbert Majoni

Zimbabwe Open University

Felix Chikosha

Zimbabwe Open University

Abstract

African nations are now emphasising the importance of scientific research and innovations in a bid to increase the pace of industrialisation. Through institutions of tertiary education, the countries are developing initiatives aimed at the creation of capabilities for industrial innovation. The most frequently used policy instruments for improving universities' contribution to innovation include promoting student innovation, encouraging faculty innovation, actively supporting university technology transfer, facilitating university-industry collaboration, and engaging in local economic development efforts. The potential contribution of universities to industrialisation can never be underestimated. There are various avenues through which universities can contribute to industrialisation, but the major ones are spin-offs, patenting of technologies, and science parks and incubators. Whilst recognising the importance of universities in facilitating industrialisation, hurdles have been noted that weaken university-industry links. These barriers include reservation on the part of universities, information gaps, conflict between the private and public domains of knowledge, national policy gaps, and funding constraints. Against this backdrop, there are contingencies that may assist university-industry links to work and remain sustainable. These include necessity, recognition and reciprocity, efficacy and efficiency, stability, and legality and legitimacy.

Keywords: innovation, industrialisation, spin-off, science parks, incubation hubs, university-industry collaboration, technology transfer

***

9.0 Introduction

This chapter concerns the role of ODeL institutions in fostering innovation and industrialisation. Working definitions of innovation and industrialisation are provided, and emphasis is placed on the role ODeL universities play in modern innovation and industrialisation processes. Frameworks for industrialisation and innovation are first elaborated, followed by policies enhancing universities' contribution to innovation. Thereafter the contribution of universities to industrialisation and barriers to university-industry links are outlined. The last section discusses the strategies for facilitating university-industry collaboration.

9.1 Definition of Innovation

The term 'innovation' is used widely in various disciplines. Hence, there is no commonly agreed definition, and as a result, the definition of innovation has remained elusive (Baregheh, Rowley & Sambrook, 2009). Literature is full of various definitions of the term innovation, but the challenge lies in which definition to use in the light of what universities do and think of as innovation. The bulk of the definition is drawn from industry and business with nothing coming from distance education universities or higher education in general (Silver, Hannan & English, 1997).

Innovation has been defined as the act or process of making something new or changing the way of doing something (Goldman, 1992). Innovation is also defined as the creative exchange, evolution, and application of new ideas to produce goods and services. In the context of business and industry, innovation has something to do with improvement as well as establishing something new or doing something differently (Ross, 2001; Murray, 2001). This implies innovation involves the conception, adoption, and implementation of new ideas. Innovation is part of a creative process that involves the application and implementation of new ideas, practices, or interventions. ODeL institutions as universities have a part to play in innovation and industrialisation, and therefore, ODeL universities should be the agency of innovation. However, it should be noted that innovation is associated with new ideas, new services, or new practices, which are in most cases, unique or original. While innovation is new to a person or institution, it can be a common practice in other institutions or countries. Hence, the extent to which an idea, service or practice is new depends on the environment or country whether they have come across that idea. (Hannan & Silver, 2000; Jenniskens, 2000). Innovation can be viewed in terms of the rate and degree to which it can influence change. Change can be rapid or gradual. (Silver, Hannan & English, 1997). It is impossible to industrialise without being innovative. Innovation embraces industrialisation and paradigm shifts to bring about new theoretical frameworks. In general, innovation involves the creation or adoption of given ideas and practices. Innovation can bring about positive or negative outcomes. New ideas practices and services arise from creative invention to improve the existing situation practice or service, resulting in change (Ng'ethe, 2003).

9.2 Driving Forces of Innovation

Innovation should have initiators and beneficiaries, who could be individuals, departments, or institutions, in response to internal or external factors, such as government policy or institutional policy (Ng'ethe, 2003; Silver, 1998). The driving forces of innovation include, among others, contextual factors such as social, economic, political, and cultural factors (Ng'ethe, 2003). The pervasive forces of globalisation, internationalization, and information communication technologies have driven ODeL institutions to innovate.

How institutions respond to environmental pressures brings about innovation. Contextual factors promoting innovation include massive numbers of student enrolments, rapid technological advances, emergence of knowledge societies, globalisation, economic recession, and financial challenges in higher education (Ng'ethe, 2003). Universities have been recognised as having the potential to contribute significantly to national socio-economic development (Sanyal, 1995). Hence governments have invested and raised interest heavily in research and innovation in universities. The cold war and the launch of the Russian Sputnik in 1958 spurred the United States government to invest in research and industrialisation in its universities (Ben-David, 1977).

Globalisation has also been a driver of innovation and change. The rapid development in information communication technologies has stimulated innovation in teaching and learning in Open distance e-learning institutions (Silver, 1998). World markets and the global economy have brought new meaning to the survival of institutions. Universities now require continual innovation through knowledge production to improve and develop new products and services to survive (Ng'ethe, 2003; Ekong & Cloete, 1997).

9.3 Building on Innovation Environment

ODeL universities have a pivotal role to play in the challenging restructuring process that the African economy is undergoing. The ability to develop and exploit new technologies, as well as understanding how technology and society interact, are all critical success factors that ODeL institutions can contribute to in this ongoing process of change. Various factors contribute to the success of innovation in an online university context. These include the innovation culture in a university, quality databases, innovation policies, and regulations, as well as research personnel. The university innovation culture is made up of the values and beliefs of university senior management, faculty research, students and administration staff based on tradition and communicated verbally and by action (Christensen & Eyring, 2011). The innovation culture of a university is a prerequisite for successful innovation (Amabile, 1998). The virtual infrastructure of the university should provide direct access to the latest information related to the university, such as research education and innovative activities (Amabile et al. 1996). Participation of different agents of innovation, such as lecturers, students, researchers, and administration staff, play a critical role in promoting innovation (Haynes, 2002; Jones, 2010).

The incentive programme can be put in place to reward researchers and innovators in an institution. A university needs to put in place an innovation policy to encourage researchers to set up companies that promote innovation (Brewer & Tierney, 2010). University management needs to have an innovative and entrepreneurial IP approach to education and research. There is a need to put in place reward systems for innovation and industrialisation (OECD, 2011). The success of innovation is the department interplay of several components namely the individual.

9.4 Industrialisation

Industrialisation involves the processing of raw materials and resource extraction by manufacturing and service activities (Bailey, 2002). Industrialisation started in the 1760s with the steam engine and the mechanisation of factors. Industrialisation has been closely associated with technological advancement. Industrialisation is a process of building up the capacity to convert raw materials into new products and putting in place the system that enables production to take place.

The context in which a country industrialises depends on the innovative capacity to exploit the existing resources. Industrial activities are divided into various components, such as primary industry, agriculture forestry, and mining, among others. The secondary industry involved the processing of raw materials, and the manufacturing tertiary sector is where they provide services, which include wholesale, retail, transportation, fiancé, and insurance and construction industry. The tertiary industry deals with the part of a country's economy concerned with the provision of services. Universities and other educational institutions fall under the tertiary industry sector.

The type of education promoted by governments has consequences for industrial development. For example, an education system that places priority on scientists and engineers is likely to have a better chance of promoting industrial progress than one that focuses on producing artists. In this regard, the new approach to industrial policy recognises the need to redirect policy and resources towards the development of appropriate human capital (UNIDO, 2011).

Stressing the link between higher education and industrialisation, Jackson (1990) stated that the first industrial revolution with its increasing demand for manpower with specialist skills to sustain it led directly to the establishment of the great technical institutes in this part of Northern England reflected in the present day by the huge concentration of higher and further education institutions in Greater Manchester.

University-industry partnerships are increasingly regarded as crucial for development in Africa. Higher education institutes must become more relevant to economic and social demands and partnering with industry is a way of achieving this, while supporting regional and national economies (Creso, 2013). Ultimately, most of the technological advances that have economic consequences can be traced indirectly or directly to universities, either through the training provided, the knowledge spillovers, the actual research conducted, or through URLs that enabled firms and faculty members to collaborate in the development of technologies.

9.5 Lester's Industrial Transformation Typology

According to Lester (2005), economies develop when firms can adapt and apply new technologies in their production processes to generate new products or services continuously over time. Universities' role in innovation processes hinges on the kind of industrial transformation occurring in the economy. Lester's industrial transformation typology includes indigenous creation, industrial transplantation, industry diversification, and industry upgrading.

Indigenous creation involves the establishment of an entirely new industry without any link to existing technology in the local economy. In other words, it is the emergence of an ultra-new science-based industry without any linkage to the existing local technological assets. Under this transition, typical university activities involve the facilitation of new business formation through incubator programs, the development of favourable licensing regimes, and matchmaking between academic scientists and local entrepreneurs.

Industrial transplantation occurs when an existing industry is imported from another area into a new locality. In this context, the industry may be old in its place of origin, however, to the destination region, it constitutes a new development. In this transition, key university functions entail the development of new study programmes, upgrading of existing curricula, and flexible learning programs to meet the human capital needs of the new industry.

Industry diversification refers to the conversion of a declining industry's technologies to form a relatedly new industry. It is the harnessing of a declining industry's technological assets to develop a similar but new industry in its place. Universities' key roles in this process are twofold. First, as knowledge integrators, by connecting previously separate technological activities. Second, as legitimacy promoters of the new industries.

Upgrading of existing industries denotes the enhancement of an industry's technological base through improvements in production technologies or the introduction of new products or services. These innovative add-ons give an existing or matured industry a face-lift in order to sustain its competitiveness. Universities support this transition by increasing problem-solving interactions with industry. Another role is by providing relevant programs and continuous education and helping industry leaders search for and adopt global best practices.

9.6 Frameworks for Analysing the Contribution of Universities to Innovation

There are two main frameworks used in the literature to analyse the contribution of ODeL universities to innovation. These are (i) the National Innovation Systems/Triple Helix and the (ii) Holistic innovation system framework.

9.6.1 National Innovation Systems and the "Triple Helix"

The pivotal role of universities in innovation systems is enshrined in the 'Triple Helix' concept of university, industry, and government interactions. The 'Triple Helix' concept of university, industry, and government interactions rose to prominence in the second half of the 1990s, largely due to the works of Etzkowitz & Leydesdorff (1997) and Etzkowitz (1998). In Leydesdorff & Etzkowitz's models, universities are considered as relevant and distinctive actors, contributing to the innovative potential of societies. This holds particularly for basic research, which is characterized by high levels of technological and market uncertainties and long lead times. Universities are considered as distinctive actors in contributing to the innovative potential of societies. Private investors tend to refrain from basic research, leaving universities and public research institutes uniquely positioned to produce science-based knowledge upon which the development of new products, processes and services can build. At the same time, an effective contribution to the capacity of an innovation system requires that universities not only create ideas that can be commercialised but also be willing to become involved in the process of transferring research ideas toward commercial success.

The Triple Helix framework can be successfully implemented to encourage a collaborative approach between the government, industry, and ODeL institutions. Online conferences and summits would bring together community leaders, educators, locals, and the government to develop strategies to create innovations and enhance industrialisation. Triple Helix theory implies an enhanced role of ODeL institutions in technological innovations.

9.6.2 Holistic Innovation System Framework (Moore & Ulrichsen, 2010)

Moore and Ulrichsen (2010) premised the innovation system framework on the idea that innovation is a continuous learning process involving the application of knowledge, pre-existing or otherwise new to the context. According to Moore & Ulrichsen (2010), effective engagement of higher education institutions with the potential users of their outputs through knowledge exchange mechanisms leads to economic and social development. The framework is more relevant to ODeL institutions as they use innovative online channels to deliver knowledge.

9.7 Policies Enhancing Universities' Contribution to Innovation

To enhance the contributions of university-based research to innovation and industrialisation, African governments should implement policies that foster innovation and industrial advancement. Most of these policy initiatives share the premise that universities support innovation in the industry primarily through the production by universities of "deliverables" for commercialisation. The EDA (2013) stipulates that the most frequently used policy instruments for improving universities' contribution to innovation include:

> ➢ Promoting student innovation
> ➢ Encouraging faculty innovation
> ➢ Facilitating university-industry collaboration, and
> ➢ Engaging in local economic development efforts

9.7.1 Promoting Student Innovation and Entrepreneurship

ODeL institutions are investing heavily in the development of their students' entrepreneurial skills. The universities are investing both in formal programs as well as in extra-curricular activities to channel students' interest in solving global problems through entrepreneurship. Examples of formal programs include degrees and certificates in entrepreneurship, while examples of extra-curricular activities include business plan contests, entrepreneurship clubs, and start-up internships.

Courses and Degree Programs in Innovation and Entrepreneurship

ODeL universities can provide courses and continuing education to firms, whilst industry employees can provide lectures at the university. Many universities are seeing an increase in student demand for innovation and entrepreneurship, broadening course and program offerings. Entrepreneurship courses and programs equip students with a wide range of valuable skills, including business plan development, marketing, networking, creating "elevator pitches," attracting financing, and connecting with local business leaders.

Experiential Learning

Experiential or applied learning in innovation and entrepreneurship has spread outside of business schools and moved into the fine arts, science, and engineering programs. ODeL universities should support specialised internship programs focused on entrepreneurship education and technology innovation that match students directly to start-up projects, technology transfer offices, venture capital firms, and industry. This variety of educational opportunities allows students to address real-world challenges in a supportive educational environment.

Competitive Opportunities

Competitions are an excellent way to actively engage faculty and students in the learning process. Business plan competitions are geared toward teaching students how to think outside the classroom, fostering collaborations across disciplines and increasing access to businesses. Competitions provide an exciting platform for students to learn practical skills, such as how to craft a business plan, access venture funding, and pitch ideas. Sequential competitions build upon project ideas, ultimately leading to complete business plans that are ready for possible funding from investors.

Entrepreneurial and Innovation Collaboration Spaces

Entrepreneurial and innovation "living spaces" are a unique trend in motivating student involvement outside the classroom setting. These spaces use the power of proximity to promote student engagement in developing innovative ideas and starting businesses. Some universities are embracing the entrepreneurial dorm, whereas others are expanding this concept to promote entrepreneurial clusters, within the university and sometimes stretching into local communities. Entrepreneurial spaces facilitate student access to learning and networking opportunities with local entrepreneurs and innovators. These spaces also host a variety of student entrepreneur clubs that serve as a premier resource for aspiring student entrepreneurs and foster a community of like-minded peers. These clubs are geared toward building financial literacy and leadership skills, as well as encouraging students to pursue commercialisation opportunities for innovative ideas and technologies.

9.7.2 Encouraging Faculty Innovation and Entrepreneurship

The EDA (2013) contends that universities are putting in place a series of policy changes to encourage more faculty entrepreneurship, which in turn will complement student entrepreneurship. These changes include greater recognition of faculty entrepreneurs, integrating entrepreneurship into the faculty tenure and selection process, and increasing faculty connections to outside partners -

through externships, engagement with business, and targeted resources for start-up creation.

Faculty and doctoral graduate students conduct the research powering many of the innovations that spawn high-growth start-ups. Faculty entrepreneurship policies are designed to connect research to market and societal relevance and to find solutions to real-world problems. Universities are encouraging faculty entrepreneurship by creating flexible workplace policies, financial awards, and making seed funding available to faculty, researchers, and graduate students, as tools for retention, revenue, income supplementation, and to keep faculty motivated and engaged. It is also a reflection of a larger desire among a new generation of faculty to be more relevant to the world around them.

The Changing Innovation Cultures

Institutions need to hire faculty who are interested not only in the advancement of their academic areas but also in pursuing commercial applications for their technologies or engaging in entrepreneurial activities that correlate with their academic disciplines. New faculty orientations often include workshops and training to help faculty navigate technology transfer offices and find the resources available to them on campus. Universities also offer faculty training in areas such as professional mentoring, prototype development, business planning, and market testing.

Rewarding Faculty Innovation and Entrepreneurship

Online universities need to acknowledge faculty achievements in innovation and entrepreneurship. These acknowledgements include campus-wide prizes and award ceremonies that bring the faculty community together to recognise and learn about the accomplishments of their peers across academic disciplines. Awards such as "Innovator of the Year" and "Faculty Entrepreneur of the Year" are popular as they reward faculty for achievements that reach beyond traditional research and teaching accomplishments. Universities are updating tenure and sabbatical leave guidelines to encourage faculty to pursue collaborative and entrepreneurial endeavours, such as launching a start-up company. Providing leave to pursue entrepreneurial activities increases the potential for the successful technology development and commercialisation of research while adding to faculty's understanding of the commercialisation process, enabling them to incorporate new material into student instruction.

Supporting Collaboration

Universities are providing additional resources to encourage collaboration with local communities and industries. A few universities have hired individuals, or create teams, to connect faculty with similar interests and research goals often reaching across academic departments to share information and experience on creating start-ups, licensing technology, and collaborating with industry. This cross-disciplinary effort helps share information on best practices and spurs new ideas for developing and commercialising new products.

Universities are also inviting community leaders and local entrepreneurs to become more involved in the development of technology and start-up companies. A few universities have developed programs to link experienced entrepreneurs with faculty to assist in the start-up process, development, and longevity. In most cases, faculty returns to teach and continue research, allowing the non-university collaborative partners to take over the leadership role and continue to develop and expand the companies. Entrepreneurs also serve in a mentoring role, helping faculty to identify and further develop commercialisation opportunities.

Engaging With Industry

The unit is engaging more with industry to obtain research and technology development ideas, capital, and other types of support. Many universities host events to bring the unit/department, industry, angel investors, and venture capitalists together for networking opportunities. These events give the industry an early look at R&D activities on campus while providing the unit with networking and funding possibilities. Examples of such events include online seminars and workshops.

9.7.3 Facilitating University-Industry Collaboration

Collaborative research by ODeL institutions involves research projects carried out by university researchers. These projects are normally partially or fully funded by industry, ODeL institutions can offer contract services and academic consultancy to firms. As such, where firms face a concrete firm challenge, they may contract the university to conduct research. University-industry partnerships are essential for further developing ideas and technologies derived from university research. These partnerships are crucial for directing investment toward commercially promising research and helping to bridge funding gaps that often exist at the technology development and marketing stages. Conferencing and networking between ODeL researchers and industry representatives. Through online meetings are important for developing and maintaining university-industry collaborations. Universities and industry have found that working together is mutually beneficial because knowledge and resources are shared to achieve common goals. Industry benefits from greater and earlier access to scientific expertise, intellectual property, and commercial opportunities, while universities benefit from enhanced educational opportunities for faculty and students, revenues from successful licensing agreements and ventures, and local and regional development.

The EDA (2013) points to those universities constantly looking for ways to connect their research and students' education to emerging industry interests. In recent years, universities in developed countries have put greater emphasis on supporting start-up companies while continuing to engage established companies that have traditionally been their licensing partners. To facilitate greater collaboration and innovation, universities are opening their facilities, faculty, and students to businesses (small and large) in the hopes of creating greater economic value. Universities need to strategically partner with companies, offering internships and externships, sharing facilities with start-ups, such as accelerators, and creating venture funds and incentive programs funded by industry, all of which drive increased innovation and product development by university students, faculty, and staff.

Sharing Resources and Knowledge

ODeL universities can have online laboratories that could be used for both the training of students and researching for industry. Such laboratories will be an avenue to fulfill the research goals which may to enable a reduction in climate gas emissions. As government resources are becoming limited, universities need to seek various channels of support for technology development and industrialisation as well as commercialisation, particularly for the business world. Universities can create "front-door policies" to easily engage private industry. Universities have a wealth of resources available to industry, including human and intellectual capital, and research and development (R&D) infrastructure. So, the front-door policies, web-portals, and easy-to-navigate licensing policies all expedite the ability of private industry and start-ups to identify university R&D with commercial potential earlier and open up opportunities for companies to easily commence strategic partnerships with universities. Companies of all ages, sizes, and geographic proximities are benefiting from this invigorated support from universities.

Research mobility, which includes both permanent and temporary assignments of university researchers working in the industry, can be another way ODeL institutions can influence industrialisation. Research mobility is important because these individuals will act as "boundary spanners" between universities and industry actors, as these individuals are knowledgeable about both the university and industry sectors (Rosli & Sidek, 2013). ODeL institutions can have personnel linking with industry online in the process of creating better relations between university and industry partners.

Universities, as hubs of innovation and entrepreneurship, are developing creative ways to draw industry partners to campus. Emerging trends to increase industry presence on campus and facilitate conversations on new ideas and technology include web portals that provide industry with access to university resources, networking events, such as breakfast forums and casual roundtable discussions, and structured/intensive student and faculty internships in the private sector. In the USA, industry speaker series is another popular tool for engaging university and industry scientists in discussions of commercialisation opportunities available in the private sector.

An emerging trend points to the use of targeted websites and social media around current research project information, patent licensing opportunities through online databases, and the creation of network banks of past campus-wide efforts and partnerships. Some universities have implemented an external-facing portal or an open web-based database that provides content on innovation and commercialisation processes to self-registered users and business partners. Others have developed tools like Source Link - online tools as tools to highlight educational resources on campus so that businesses can easily find university experts of interest to them. These portals house all relevant information in one location, which reduces search times and increases efficiency in identifying potential commercial opportunities. By increasing openness and transparency, the industry can easily access university resources and information without having to search through multiple university records.

Accelerators

Accelerators are partnerships between universities and companies that are designed to fast-track the innovation and commercialisation process by providing access to world-class scientific facilities, technical personnel, and testing and diagnostics equipment resources not readily available to many start-ups. Some accelerators focus on helping companies in the post-incubation period, such as meeting the technical needs of start-ups and bridging the funding gap.

Guidance on Intellectual Property Rights and Royalties

As more university researchers partner with the industry for financial R&D support, negotiating a functional IP policy is becoming an important issue. To increase these partnerships, some universities have developed a standard policy and agreements that they use with all industry collaborators. These policies guide decisions on issues such as rights to IP and division of royalties. Many universities also are creating standard forms that outline university and industry responsibilities and profit-sharing.

9.7.5 Engaging With Local Economic Development Efforts

Universities should be active partners in local economic planning and revitalisation efforts. Universities have taken varied approaches to advance state, regional, and local economic development, and growth objectives, including:

Encouraging Direct University Participation in Local Businesses and Communities

Universities are encouraging student and faculty education, innovation, and entrepreneurial pursuits that revitalise local businesses and address other local development needs. Faculty members also support local communities through teaching, mentoring, and initiatives to advance innovation and economic development goals. Many university programs are working to foster dialogue between faculty and the local community to tackle local challenges. As faculty engage in R&D, they increasingly collaborate with regional stakeholders to push technology development forward and open the door to viable market opportunities locally. These efforts have led to long-term partnerships with local communities.

Collaborating With Local Governments, Industry, and Other Stakeholders to Develop Comprehensive Approaches for Innovation and Economic Development

Universities are engaging in long-term, dedicated innovation and entrepreneurship efforts that promote economic development. They are working closely with community stakeholders, government, companies, venture capitalists, entrepreneurs, and workers to improve access to university-based assets and to implement regional innovation and economic strategies. Universities use a variety of collaborative mODeLs, including research parks, university corridors, start-up accelerators, shared laboratory space, incubators, and innovation and manufacturing clusters. These venues bring together infrastructure and intellectual capital to address innovation and business challenges and to develop local economies. These efforts provide a cost-effective and productive means for conducting research, developing technology, and spurring new markets and businesses.

Start-up incubators and accelerators hosted by universities serve as powerful places for local community members to start new companies and solve pressing local and national innovation and commercialisation challenges. Incubators focus on addressing local community issues, such as supporting local startups, by providing mentorship and technical support, thus contributing to local economies.

Linking Local Communities to Support Networks

ODeL institutions can play a predominant role in linking local businesses and community leaders with national support networks to expand the pool of available resources. Universities hold a unique position in local communities. They can provide online platforms where all stakeholders, including researchers, venture capitalists, companies, entrepreneurs, consultants, and regional authorities and organisations, can come together to tackle critical local issues. Several university economic development efforts have targeted underserved communities, such as programs supporting SMEs to help increase economic development opportunities across the region.

9.8 The Contribution of Universities to Industrialisation

Veugelers & Rey (2014) contend that governments have become increasingly active in pressing universities within their jurisdictions to contribute to local economic development. Beyond the direct impact from universities, their presence may also attract other key economic resources to the region, including firms and workers, educated or not, who may want to locate close by, as well as financiers, entrepreneurs, and others seeking to exploit new business opportunities emanating from the campus.

9.8.1 Technology Transfer Model: Licensing and Spin-Offs

At present, the major focus in the contribution of universities to industrialisation is on technology transfer, more particularly patenting, licensing, and spin-offs. Universities are encouraged to transfer their laboratory discoveries by patenting and licensing intellectual property to local firms.

Spin-Offs

University entrepreneurial activities provide critical organisational skills to students, and at the very best, may result in a university spinoff. Academic entrepreneurship or spin-offs are a source of new firms and jobs and can be a significant revenue source for regions. Spin-offs from university or publicly funded research institutes can be important both as new material forces in the region and as vehicles for regional technology transfer. Universities do not only have an impact on new firm creation through their own spin-offs, but they also correlate with other start-ups (Veugelers & Rey, 2014). Through Academic spin-offs, ODeL graduates develop technologies through a company they own, which are often the outcomes of research conducted by these academics.

Patenting of Technologies

ODeL institutions can influence industrialisation through patenting. This involves the selling of Intellectual property (IP) generated by ODeL institutions to industry. Universities should lobby the state to promulgate laws relating to patenting of technologies to give researchers intellectual property rights over scientific findings arrived at with the use of public funds. IP regards the policy to promote the transfer of university-developed technology to industry. There should be clear-cut regulations on who should have intellectual property rights (IPR) on technology developed by the university in collaboration with industry

(EDA, 2013). To increase transparency and encourage industry cooperation, universities are establishing unified and structured IP policies. These policies guide decisions on issues such as rights to IP and division of royalties. These new IP strategies reduce uncertainty, alleviating the financial concerns that surround university-industry partnerships.

9.8.2 Science Parks and Incubators

A science park adjacent to the university generally requires government backing. Universities should help in the development of industrial clusters in such customized parks (Veugelers & Rey, 2014). Universities should set up incubators to nurture firms that can be spun off, sometimes with the help of venture capital provided by the university or with the help of university connections. Some of these ventures provide the university with large returns on invested capital. The government can also entice the development of such clusters through funding or tax credits. Science-intensive sectors such as pharmaceuticals have strong complementarities with basic academic research by ODeL institutions. Companies' R&D will be able to utilise research publications by ODeL institutions.

9.9 Barriers to University-Industry Links

There are three clusters of barriers to these links. The first relates to policies, the second to the universities, and the third to industry (Mihyo et al., 2011).

9.9.1 Reservation on the Part of Universities

Some universities feel it is not within their mandate to engage in academic entrepreneurship. The traditional laws establishing public universities cater to teaching, research, and community engagement. There is the risk that if universities get involved too much in the research agendas of industry, they may neglect the university's core business and teaching.

9.9.2 Information Gap

Not many companies know about the research outputs or activities of various departments in most universities. Very few universities post abstracts of staff and graduate students' research output on their website. Fewer post biographies of their staff on their websites. Annual reports in many cases do not indicate research profiles of departments or research output of staff. Similarly, very few universities have a comprehensive view of the needs and activities of industries in their locality, country, or region. This information gap limits the potential for university-industry links.

9.9.3 Conflict Between the Private and Public Domains of Knowledge

For academics, knowledge is a public good that should be disseminated widely and easily accessed. The publicity increases recognition for researchers and the relevance of universities to society. For industry, knowledge is a private commodity. This conflict of perceptions also extends to issues of intellectual property rights. At the university level, academics feel they have the right to own the intellectual property rights arising out of their research. On the other hand, universities feel they should own these rights even if they have not funded the research. This has been a source of contestation.

9.9.4 Policy Gaps

At the national level, most policies dealing with science, technology, and innovation mention university-industry links but do not give guidelines on funding modalities, support systems, or quality assurance. Within these policies, funding for universities is not covered, and support for R&D in industries through tax and other incentives is missing. For universities to transfer or share knowledge with industry, the latter should have R&D activities and researchers of its own.

9.9.5 Funding

Universities have funding constraints, and as a result, cannot stretch their capacity to undertake core functions and at the same time support industry for innovation. Most technology development initiatives and networks, such as the innovation clusters project, are very dependent on donor funding. The funding from universities is not enough to enable them to commit full-time staff resources and equipment to innovation projects. It would help universities if governments and industries increased core support for these centres or projects.

9.10 Facilitating University-Industry Collaboration

It is important to identify what helps university-industry links work and remain sustainable. Whilst universities are facing funding, knowledge, and resource constraints, industry has the resources that they need if they can prove that they have the capacity and the quality that industries can rely upon. Ankrah (2007) suggested five contingencies that may assist university-industry links to work and remain sustainable. They include necessity, recognition and reciprocity, efficacy and efficiency, stability, and legality and legitimacy

9.10.1 Necessity

Necessity will push all actors to look for competitive advantage and the industry will need new knowledge. This knowledge cannot be generated within industry alone. Synergies with universities think tanks and consulting firms are inevitable. These partners, on the other hand, are facing funding, knowledge, and resource constraints, and industry has the resources that they need if they can prove that they have the capacity and the quality that industries can rely upon.

9.10.2 Recognition and Reciprocity

For links to work, there's a need for recognition and reciprocity among the players. Universities need to earn recognition and reciprocity from the industry by sharpening capabilities and producing quality of research outputs. On the other hand, the industry must win the recognition and respect of governments and universities. An industry that has no R&D, research programme, equipment, materials or data, and information will not attract incentives from governments or partnerships in technology development from outside firms.

9.10.3 Efficacy and Efficiency

Efficacy and efficiency are shaped by time and cost. If research processes take too long to produce results at a very high cost, contracts are not renewed and links take a short duration. Links normally start with informal activities and mature into long-term engagements. To manage this transition, universities have adopted strategic interventions that can enhance their efficiency. Delivery on time, prioritisation of projects, managing costs effectively, and improving their credibility can enable them to get long-term contracts.

9.10.4 Stability

Stability is crucial in any relationship. Staff retention problems within universities are undermining their credibility in these links. Universities need to develop human resource strategies that can provide the basis for assurance that once a project is launched, the same team will see it through to the end. The long-term formal links are possible only with universities in which research capacity is not only available and strong but stable and reliable and where leadership succession is assured.

9.10.5 Legality and Legitimacy

Legality and legitimacy deficits can weaken collaboration. The contested terrain of intellectual property rights within universities (academics and their employers) and between them and industry needs to be resolved through contract systems that accommodate the conflict of interests between actors. At the same time, it is crucial to accept that academics value recognition, and for most of them, the presentation of findings at prestigious conferences is more motivating than other gains. Their legitimate right to publish and disseminate needs more space in collaboration arrangements than is currently the case.

9.11 Summary

This chapter concerns itself with the role of ODeL institutions in fostering innovation and industrialisation. Universities are very important centres of innovation that can bring industrial advancement to countries. To properly position themselves as leaders in innovation, African universities need to make changes to their way of doing business. They must make important changes in their programmes to embrace innovation and industrialisation issues in their research and teaching agenda. Such changes, however, need not only occur in curricula but also in teaching approaches and engagement with basic and applied research aimed at resolving today's societal ills. Teaching must embrace new participatory and problem-solving elements to contribute towards innovation, and industrialisation. Furthermore, universities must engage with the main end-users of their services, communities, and industries. Frameworks for innovation are discussed as well as university policies that contribute to innovation. The contribution to industrialisation by universities is also detailed, as are the barriers to innovation. Lastly, recommendations to facilitate university-industry collaboration were put forward.

9.12 References

Amabile, T. M., Conti, R., Coon, H., Lazenby, J., & Herron, M. (1996). Assessing the work environment for creativity. *Academy of Management Journal, 39*(5), 1154–1184.

Amabile, T. M. (1998). How to kill creativity. *Harvard Business Review, 76*, 77–87.

Ankrah, S. N. (2007). *University-Industry Inter-organizational Relationships for Technology/Knowledge Transfer: A Systematic Literature Review.* Leeds University Business School. https://www.researchgate.net/journal/SSRN-Electronic-Journal-1556-5068

Bailey, T. (2002). *Innovations in Higher Education: Problematising the International Trends in The African Context.* Cape Town: Education Policy Unit, University of the Western Cape.

Baregheh, A., Rowley, J., & Sambrook, S. (2009). Towards a multidisciplinary definition of innovation. *Management Decision, 47*(8), 1323-1339.

Ben-David, J. (1977). *Centers of Learning: Britain, France, Germany, United States.* New York: Mcgraw-Hill Book Company.

Brewer, D., & Tierney, W. (2012). Barriers to innovation in the US education. In Wildavsky, B., Kelly, A. and Carey, K. (Eds.), *Reinventing Higher Education: The Promise of Innovation* (pp.11-40). Cambridge, MA: Harvard Education Press.

Christensen, C. M., & Eyring, H. J. (2011). *The innovative university: Changing the DNA of higher education from the inside out.* San Francisco: Jossey-Bass.

Creso, M. (2013). *Perspective of Industry's Engagement with African Universities.* http://www.aau.org/sites/default/files/University.

Economic Development Administration (EDA). (2013). *The Innovative & Entrepreneurial University: Higher Education, Innovation & Entrepreneurship in Focus.*

Ekong, D., & Cloete, N. (1997). Curriculum Responses to A Changing National and Global Environment in An African Context. In *Knowledge, Identity and Curriculum Transformation in Africa.* Cape Town: Miller Longman.

Etzkowitz, H., & Leydesdorff, L. (1997). Introduction to special issue on science policy dimensions of the triple helix of university-industry-government relations. *Science and Public Policy, 24*(1), 2-5.

Etzkowitz, H. (1998). The sources of entrepreneurial science: cognitive effects of the new university-industry linkages. *Research Policy, 27*(8), 823-835.

Goldman, J. L. (1992). *Webster's New World Dictionary.*

Hannan, A., & Silver, H. (2000). *Innovating in Higher Education: Teaching, Learning and Institutional Cultures.* Philadelphia: Open University Press.

Haynes, J. (2002). *Children as Philosophers. Learning through Enquiry and Dialogue in the Primary Classroom.* London: Routledge Falmer.

Jackson, R. (1990). Higher education, industry and the economy. *The Vocational Aspect of Education, 42*(112), 39-42.

Jenniskens, I. (2000). Government Steering and Innovations in University Curricula. In Kalleberg, R., Engelstad, F., & Brochman, G. (Eds.), *Comparative Perspectives on Universities.* Stanford, Connecticut: Jai Press Inc.

Jones, B. F. (2010). Age and Great Invention. *Review of Economics and Statistics, 92*(1), 1-14.

Lester, R. K. (2005) *Universities, Innovation, and the Competitiveness of Local Economies.* A summary report from the Local Innovation Systems Project – Phase 1, Local Innovation Systems Working Paper 05-005, MIT-IPC, Cambridge, MA.

Mihyo, P. B., Hammond, A. B., Makhoka, A. O., & Tjihenuna, U. G. (2011). *The Role of Tertiary Education Institutions in the Development of Technical and Technological Capabilities for Employment Creation in Eastern, Southern and West Africa: Selected Case Studies.*

Moore, B., & Ulrichsen, T. (2010). *Towards a holistic approach to higher education policymaking in Africa: UK and US evidence on the infrastructure and institutions enhancing the socio-economic returns to higher education.* http://events.aau.org/userfiles/file/corevip11/papers/barry_moore_et_al_Creating_AHES.pdf

Murray, J. Y. (2001). Strategic alliance-based global sourcing strategy for competitive advantage: a conceptual framework and research propositions. *Journal of International Marketing, 9*(4), 30-58.

Ng'ethe, N. (2003). *Higher Education Innovations in Sub- Saharan Africa: With Specific Reference to Universities.*

OECD. (2011). *Education at a Glance 2011: OECD Indicators.*

Rosli, M. M., & Sidek, S. (2013). The Impact of Innovation on the Performance of Small and Medium Manufacturing Enterprises: Evidence from Malaysia. *Journal of Innovation Management in Small & Medium Enterprises.*

Ross, M. (2001). *The University: Anatomy of Academe.* New York: Mcgraw-Hill Book Company.

Sanyal, B. C. (1995). *Innovations in University Management.* Paris: IIEP, UNESCO.

Silver, H. (1998). *The Languages of Innovation: Listening to the Higher Education Literature.* Working Paper No. 1, Innovations in Teaching and Learning in Higher Education Project. Plymouth: University of Plymouth.

Silver, H., Hannan, A., & English, S. (1997). *Innovation: Questions of Boundary.* Working Paper No. 2: Innovations in Teaching and Learning in Higher Education Project. Exmouth: University of Plymouth.

United Nations Industrial Development Organization (UNIDO). (2011). *Economic Development in Africa Report.*

Veugelers, R., & Rey, E. D. (2014). *The contribution of universities to innovation, (regional) growth and employment.* EENEE Analytical Report 18. http://www.education-economics.org

Chapter 10

Organisational Climate and Development in ODeL Institutions

Rittah Kasowe

Zimbabwe Open University

Abstract

This chapter aims to inform ODeL institutions of individual transformation and the accompanying tension of mergers on the organisational climate and the influence thereof on HEI sustainability. The concept of organisational climate, its development climate levels, models and influences, dimensions, determinants, structure, and processes will be discussed. Apart from the mentioned aspects, the roles of organisational climate variables, notwithstanding culture, will be articulated while also focusing on the well-being of employees, their work performance, and ultimately, the institutional performance. The chapter provides a leeway for ODeL institutions to improve their organisational climate to enter a new era of globalisation.

Keywords: Climate; Development; Open and distance e- learning

***

10.0 Introduction

This chapter aims to inform ODeL institutions of individual transformation and the accompanying tension of mergers on the organisational climate and the influence thereof on HEI sustainability. Furthermore, it describes extensively the concept of organisational climate, its development climate levels, models to be used and its influences, dimensions and determinants, structure, and processes in ODeL institutions. Apart from the mentioned aspects, the roles of organisational climate variables, notwithstanding culture, will be articulated for ODeL institutions to improve organisational climate.

10.1 The Concept of Organisational Climate

Organisational climate is seen as the employees' perception of the organisation's policy, practices, and procedures, both formal and informal (Širca, Babnik &

Breznik, 2013). Very few studies are designed to investigate the causal path of the effect of innovation on organisational performance systematically by examining the influence of organisational climate.

Altman (2000) indicates that the perception of the organisation is reflected in the way the employees describe their workplace. Thus, organisational climate is a collective concep, determined by the employees' perception of the organisation as well as their perception of organisational processes and engagement. It is a set of characteristics that describe an organisation and that (a) distinguish the organisation from other organisations (b) are relatively enduring overtime and (c) influence the behavior of people in the organisation". Organisational climate is a set of specific features of the organisation inducing the manner of its conduct towards workers and the environment (Hershberger, Lichtenstein & Knox, 1994). It is a set of characteristics of organisational situations that are relatively permanent effects of the operation of social organisation, shaping organisational behaviour motives of those employees (Bratnicki, Krys & Stachowicz, 1988). Organisational climate entails the characteristics for a given institution set of norms conditioning employee behaviour. It results from both objectively functioning organisational processes, as well as their subjective feelings. These two images overlap each other and set the frame of employees' conduct in a given organisation (Potocki, 1992). The concept of organisational climate refers to a set of organisational practices, objectively evaluated, which influence attitudes, values, and perceptions of the people who are part of it, as well as productivity and interpersonal relations highlighted by them. It is the quality of the organisational environment perceived or experienced by the members which influences their behaviour. Climate acts as a motivation in the organisation and that climate determines the reliability of the organisation. Organisations tend to attract and keep people who adjust to their climate so that their standards are preserved. Therefore, it follows that the climate will be an important variable, because of its influence, not only on organisational phenomena, but also on the behaviour of individuals when integrated in the organisational context.

10.2 The Concept of Organisational Climate in ODeL Institutions

Organisational climate in ODeL institutions refers to a set of attributes which can be perceived about the organisation and/or its subsystems, and that may be induced from the way that organisation and/or its subsystems deal with its members and environment (Shreedevi Shintri & Bharamanaikar, 2017). Organisational climate (OC) plays an important role in the innovation of an ODeL institution. In addition, innovation has become critical for ODeL employees in an increasingly complex and challenging e-learning and teaching environment. The economic and cultural environments as well as the institutional and individual variables are determinants of the ODeL organisational climate. The constant satisfaction of individual needs and emotional balance is the main motivation for the behavioural development of the individuals, being the process that leads to the construction of the organisational climate. Motivation - at an individual level - leads to the organisational climate. Thus, the organisational climate is closely related to the degree of motivation of the employees, given that when there is great motivation among members, the motivational climate rises and translates into satisfaction, energy, interest, and collaboration relationships. Human needs arise from the interaction with the environment, with motivation as a dynamic component in human behaviour. No matter how much motivation an internal process to the individual is, it is concluded, however, that the environment contributes to its evolution, since it is from it that individuals build their reality. The satisfaction of individual needs, which may be either physiological or safety-related (vegetative needs) as well as social, esteem, or self-fulfillment related (higher needs), rely heavily on the interpersonal relationships with people who are in higher hierarchical levels (leadership), who are responsible for understanding the motivation of individual employees, as well as their needs and the consequent behavioural adjustment of the individual. Academics in ODeL universities are also people who are continually prompted to adjust to a variety of situations to meet their needs and maintain an emotional balance. This adjustment requires not only the satisfaction of physiological needs or safety but also the need to belong to a close social group for self-fulfilment. Hence, it turns out that the organisational climate is closely linked to the degree of the employees' motivation in this era of technological use in their work. When there is a high degree of motivation, there is a climate of satisfaction, interest, and collaboration in ODeL institutions. Conversely, when there is frustration or barriers to the satisfaction of needs, the organisational climate tends to be worse, characterised by apathy states, sometimes leading to depression. The concept of organisational climate translates the environmental influence on the motivation of ODeL employees and can be described as the quality of the organisational environment regarded by employees.

10.3 Characteristics of Organisational Climate in an ODeL Institution

Creative organisational climate in an ODeL institution is one of the most important elements that play an important role in the development of creativity. Climate is what members of the organisation experience, and culture reflects the values of the organisation. The climate is a variable determined by organisational and psychological processes, which, in turn, affect the overall performance and good results of the organisation. (Schneider, et al., 1996). Giri & Kumar (2007), in their research, observe that organisational climate has a significant impact on job satisfaction and productivity. Therefore, the climate can be a modifier that increases or decreases the effects of the entity. In ODeL institutions, the processes include group problem-solving, decision making, communication, and coordination. Therefore, organisational climate factors (e.g., the external environment in which the organisation operates, the resources available within the organisation, as well as its culture and management practices) can play an important role in bringing organisational creativity, including the employee (Kuenzi & Schminke, 2009). Meanwhile, the psychological processes include learning in the organisation, individual problem solving, creating, motivating and commitment (Ekvall & Britz, 2001).

Figure 10.1: Mechanisms of Shaping Organisational Climate in ODeL Institutions

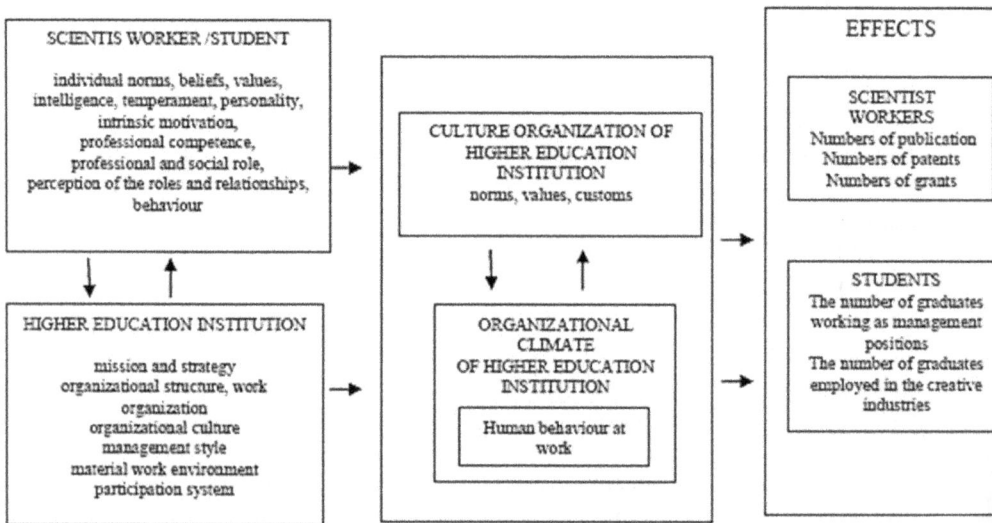

SCIENTIS WORKER /STUDENT		EFFECTS
individual norms, beliefs, values, intelligence, temperament, personality, intrinsic motivation, professional competence, professional and social role, perception of the roles and relationships, behaviour	CULTURE ORGANIZATION OF HIGHER EDUCATION INSTITUTION norms, values, customs	SCIENTIST WORKERS Numbers of publication Numbers of patents Numbers of grants
HIGHER EDUCATION INSTITUTION mission and strategy organizational structure, work organization organizational culture management style material work environment participation system	ORGANIZATIONAL CLIMATE OF HIGHER EDUCATION INSTITUTION Human behaviour at work	STUDENTS The number of graduates working as management positions The number of graduates employed in the creative industries

Source: Sokol, Gozdek, Figurska, & Blaskova 2014

The mechanism of shaping of organisational climate of ODeL higher education institutions and their influence on students' and scientist workers' creativity.

Uncommon in the world is it to examine the organisational climate of ODeL higher education institutions as a source of creativity of students, administrative staff, and lecturers. This seems to be very interesting issue because the ODeL education system should create chances and opportunities to develop creative competence. It is the degree of orientation of the institution and staff employed there, including degree of their creativity, that will enhance their competences, enabling them for creativity and employment in the creative sectors (see Fig 10.1 above). The modern trend of the world economy sees creativity as a resource, values that determine development of the institutions, their ministries the country, or region level. (Sokol et al., 2014).

10.4 Model of Organisational Climate in ODeL Institutions

A model of how the climate within an organisation develops and influences job behavior is suggested. The influences on climate (the external environment, differences in the structure of the organisation, and personal differences in the style and behavior of management) are moderated by the norms of the group of which the employees are members, as well as the individual's tasks and personality, to produce, in effect, three types of organisational climate. The individual has a perception of the climate that exists within the institution. To the extent that this is shared by the other employees in their departments, a group climate is formed. Where there exists a collective perception within the property, an organisational climate can be described, one that is generally agreed on to be descriptive of the operation. The individual then develops in his or her mind a map of the perceived climate, which acts as a screening device to reinforce that perception. Research has shown, for example, that the longer an individual has been working within a certain climate, the more difficult it is to change that person's perception of it. Based on the individual, group, and organisational climates, employees develop expectations that are moderated by their ability, and personality affects motivation, satisfaction, and job performance.

10.5 External Influences on Organisational Climate

The external environment surrounding the institution influences the type of climate that is appropriate. We can speculate, for example, that the availability of labour will help shape the extent to which the institution values employees. When the competition for employees is stiff, management will adopt a stronger employee orientation than when labour is plentiful.

10.6 Organisational Influences on Organisational Climate

There is an assumption that close physical proximity between employees and management will produce greater employee identification with management goals and objectives. Additionally, some feel that a smaller property will produce a greater feeling of teamwork than a larger operation. The results of research on the effect of size on organisational climate are mixed. While increasing size might reduce job satisfaction of employees, size alone is not a decisive determinant of organisational climate.

Considering that ODeL institutions rely most heavily on the use of technology in its delivery, it can be argued that there is a significant relationship between climate and types of technology. ODeL institutions that use small batch and process technologies perceive more favorable climate than using mass production techniques. ODeL institutions have highly bureaucratic structures and are more likely to be perceived as closed system with a less satisfactory climate. In some cases, employees feel they have more individual autonomy to be considered by the institution. Their perception of climate is perceived in a situation when the ODeL institutions have an orientation toward students rather than employees.

10.7 Personal Influences on Organisational Climate

In ODeL institutions, employees as individuals bring with them biases toward seeing what them is around. Individuals who grew up inherently suspicious of management will tend to see negatives in everything management does. They may view things differently from other employees who were raised to believe that management is always right. Thus, employees' personalities influence organisational climate.

10.8 Moderating Influences on Organisational Climate

In ODeL institutions, the external influences on climate are moderated by several factors. For example, those perceptions of climate vary among employees at different levels in the management hierarchy. Perceptions are also influenced by the type of work that employees perform and their characteristics. At this level, there are also external individual factors that moderate the link between climate and work behavior, and one is the ability of the individual employee. In an innovative climate, employees who have the skills to produce in an unstructured setting will be more productive than those of lesser ability. Another factor is the employee's personality. Those with a high need for order perform better in a highly structured climate, while those with a high need for autonomy perform better in an environment in which decision-making is decentralised. Understanding of the dimensions will help in well-structured, organised study of climate and can be further applied to assess the impact of these dimensions on various HR and organisational behaviour aspects like employee performance, employee motivation, job satisfaction, occupational stress, employee commitment, employee morale, employee behaviour, team effectiveness, and organisational efficiency (Shreedevi Shintri & Bharamanaikar, 2017).

In ODeL institutions, employees are motivated by many different factors. Some are internal factors, such as a need for power or achievement; others are connected to the work itself, such as the desire for challenging work; while still others are influenced by a supervisor or manager, such as the need for feedback or praise. There are certain things that an individual manager can do little about; for example, pay and benefits. The management can directly influence other things, such as recognizing employee achievements and giving some decision-making authority. For employees who place great importance on the work situation, certain dimensions of climate are more important. Such employees prefer task-oriented management actions that seek to get the organisations moving. They also enjoy friendly social relationships while not wishing to be burdened with what they consider merely busywork. For those who see the work situation as being less important, the emphasis sought is on maintaining pleasant relationships while reducing dissension and disruption.

10.9 Dimensions of Organisational Climate in ODeL Institutions

10.9.1 The Forum Corporation

Organisational climate can be categorised in seven dimensions, or key aspects. A well-respected model is that of the Forum Corporation. The Forum model describes the climate of an organisation in six dimensions: three dealing with performance, three with development. The performance dimensions are *clarity, commitment,* and *standards.* The development dimensions are *responsibility, recognition,* and *teamwork.*

10.9.2 Clarity Performance Dimension

Clarity refers to how well the employees understand the goals and policies of the ODeL institutions, in addition to how clear they are about their own work. It is the feeling that things are organised and run smoothly, not confused. If they feel unclear about what they should be doing relative to others in the operation, they will have a low score on this dimension.

10.9.3 Commitment Performance Dimension

Commitment is the extent to which employees feel continually committed to achieving the goals of the institution; the extent to which they accept ODeL institutions' goals as being realistic; the extent to which they are involved in the setting of such goals; and the extent to which their performance is continually evaluated against the goals of the operation. ODeL institutions have certain goals, such as return on investment, student satisfaction, and employability. These goals are achieved (or not achieved) by the efforts of the employees. Institutional goals can be met only if academic staff/employees are in some way committed to achieving them. The greater the commitment, the more likely it is that the objectives will be achieved.

10.9.4 Standards Performance Dimension

Standards measure the degree to which employees feel that management emphasises the setting of high standards of performance and the extent to which they feel pressure to improve their performance continually in ODeL institutions. To achieve that student's benefit, concessions are made in the areas of student service, equipment maintenance, and employee training and development. Employees, those who have been with the operation for an extended time, may feel that standards toward the students have been slipping. This will influence how they feel toward the institution and may well affect their performance.

10.10 Development Dimensions

10.10.1 Climate Development Dimension

Among the development dimensions of climate, responsibility is the feeling employees have that they are personally responsible for the work that they do, that supervisors encourage them to take the initiative, and that they have a real sense of autonomy. The employee who must check with the boss before he or she can do anything does not have this. Some supervisors, while complaining that their subordinates will not leave them in peace and will not make decisions for themselves, do not encourage employee initiative. They criticise employee decisions without being constructive; they will not tolerate employee opinions that differ from theirs. One explanation for this behavior is that the supervisor, while critical of the employees' lack of initiative, wishes to keep a close check on them. This paternalistic feeling comes from the belief that if employees can make decisions and initiate actions without them, the supervisors will not be needed. The way this type of supervisor feels needed is to force employees to check with him or her about even the most minute details of a job.

10.10.2 Recognition Development Dimension

The second development dimension is recognition: the feeling that employees are noted and rewarded for doing good work rather than receiving criticism and punishment as the predominant form of feedback. In a climate such as this, where rewards and recognition outweigh threats and criticism, there is a promotion system in place that helps the best person rise to the top, and the organisation has a reward structure related to the excellence of performance. It sometimes seems, however, that the only feedback employees get is when something is amiss. When we hear: "The manager wants to see you," most of us will immediately think: "What did I do wrong?" A major reason is the idea of management by exception. Under this accounting term, targets are set and, if met, the property is on target and no remedial action need to be taken. Thus, if things are going well, the manager, who has many demands on his or her time, will pass over that department to concentrate on the problem areas. Under this type of climate, in fact, employees may perform negatively to receive some feedback, even if it is criticism. The fact is that an absence of feedback (extinction is the psychological term) is more punishing than punishment.

10.10.3 Teamwork Development Dimension

Teamwork is the third development dimension. This is the perception of belonging to an organisation that is cohesive, one where people trust one another, and where employees feel personal loyalty and the sense that they belong to the organisation. It is the feeling of working together, rather than 'us versus them,' whether that be management versus workers or kitchen versus dining room. We all like to feel that we are part of a winning team.

10.10.4 Work Behavior Dimension

Numerous studies have found a correlation between organisational climate and job performance. Climates seen as supportive have produced higher performance than those perceived as less supportive. Employee-centered climates have not always led to higher performance levels. One major factor seems to be the consistency with which climates are perceived. Employees who perceive that a climate is always rules-oriented or always employee-oriented perform better than in situations in which the climate perception changes. That link is not as clear or as persuasive, however, as the relationship between climate and job satisfaction. Supportive climates lead to job satisfaction. However, is there a link between job satisfaction and job performance?

10.11 Determining Factors of Organisational Climate in ODeL Universities

Chiavenato (2009) highlights that there are two situational or environmental motivation determining factors: expectancy and incentive value. Expectancy has to do with the subjective probability of needs satisfaction - or its frustration and incentive value relates to the amount of satisfaction or frustration because of the verified person's behaviour. The organisational climate is well understood as the quality of the organisational environment observable by members of the organisation, and that influences people's behaviour. It comprises a broader and more flexible framework on the environmental influence on motivation "In fact, the organisational climate influences people's motivational state and is influenced by them" (Chiavenato, 2009).

Both leadership styles and the organisational structure are important for the organisational climate, as they influence individual behaviour according to the needs of affiliation, power, and achievement in the organisation. The leaders are particularly relevant figures in promoting courage and brave organisational climates through the contagion effect, representing the emotional and moral muscle that permits facing difficulties and pursuing ambitious new missions. Moreover, the interpretation of the individual perception of his work situation and of the leadership style interaction should also be emphasised and what this might mean in terms of individual satisfaction or organisational productivity.

In short, leaders also promote an organisational climate of psychological safety that induces people to take the initiative, take risks, learn from mistakes, innovate, and reacquire their self-esteem, leading them to focus their energy on important tasks and challenges. Subsequently, there are seven organisational climate categories:

- Leadership (power).
- Responsibility (power).
- Organisational Clarity (realisation).
- Performance standards (implementation).
- Rewards (affiliation).
- Human warmth (affiliation).
- Support (affiliation).

In this context, the organisational climate is understood as the perception that seeks to measure the collaborators' grounds for satisfaction and the reasons for discomfort so that it builds a work environment that strengthens the relationships of the collaborators with the organisation, with their colleagues, with their teams, and with their leaders, always looking for membership, motivation, and the commitment of their staff. Other authors, such as Litwin and Stringer (1968), conclude that distinct organisational climates can be created by variation in the organisational leadership style (Manuela et al., 2014).

10.12 Psychological climate of ODeL institutions

According to (Sokol et al., 2014), organisational climate can be categorised into four dimensions, namely: (i) autonomy; (ii) structure; (iii) remuneration; and (iv) consideration, warmth, and support. These dimensions determine the psychological climate of an organisation, which is the individual's experience or perception of the organisational climate (Isaksen et al., 2001). The psychological climates in ODeL institutions are, however, also influenced by the workgroup to which the individuals belong, the task for which the individuals are responsible, and the individuals' abilities and personalities (Field & Abelson, 1982). From the psychological climate, individuals form a cognitive map and define their personal expectations, which in turn determine their work behaviour. Even though Tierney (1999) is of the opinion that organisational climate develops in a social way, organisational climate is a specific combination of situational variables, which can be categorised into three factors, namely: external influences; the organisation's history; and management (Sokol et al., 2014). Literature reveals that there is the combination of external and organisational factors and their influence on the organisational climate. External factors include the physical as well as the sociocultural environment (transforming factors), while organisational factors involve transactional factors, such as centralisation, configuration, formalisation, standardisation, size, structure, technology, management behaviour, leadership patterns, control, and remuneration (Isaksen et al., 2001). Hence, ODeL institutions ought to take cognisance of these factors to create conducive climates. The psychological climate is derived from the psychological contract, which is based on a process of mutual expectations that the individual and the organisation develop through the cooperation promoted by the managers. It is a set of mutual expectations that relate to work (performance), roles, confidence, and influence, established by tacit arrangement, but about which there is an agreement. A psychological contract arises with the development of work relationships and specifically when the worker performs his functions voluntarily. A psychological contract is a mental model that people use to frame labour commitments and establish trust relationships with the organisation, revealing an implicit set of expectations always operating between the members of an organisation. It sets expectations about behaviour that go together with all the performance, and it is expected that the management treats its employees fairly, facilitating acceptable working conditions for a good performance, communicating clearly what is a fair working day, and giving them an indication of how the employee is performing his obligations; and those employees comply, demonstrating a "good attitude and loyalty" towards the organisation. Psychological contracts can be summarised in the past and emerging forms of the employment relationship as shown in Table 10.1 below:

Table 10.1: Past and Emerging Forms of the Employment Relationship

CHARACTERISTICS	RECENT PAST	EMERGING
FORMS		
Focuses	Security; continuity; loyalty	Change; future employability
Form	Structured and predictable	Flexible, open to renegotiation
Values	Tradition; equity; social justice; socioecon omic class	Market forces; skills and knowledge; added value
Employer Responsibility	Continuity; security; training; career prospects	Equity: reward for value added
Employee Responsibility	Loyalty; attendance; compliance with rules; positive performance	Proactive capability; innovation; excellent performance levels
Contractual relationships	Formalized	Individual responsibility, career development through new skills and training
Career Management	Responsibility and Organization; internal careers planned and directed by the HR department	Individual responsibility to manage / negotiate their services (internally and externally)

Source: (Sokol et al., 2014).

10.13 Determinants Shaping Organisational Climate in ODeL Higher Education Institutions

Organisational climate in ODeL higher education institutions determine the level of creativity for academic teachers, administrative staff, and students. However, there are some guidelines as to the factors shaping them to the conducive development of creative attitudes or restricting them. These factors are:

Relationship support of colleagues: Relationships in the institution need to be characterised by trust, openness, humour, and good communication, therefore allowing colleagues to support and stimulate each other to work.

Support of lecturers and administrative staff: Relations with regards to ODeL higher education institutions should be based on trust and openness, a certain degree of autonomy, and the creation of conditions conducive to the development.

Positive relationships with lecturers: Perceptions of direct superiors should support new and innovative ideas.

Positive interpersonal exchange: The academic community ought to be seen as 'being together'; forming a coherent whole and not experiencing significant conflicts.

ODeL higher education institutions environment resources/time: Perception of the university as having and wanting to use the resources to support and strength implementation of creative ideas for the generation of new ideas is also needed – timorously.

Safety: Academic communities should feel that they can openly talk about their new ideas without be ridiculed or punished; trust and guarantee of safety becomes a priority.

Motivation: Motivation should be aimed at strengthening the processes related to creativity and aspiration for it.

Orientation on reward: Rewarding creativity needs to be properly selected in an incentive system manner so that prizes do not become a factor that inhibits the creative process.

Autonomy / independence: Perception of university workers and students need to have the freedom and flexibility to carry out their tasks.

Risk-taking: Treatment of new situations ought to be treated as a source of inspiration, and new challenges being accommodated.

Stress: The level of stress conditions the creative processes and openness and willingness to exchange information between each other and between scientist workers and students need to be accepted.

Flexibility and adaptability: Each adaptation to new conditions and tasks has to be taken as a challenge.

Diversity and tolerance for it: There is room for tolerance in higher education institutions for diversity and innovation. These factors determine creativity while allowing notice in diversity and otherness problems that do not exist when dealing with uniformity.

Participation: Students need to participate in creative processes. Hence, communication between academic teachers and students must be clear, open, and efficient.

Systems and processes: University systems and processes enhances those conditions that are conducive to the development of creativity

Intellectual stimulation: Making collaboration through open discussion, debate, and virtual team discussions.

Organisational integration: Perception of higher education institutions be seen as integrated externally (with the environment) and internally (e.g., the teams within the organisation).

10.14 Structure and Processes for Organisational Climate in ODeL Higher Education Institutions

The first factor, which plays an important role in the creative process of a university, is the support of colleagues understood as a colleague's desire (researchers and students) for cooperation and mutual assistance. This can be done through mutual motivation or the formation of a healthy competitive environment. Assistance and support in this context also refer to the exchange of knowledge, skills, and ensuring encouragement. Also, it is important to support students through their academic teachers. This is a direct responsibility of the scientist workers, as well as their creative competence. In addition to the climate for creativity, it is important that academic teachers:

- become role models for their colleagues, especially students.

- let students a certain freedom in decision-making and action and limiting excessive control, which assure learners the autonomy in action.

- assure adequate support for students (not just mental) and encourage students to undertake creative activities.

- assure a kind of style of teaching in higher education institutions that will act motivationally on the work of other research workers and students.

Relevant to organisational climate oriented on creativity are the relationships between the lecturers, administrative staff and students, and interpersonal exchanges. Lecturers and the entire staff's actions in an ODeL institution should not only be limited to control. Relationships should be based on trust, openness, and security. Students should not feel the threat from the academic workers and other students proposing new ideas. Academic communities should be seen as 'being together,' forming a coherent whole, without experiencing significant destructive conflict. West (1990) found that a sense of security has a positive effect on the level and number of new ideas. People are often more willing to present their ideas to a greater extent when they feel they will not be ridiculed or punished. These same guidelines should apply to the relationship between the collaborating scientist workers. Also, motivation reflects the emotional involvement of the academic community in its activities and the ability to achieve the objectives (Ekvall, 1996). Proper motivation oriented on the creation of creative ideas occurs when people experience joy and feel useful at work.

Autonomy factor means to preserve the independence of the institution with regards to contacts; sending and receiving information; discussion of issues and alternative solutions; and taking initiative and making decisions through created platforms. Organisational climate that supports the autonomy to achieve clearly defined objectives will likely to be more effective in terms of creativity, than the institution, which is not thus focused on the development. Environment of freedom and autonomy more likely adapts to intrinsic motivation, which is a key factor in promoting creativity. Excessive control either empowers employees and students or hinders creative performance. This can be in control of decision-making, control the information flow, and even the perception of control in the form of loyalty systems, which places too much emphasis on increasing motivation. Climate of an ODeL higher education institution, which promotes primarily control and not co-partnership, reduces creativity and innovation. Another important factor influencing organisational climate is the level of stress that is associated with the study and performance of scientific work. Also important is so-called time pressure, which can affect disorganising on the creative process. If the atmosphere in the academic environment is unfriendly and causes stress for researchers and students, then level of creativity is limited. First, one of the characteristics of the climate is that employees and students should be encouraged to be creative and giving new solutions. The entire structure of ODeL higher education institutions should be focused on teaching students creative behaviours in the use of technology, so desirable in today's world. Academic lecturers as representatives of the creative class should show by their work and thereby encourage students to be creative. In an ODeL high education institution, staff and students should be provided with techniques and methods for stimulating creativity that will support e-learning education.

Flexibility and adaptability as other factors are the components that also play an important role in shaping creative organisational climate. ODeL institutions, to be creative and innovative, need to quickly and proactively respond to the ambient turbulence and requirements of globalisation with regards to technology and education that is e-learning. This is especially important in today's world economy, where the variability of the operating conditions is greatly enhanced. It is worth noting that the appropriate organisational climate supporting creativity in ODeL higher education from the diversity, which is so important to enable them, form creative ideas. Diversity in ODeL higher education institutions can be interpreted differently. Namely, we can talk of diversity of opinion, staff, students, and space. Each of these elements influences the level of creativity. It is worth noting that intolerance differences deny diversity and thus blocking it. In addition, students should participate in the creative processes at the university. This may apply to participation in research and development of 5.0 that is innovation and industrialisation projects and students' scientific associations. This allows students to establish a closer relationship with academic employees and benefit from their knowledge and experience and create a link to the partnership and shared responsibility. Organisational systems and processes are those conditions that are conducive to the development of creativity. The development process is related to the work of, inter alia, access to knowledge at the university. Library systems should be developed that the students or researchers may use them at any time. Also, the system in the form of e-learning and intranet should be developed, since this is the modus of operando in ODeL institutions. Students and researchers should be free to communicate with regards to the flow of knowledge if creativity is formed at the university as competence.

Organisational integration is a multidimensional concept, but in its basic level, considers the level of cohesion and unification, referring not only to those working in the institution but also the students, which provides a smooth and effective functioning. Intellectual stimulation making through cooperation in teams (student-student, student-lecturer, or lecturer-lecturer) have a positive influence on each other, adding to the creative process. It does so through open discussion and debate via e-learning platforms.

10.15 Role of Organisational Climate in ODeL Institutions

Organisational climate surveys offer organisations and their employees a snapshot in time of employee evaluations of their work and institution. Individual employee perceptions or work and organisation are aggregated to indicate the organisational climate. Unlike organisational culture, which is more deep-seated behaviour based and resistant to current events, organisational climate is more voluble and based on perceptions of events at a point in time such that climate may be regarded as an expression or subset of culture; a relevant analogy equates culture to the 'meteorological zone' in which the organisation resides while climate represents the 'daily weather'. Climate is obviously more easily captured and measured than culture, and so its value lies in allowing management and employees to understand internal strengths and weaknesses and act where necessary. Climate surveys further offer a voice to employees and provide a means of measuring attitudinal change over time. Organisational climate is measured quantitatively through questionnaires although some qualitative studies have been undertaken.

Variables Affecting Organisational Climate in ODeL Institutions

There are five variables that have a definite effect on organisational climate in ODeL institutions. These variables include the following:

- Support from the organisation, including remuneration, recognition, administrative support, and support mechanisms (Isaksen et al., 2001).

- Leadership, quality of supervision, effective and fair management practices, effective communication, participation in decision-making by all members, and effective labour management (Sokol et al., 2014).

- The nature of the interpersonal processes in the organisation (Altman, 2000).

- Role and post characteristics (Mader, Scott & Razak, 2013).

- The effect of the external environment on the individual as well as the organisation.

These variables influence the organisational climate within ODeL higher education institutions.

10.16 Organisational Climate and Organisational Culture in ODeL Institutions

Lack of understanding about the role of organisational culture in improving management and institutional performance inhibits the ability to address the challenges that face higher education and confounds the ability to create and maintain global partnerships. ODeL institutions might face increasing complexity and fragmentation. As decision-making contexts grow more obscure, costs increase, and resources become more difficult to allocate, leaders in the institution of higher education benefit from understanding their institutions as cultural entities. They need to recognize that those with whom they will work with on a global partnership will have a culture different from their own. The point is certainly not that one organisational culture is better than another, but instead that working across cultural boundaries is necessary for any leader involved in global partnerships.

Leaders should make decisions. These decisions, however, need not engender the degree of conflict. Indeed, properly informed by an awareness of culture, some decisions may contribute to an institution's sense of purpose and identity, and will facilitate the ability to create and maintain global partnerships. Moreover, to implement decisions, ODeL institutions' leaders and management must have a full, nuanced understanding of their organisation's culture. Only then can they articulate decisions in a way that will speak to the needs of various constituencies and marshal their support. Without an understanding of one's own culture, the ability to create connections with another organisation's culture becomes that much more difficult.

Cultural influences occur at many levels, within the department and the institution, as well as between universities when they work with one another, regardless of whether the companion organisation is in the same country or abroad. Because these cultures vary dramatically, a central goal of understanding organisational culture is to minimize the occurrence and consequences of cultural conflict and help foster the development of shared goals. Studying the cultural dynamics of educational institutions and systems equips ODeL institutions to understand and, hopefully, reduce adversarial relationships. Equally important, it will enable to recognise how those actions and shared goals are most likely to succeed and how they can best be implemented.

One assumption of this chapter is that often, more than one choice exists for the decision-maker; one simple answer most often does not exist. No matter how much information we gather, frequently, we can choose from several viable alternatives. Culture influences the decision. Effective administrators understand that they can take a given action in some institutions but not in others. They are less aware of why this is true. Bringing the dimensions and dynamics of culture to consciousness helps ODeL leaders assess the reasons for such differences in institutional responsiveness and performance. This will allow them to evaluate likely consequences before, not after, they act. An understanding of the cultural determinants of an organisation enables a decision-maker not only to understand their organisation but also those with whom they will enter into a global partnership.

It is important to reiterate that an understanding of organisational culture in ODeL institutions is not a panacea to all administrative problems or a certainty that global partnerships will always be successful. An understanding of culture, for example, will not automatically increase enrolments, increase research grants, or increase the number of global partnerships that get formed. However, in ODeL institutions, administrators' correct interpretation of the organisation's culture can provide critical insight about which of the many possible avenues to choose from is best when deciding about how to increase enrolment, whether to undertake a particular approach to increasing research output, or how to improve global partnerships. Indeed, the most persuasive case for studying organisational culture is quite simply that we no longer need to tolerate the consequences of ignorance, nor, for that matter, will a rapidly changing environment permit us to do so. By advocating for a broad perspective, organisational culture in ODeL institutions encourages practitioners to:

- consider real or potential conflicts, not in isolation but on the broad canvas of organisational life

- recognise structural or operational contradictions that suggest tensions in the organisation

- implement and evaluate everyday decisions with a keen awareness of their role in and influence upon organisational culture

- understand the symbolic dimensions of ostensibly instrumental decisions and actions

- consider why different groups in the organisation hold varying perceptions about institutional performance.

Many administrators intuitively understand that organisational culture is important; their actions sometimes reflect the points mentioned above. A framework for organisational culture in an ODeL institution provides administrators with the capability to better articulate and address this crucial foundation for improving organisational performance in general and in global partnerships.

When anthropologists conduct fieldwork to better understand the culture of a society or a collective group, they are equipped with disciplinary-specific terms, such as "fictive kinship," that define commonly encountered phenomena. These terms are not only intelligible to other anthropologists but they are deemed crucial for a thorough description and analysis of a given culture or cultural activity. For an understanding of ODeL institutional cultures in higher education, it is therefore useful to pinpoint similarly important phenomena and provide a working terminology that can serve as the basis for a conceptual framework. Six such terms define an organisation's culture at a university: mission, socialization, information, strategy, leadership, and environment. In what follows, I provide a thumbnail definition of these terms in relation to how to think about global partnerships.

- *Mission:* A mission is succinct, clear, and orients the institution to its primary roles in society. If global partnerships are a central part of a university's role, then one expects to see mention of international outreach and involvement.

- *Socialisation:* Socialization pertains to how new members are oriented to the mission and functions of the institution. Socialization is not a static concept and changes and adapts as individuals enter and exit the organisation. If global outreach is important, then individuals will be socialized in a manner that enables them to learn more about than their discipline, country, or institution.

- *Information:* The material that individuals receive and the way it is conveyed pertains to this term. If the organisation honors global partnerships, then a significant communicative symbol pertains to all of the members receiving information and updates about international engagements.

- *Strategy:* Any organisation will have an implicit or explicit plan about the direction the organisation is taking; if global partnerships are important, then they will be one key component of a university's strategic plan.

- *Leadership:* The board, university president, and senior administrators are obvious actors who are key in the direction the university will take. Global partnerships should have someone who oversees the strategic direction the university takes as a member of the senior leadership team.

- *Environment:* ODeL institutions have a variety of geographies that can define their sphere of influence. A local institution may define nothing more than the city or town where it is located. Regional universities may have a broader geographic region but define their clientele and outreach as a region within the country. A university that desires long-standing and impactful global partnerships will see its environment in much broader terms. Nevertheless, a university need not be as broad as defining "the world" as its environment. Instead, for strategic reasons, the institution may focus on one area, such as Southern Africa or the whole of Africa. By focusing on this manner, the organisation helps frame what is and is not of importance to the university's members.

10.17 Summary

The ODeL institutions have been moving through a period of rapid change, even more so within the Southern African context and the world due to the transformation of the countries in general. Transformation and mergers lead to individuals experiencing a feeling of loss, whether it is a loss of identity or their sense of belonging to the organisation. Furthermore, individuals may feel that their personal and professional values are under threat and therefore may experience a fear that the teaching standards will be compromised and that they may fail to achieve customary levels of excellence. This chapter aimed to inform ODeL institutions of individual transformation and the accompanying tension of mergers on the organisational climate and the influence thereof on HEI sustainability. The concept of organisational climate, its development climate levels, model and its influences, dimensions and determinants, structure, and processes have been extensively discussed. Apart from the mentioned aspects, the roles of organisational climate variables, notwithstanding culture, have been articulated. Although universities have always had unique cultures, I have suggested that rather than aiming at maintaining the status quo, the culture now needs to shift towards innovation. It was highlighted that organisational climate is not only related to the employees' attitudes towards work but also to the well-being of employees, their work performance, and ultimately, to the institutional performance. The chapter provided a leeway for ODeL institutions to improve their organisational climate in order to create a more stable and sustainable work environment to improve their operations as one of the pillars of sustainability in an effort to enter a new era of globalisation.

10.18 References

Altman, R. (2000). Forecasting your organizational climate. *Journal of Property Management, 65*(4).

Bratnicki, M., Krys, R., & Stachowicz, J. (1988). *The organizational culture of companies.* [Study shaping the process of change management]. Ossolineum: Wroclaw.

Chiavenato, I. (2009). Recursos Humanos: *Capital Intelectual das Organizações. Elsevier, Rio de Janeiro.*

Ekvall, G. (1996). Organizational Climate for Creativity and Innovation. *European Journal of Work & Organizational Psychology, 5*(1), 105-123.

Field, R. H. G., & Abelson, M. A. (1982). Climate: A Reconceptualization and Proposed Model. *Human Relations, 35*(3), 181–201.

Giri, V. N., & Kumar, B. P. (2007). Organizational commitment, climate, and job satisfaction: An empirical study. *IUP Journal of Organizational Behaviour, 6.*

Hershberger, S. L., Lichtenstein, P., & Knox, S. S. (1994). Genetic and Environmental Influences on Perceptions of Organizational Climate. *Journal of Applied Psychology, 1.*

Isaksen, S. G., Lauer K. J., Ekvall G., & Britz, A. (2001). Perceptions of the best and worst climates for creativity: Preliminary validation evidence for the Situational Outlook Questionnaire. *Creativity Research Journal, 13*(2), 171–184.

Kuenzi, M., & Schminke, M. (2009). Assembling Fragments Into a Lens: A review, critique, and proposed research agenda of the work climate literature. *Journal of Management, 35*(3), 634-717.

Mader, C. Scott, G. & D. A. Razak. (2013). Effective change management, governance and policy for sustainability transformation in higher education. *Sustainability Accounting, Management and Policy Journal* 4(3), pp. 264–284.

Mikula, B. (2000). Organizational climate and organizational culture: An attempt to systematize concepts. Scientific Papers MWSE, Tarnow, 3.

Manuela, N. M., Araújo, C. &, Couto João, P. A. (2014). Higher Education Institution Organizational Climate Survey. *International Journal of Advances in Management and Economics, 3*(1).

Potocki, A. (1992). *Selected methods of humanization of work.* Wrocław: Ossolineum.

Širca, N. T., Babnik K., & Breznik, K. (2013). Towards organisational performance. Understanding human resource management climate. *Industrial Management and Data Systems 113*(3).

Schneider, B., Brief, A. P., & Guzzo, R. A. (1996). Creating a climate and culture for sustainable organizational change. *Organizational Dynamics, 24*, 6-19.

Shintri, S., & Bharamanaikar, S. R. (2017). A theoretical study on evolution of organisational climate theories and dimensions. *International Journal of Science Technology and Management, 6*(3).

Sokol, A., Gozdek, A., Figurska, I., & Blaskova, M. (2015). Organizational climate of higher education institutions and its implications for the development of creativity. *Procedia - Social and Behavioural Sciences, 182*(3), 279-288.

Tierney, P. (1999). Work relations as a precursor to a psychological climate for change. The role of work group supervisors and peers. *Journal of Organizational Change Management, 12*(2).

West, M. A. (1990). The social psychology of innovation in groups. In: M.A. West, J.L. Farr (Eds.), *Innovation and Creativity at Work: Psychological and Organizational Strategies.* Chichester, England: John Wiley.

Chapter 11

Programme Management, Implementation and Evaluation Practices in ODeL Universities

Richard Bukaliya

Zimbabwe Open University

Abstract

Successful programmes in any organisation hinge on how best the programmes are managed, implemented, and evaluated. ODeL programmes are no exception, as there is a need for management practices that are amenable to transformational changes, coupled with evaluation practices throughout the process of ODeL programme implementation. This having been said and done, there is a need for processes of coordination to direct and oversee implementation of said programmes to make them deliver outcomes and benefits aligned to the institution's strategic objectives. ODeL institutions, while being advised to be innovative, need to follow available practices, as there might not be any need to reinvent the wheel. This, therefore, means where existing theories are applicable, ODeL practitioners need to consider them and look for other practical ways of solving existing challenges. This chapter, therefore, discusses the tenets of programme management, implementation and evaluation practices in ODeL universities. The chapter provides both theoretical and practical insights into how ODeL institutions ought to be and are involved in programme management, implementation, and evaluation so that envisaged programmes are sustained for the betterment of society.

Keywords: Programme, Management, Implementation, Evaluation, ODel Practices

***

11.0 Introduction

Management practices that are amenable to transformational changes because of evaluation practices throughout the process of programme implementation give rise to programme success. Coordination to direct and oversee implementation of the said programmes to make them deliver outcomes and benefits aligned to the institution's strategic objectives are, therefore, important. ODeL institutions need to follow available best practices, as there might not be any need to reinvent the wheel. This, however, does not mean side-lining innovation but where existing theories are applicable, ODeL practitioners need not shun these. This chapter looks at the tenets of programme management, implementation, and evaluation practices in ODeL universities to ensure these are successful institutions. The chapter provides both theoretical and practical insights into how ODeL institutions ought to be and are involved in programme management, implementation, and evaluation practices amidst calls for reforms towards the betterment and acceptance of ODeL universities and programmes by various stakeholders.

11.1 Programme Implementation Practices

Sebba (2004) sees implementation as the process of putting into action what has been agreed upon. You notice that implementation is the phase between a decision and operation. It seeks to determine whether an organisation can carry out and achieve its stated objectives. A new programme is usually carried out by agencies that are responsible for the problem area; the decision-makers who formulate a programme may not be the implementers. You realise that when an institution develops a programme, it is the ODeL tutor who is left to do what is prescribed by the programme policy.

Implementation as the third stage of a programme cycle involves the action that will be taken to put the law into effect. Implementation viewed broadly means administration of the policy in which various actors, including you the ODeL practitioner, organisation, procedures, and techniques work together to put adopted policies into effect to attain programme goals.

Therefore, implementation encompasses those actions by public or private individuals and groups that are directed at the achievement of goals and objectives set forth in prior policy decisions meant to effectuate or bring into being given programmes. In other words, we are talking of operationalising plans through different activities meant to achieve set objectives.

11.2. Programme Management

We borrow from the definition prescribed by Schwalbe and Furlong (2013), who define a programme management as a series of initiatives and activities, that are meant to stir an undertaking as reflected in its objectives, thus contributing to a common, overall objective of the institution. Programme management is the overall management of the interrelated activities that make up the programme.

It also involves linking in with the institutional change functions within the business areas affected to ensure that the changes are properly implemented. As with project management, planning work and tasks is a key part of programme management, but the work is more closely aligned to the organisation's ongoing strategy rather than specific deliverables. Programme management often provides a layer of governance above specific projects and ensures that they are run effectively under the guidance of able individuals.

11.3. Key Aspects of Programme Management

Let us look at some of the significant aspects of programme management. I draw your attention to the five that are as follows:

- **governance:** defining the programme roles and responsibilities as well as the processes and metrics to assess its progress

- **management:** planning the overall programme, ensuring that regular reviews are undertaken and that stakeholders are engaged.

- **financial management**: costs of managing the programme need to be tracked and controls need to be put in place

- **infrastructure**: creating the right work environment to support the programme; and

- **planning**: developing a programme plan based on the specific projects, resources, timescales, and controls for the overall programme.

11.4. The National Programme Office

Due to the geographical dispersion of ODeL offices, an ODeL programme should be supported by a national programme office under a national programme leader. The national programme leader manages the programme on a day-to-day basis and coordinates all the activities to do with the programme at a national level, disseminating information to the different regional campuses to foster uniformity in the institution. The national programme leader monitors the progress of activities, and the realisation of programme plans and receives information for benefits of reviews and produces reports as defined by the chairperson of the department. The programme leader also provides and allocates resources that assist with the design of the programme blueprint and facilitates assessments for the reconfiguration of the programme if the programme has outlived its purpose. The programme leader is a centre of excellence and assists with the correct implementation of the programme's principles, governance themes and transformational flow. The leader may serve a single programme or several programmes, depending on the size or capabilities of the ODeL institution.

11.5. Approaches to ODeL Programme Management

A programme management framework can offer a governance structure and provide process models, documentation templates, and guidelines for adapting it to the specific programme. For that reason, the programme leader is required to lead the programme member and be in possession of several attributes and skills. Let us look at some of these requisite skills.

Programme leaders need strong leadership, communication, and interpersonal skills. They work with a team scattered throughout a large geographical setting. They, therefore, are required to lead the programme team. Knowledge of programme framework as well as resource allocation and programme procedures are beneficial. The programme leader should be able to advise the teams and to anticipate and solve any problems that may be encountered during the programme implementation, bearing in mind the geographical isolation of the team members.

The success of any programme depends on how well four key aspects are aligned with the contextual dynamics affecting the programme. Let us look at what has been referred to as the four P's.

- **Plan**: The planning and forecasting activities.
- **Process**: The overall approach to all activities and project governance.
- **People**: Including dynamics of how they collaborate and communicate.
- **Power**: Lines of authority, decision-makers, organograms, policies for implementation, and the like.

There are several approaches to organising and completing programme activities, including: phased, lean, iterative, and incremental. There are also several extensions to programme planning, for example, based on outcomes (product-based) or activities (process-based).

11.6. Programme Goal and Objectives

The overall goal of an ODeL programme with several projects gives direction to each individual project which will then formulate its own goal based on the overall programme objective. The project goal is a concise statement of the purpose of the project. Objectives stem from the goal and specify what the project is going to do. It is therefore important to have clear ODeL programme objectives. The more specific the programme objectives, the greater the chances are of achieving them. The acronym "SMART" is used to describe a good objective (The Global Fund, 2009). These SMART objectives are needed for any successful ODeL programme. Let us look st what SMART stands for as related to ODeL objectives.

- **Specific:** It must be clearly defined, leaving no room for ambiguity or misinterpretation of the ODeL programme objective.

- **Measurable:** It must be clearly stated in the objective of the ODeL programme what will be done and how it will be measured to determine if the project goal has been met. Setting a measurable objective makes programme evaluation easier.

- **Achievable:** Be realistic about what the ODeL programme can achieve in terms of the scale/scope of the project, the time that the programme is set to run, the human or other resources available, and the allocated budget.

- **Relevant:** Objectives are the building blocks or steps towards meeting the ODeL programme goals. They therefore need to relate and be relevant to the goals.

- **Timebound:** There is need for clarity in the objectives about the timeframe in which the ODeL programme or activities will take place.

ODeL programme objectives lead to academic programmes or courses on offer in the institution. These programmes are a result of demand to close the skills gap obtaining in a nation. As such, the courses kick off being on demand, and at saturation point, the programmes need to be phased out as they outlive their lifespan after satisfying the intended objectives. We need to look at the life cycle of any programme and see what is involved in each of the stages.

11.7. Programme Management Cycle

A programme has basically five phases that enable leadership to map the best possible direction. The five phases are initiating, planning, execution, monitoring and controlling, and closing. Let us look at each of the phases.

- **Initiation:** At this stage, the institution needs to determine why the programme is required. There is need to ascertain if it is feasible or not and what requirements are needed for the programme implementation. The course leaders need to carry out a feasibility study. A list of stakeholders and prospective beneficiaries of the course are identified, and a survey carried out to ascertain their willingness to subscribe to the programme. Upon getting positive input from the intended beneficiaries and stakeholders, programme leaders then need to take it to the next phase, which is the planning phase.

- **Planning:** In the planning phase, programme leaders need to detail the programme scope, its time frame, and potential benefits and prospective beneficiaries, such as groups of potential students.

Completeness and continuity are the major components of a successful programme plan. Outputs of this phase include a detailed programme overview, a communication plan budget baseline, programme scheduling, individual project goals, a scope document (course outline which includes the course objectives), and an updated beneficiary register. An ODeL institution needs to make use of various brains in coming up with course outlines, hence the need to involve several players at this level.

- **Execution:** The execution phase entails that programme team members who are faculty members are coordinated and guided through proper communication to get the work done, as explained in the approved programme management plan, which includes all the course outlines for the specific programme courses. Additionally, this phase also covers the proper allocation and management of other programme resources like materials and budgets. There are issues to do with massive typographical work and this needs to be budgeted for. Programme deliverables are the output of the execution phase. There is need to look at the numbers enroled for the programme and ascertain if the ODeL programme has indeed been received by all potential students.

- **Monitoring and control:** The time, cost, and performance of the programme are compared at every stage, and necessary adjustments need to be made to the programme activities, resources, and plan to keep things on the right track. Outputs from this phase include programme progress reports. Reports could include the numbers of enroled students and feedback from these students as well as employers and other beneficiaries in the communities where in-stream students and graduates from the programme are providing services.

- **Closure:** Every programme has its life span, and programme closure entails the termination of any programme that would have lived its life span. There comes a turning curve where the ODeL programme fails to attract any further meaningful numbers of students into a cohort. That is the point of the process that involves terminating the programme, reviewing the programme outputs, and transitioning them to new programme goals. The programme closeout phase offers time for both celebration and reflection. Reflections from this phase include results and what was learnt, and these could then be applied to other programmes in the future.

11.8. Importance of ODeL Programme Management

Kivunja (2015) argues that leadership is about enabling change that helps followers to contribute to this change. From this assertion, you notice that each tutor must strive to be an effective change agent for the success of any educational organisation. Without leadership, therefore, no meaningful change can be achieved in the ODeL campus. Leadership makes all the difference in success or failure of organisations. The same sentiments are echoed by Truskie (2002) when he asserts that there is a direct link between leadership, organisational culture, and performance. From all these propositions, you notice that leadership is very important as it helps influence what happens in the core business of the ODeL campus or school. All the success and failures in the ODeL teaching and learning processes rely on leadership. Outside of the ODeL campus, Fligstein and Freeland (1995) assert that the ability of organisational leaders to solve internal resource problems is a function of their abilities, knowledge, and links with the outside world. This external linkage highlights the importance of leadership to coordinate and to harmonise the structural-cultural dynamics which foster organisational development and learning in a way that makes a positive difference to the lives of learners in an ODeL setting.

As argued by Scott (1999), effective leadership is important in the effective management of educational change in an ODeL institution. In support, Fullan (2001) states that effective ODeL leaders are the key to large-scale, sustainable ODeL education reform. This, therefore, implies that without leadership, you cannot expect to find sustainable programmes in ODeL settings. All elements of restructuring of public education are are dependent on effective leadership to ensure successful implementation. This remark underpins the importance of leadership in an ODeL institution.

Cited by Kivunja (2015), Barker and Coy (2004) argue that the success or failure of cultural change in ODeL campus depends on the attitude of the leadership team. The leaders are there to champion the beliefs and values that underpin the emerging culture. The heart of the cultural change process lies the integrity of the leader, the example set by the leader and the trust established by the leader (Barker & Coy, 2004).

From the above citation, you realise a pattern in consensus among the authorities that leadership plays a key role in the structural and cultural dynamics designed for an ODEL set up. Leadership is seen as the glue that holds together the structural and cultural dynamics within an organisation through the execution of informational, interpersonal, and decisional roles (Kivunja, 2015). As Scott (1999) also adds on to this discourse by remarking that leadership is about enabling followers to bring about desired change by setting up organisational structures which enable the cultural synergies within the

ODeL context to be shared and dispersed within the ODeL organisation between and among all members involved in ODeL.

Such views then make us believe that leadership is important because it is responsible for calling for a commitment and passion from every member of the ODeL setting to contribute, which results in a positive difference in the lives of the ODeL learners and help lay the foundation which will help them develop into productive citizens who will be able to live and work productively in increasingly dynamically complex and different societies where they live.

11.9. Key Leadership Roles in Programme Management

What has evolved from our discussion above on the importance of leadership in ODeL can be acutely summarised in four main roles, namely the leader as a team leader, as policy designer, as pedagogy creator, and as a rights advocate (McCrea, 2015). Let us unpack these roles and show what they mean in as they relate to leadership in an ODeL setting.

11.10. Leading People in ODeL Settings as a Team Leader

ODeL programme leadership assists to a great extent in articulating the goals of the ODeL system. The ODeL programme team leader plays a vital role as a change agent as well as a follower at the same time. Whilst the team leader expects to lead as the captain, at some time he/she should be led by other team members in areas where he/she does not understand. It follows that being a leader does imply you know all. You agree that your main role is to assist the team to achieve victory since you have personal interest in the success of the team. By so doing, the success of the ODeL`s goals and policies involves all participants, with the leader as the provider of the vision, as team leader and the involvement of other organisational structures and resources that are then used by the team to work together for the success and sustainability of the organisation (Brundrett & Crawford, 2008). During the leadership in ODeL programmes, there is need for cooperative learning. Let us borrow from what Johnson and Johnson (2004) argue as five principles of cooperative learning in instruction and link these to the ODeL situation. The principles they advance are as follows:

- positive interdependence
- individual accountability
- equal participation.
- group processing; and
- simultaneous interaction.

Similarly, we have Kivunja (2015), who has highlighted the need for the 4Cs in instruction and we borrow these as they assist in the ODeL situation. The 4Cs are:

- critical thinking and problem-solving
- collaboration
- creativity and innovation; and
- communication.

Let us look at these issues in some detail.

- **positive interdependence:** As relates to positive interdependence, the leader should make sure that all participants work together closely such that there is the understanding that we shall "sink or swim together" (Johnson & Johnson, 2004). Johnson & Johnson (2004) argue participants in an ODeL setting realise and believe they can achieve their personal goals when the other team members also reach their goals.

- **individual accountability:** This ensures that the ODeL leader puts it across to all the staff that they have a sense of individual responsibility for the performance of the tasks and achievement of the common goals. All members should feel that they have a responsibility to contribute to the task assigned to the team because they have something valuable to offer. Where there are courses to share, the programme leader makes sure that these are shared equitably and according to specialisation.

- **providing for equal participation**: This aspect entails that every member of the team assumes an equal share of the tasks that need to be completed in the ODeL setting. The ODeL leader needs to ensure that equal opportunity is provided to the members and that each member of the team contributes to the task according to their personal best. This way, the team's goal is achieved through interaction among all members of the ODeL team.

- **group processing**: For this to be effective in the ODeL setting, the Programme Leader needs to give participants the opportunity to reflect on learning experiences during teamwork, so they better understand what happened during the cooperative activities. As members, you need to evaluate how you have achieved the set goals. There is need to discuss the overall experiences among all members and to review which actions were helpful and which ones were not. Further to that, you should decide on which actions to keep for future use, to decide on which actions to change in future teamwork, to set goals for future work, and to strategise for future success. Periodic meetings, therefore, become very useful. These could be for programme evaluation or deliberating on issues to do with other faculty related processes such as examinations.

- **provide for simultaneous interaction:** The ODeL programme leader, needs to ensure that team members engage in interpersonal and group interactions, get to know each member of the team, develop trust for each member of the team, actively listen to each member of the team, communicating clearly and accurately, take turns, use the opportunity to state ideas freely, accept responsibility to contribute and for what each member contributes, provie constructive criticism to other members of the team, accept constructive criticism from other members of the team, share tasks, engage in democratic decision-making, be sensitive to team members' different perspectives, clarify differences, accept and support each other, avoid conflict, and resolve conflict constructively, if it occurs (Kivunja, 2015).

As programme leader in the ODeL setting, the leader needs to ensure that the people exercise critical thinking all the time to maximise the rationality of their decision-making and problem-solving. They need to work collaboratively and support each other. They should also be creative and innovative in the way they engage in the programme activities.

11.11. Leading People in ODeL Settings as a Policy Designer

When the programme leader leads other personnel in an ODeL institution as a policy designer, there is need for vision for the big picture for the ODeL programme (Kivunja, 2015). As programme leader creatively influences staff and learners in ODeL campus to engage positively in the learning, teaching, educating, and growing up. Programme leaders need to bear in mind that programme designers are by profession able to critique their creations, to reflect on how their present designs are meeting client demand and to plot a different course or come up with an entirely new design to maintain relevance to the clients. The leader is tasked to originate the programme vision and for that reason as the ODeL programme leader, have not only the determination to see the proposed policies being implemented correctly, but also the patience, resilient demeanor, intellectual fortitude and organisational calm to allow any slow changes and challenges to take effect to improve the efficacy of the ODeL programmes (Kivunja, 2015).

11.12. Leading People in ODeL Settings as a Pedagogy Creator

The ODeL programme leader, as a pedagogy creator, should come up with insights that lead to the generation of new ways of teaching, learning, assessment, and curriculum development to develop "best practice pedagogy" (Kivunja, 2015). Being a creator of pedagogy involves developing or advocating learner-friendly strategies. This role involves recognition that, in the creation of pedagogy for ODeL, the students' interests must be the prime factor that influences what is created. It also recognises that students of the current digital age learn best through interconnected peer learning networks, which give them opportunities to develop and utilise their digital fluency skills. There is, therefore, a need to create a situation where students get access to technological gadgets that assist in developing creativity and communicating with peers.

11.13. Leading People in ODeL Settings as a Rights Advocate

There is talk of both students' rights and responsibilities as well as human rights in general. As rights advocate in the ODeL institution, the programme leader needs to get acquainted with the rights so that they are advanced in the programmes being led. An ODeL leader as a rights advocate is required to champion the cause of the ODeL programme at different levels (Kivunja, 2015). To begin with, the leader is required to advocate for the success of the ODeL institution. Added to that they need to advocate for the improvement in working conditions of all co-workers at the ODeL institution. Most importantly, they need to advocate for the students' rights and similarly good conditions for people in the ODeL community at large because these are the clients who provide the learners they look after. In the institution, for example, the leader ensures that staff members are given every opportunity for professional development and career advancement. Programme leaders prepare policies that protect the learners in the programme from abuse. For example, there is a need to have in place policies for the protection of students against abuse by tutors. These policies could come in form of tutorial letters and tutors' guides. Tutors' guides might be used to provide polices that make it impossible for tutors to short-change the students in tutorial delivery.

11.14. Efficient and Effective Leadership Function in an ODeL

On one hand, for an efficient ODeL programme leader, it implies that one needs to allocate and utilise educational resources in a way that optimises their use. In other words, there is neither waste nor inefficiency in the use of available ODeL resources. The resources might include course modules and guides. On the other hand, by effectiveness, we mean the extent to which organisational goals are achieved in the specified planning horizon. Hattie (2003) states that the extent to which learners achieve stated learning outcomes in an educational is what can be termed effectiveness. One can only be deemed to effective when learners in the programme are performing to expectation. There is a need to provide good quality services so that the community in which you are operating will label the leader effective. Therefore, when leadership meets the stated standards, that leadership passes the test of efficiency and effectiveness criteria in the ODeL setting.

According to Kivunja (2015), efficiency and effectiveness of leadership in an ODeL setting is judged considering the quality of service stipulated in the relevant documents for the respective jurisdiction. One may notice that issues of efficiency and effectiveness could be judged, for example, through the provision of conducive environments for the wellbeing of the students and staff in an ODeL institution, their sense of belonging, contribution to the ODeL setting, communication, and the quality of outcomes as reflected in the ODeL students produced by the ODeL institution.

11.15. Characteristics of Coordination

Coordination is a process of integration and involves an orderly pattern of group efforts on the enterprise towards the accomplishment of common objectives. This process of co-ordination at the ODeL campus is manifested through the following characteristics:

- co-ordination between individuals in a group in the ODeL campus.
- co-ordination between groups of a department in the ODeL campus.
- co-ordination among various departments of the ODeL campus.
- co-ordination among various activities and operations in the ODeL campus; and
- external coordination with communities outside of the ODeL campus.

If all the above characteristics are manifested in the leader, then coordination is a success.

11.16 Roles of the Coordinator in ODEL Programmes

Let us summarise the roles of the ODeL coordinator, first in pictorial form. Figure 11.1 below presents the coordination roles which we feel are significant in ODeL coordination.

Figure 11.1: Roles of the Coordinator in ODeL Programmes

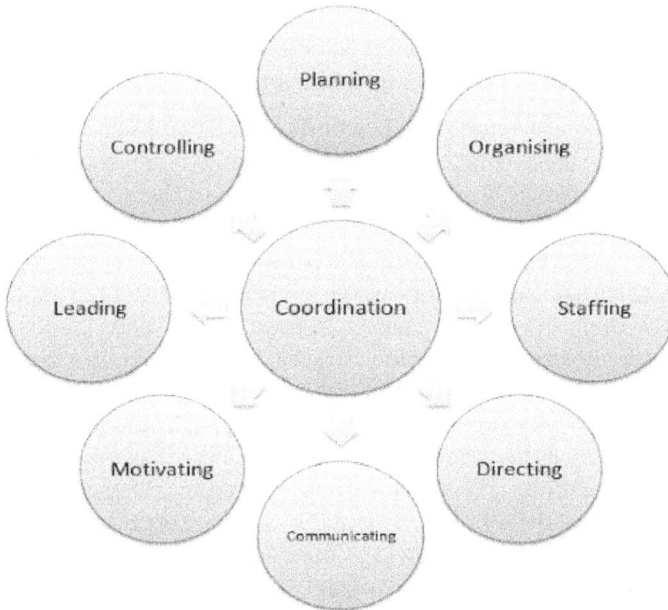

Adapted from Brech, 2002

We now want to focus on each of the roles and see what each of them entails.

We need to indicate that for the roles that we have discussed above to be effective, you need to consider certain principles. Let us look at the principles that make you effective in your policy coordination roles.

- **Planning:** By planning, we mean a function of ODeL management that involves setting objectives and determining a course of action for achieving those objectives (Waring, 2016). Planning requires that, as ODeL managers, you be aware of environmental conditions facing the ODeL campus and forecast future conditions. It also requires that ODeL managers be good decision-makers (Lamond, 2004). The planning process begins with environmental scanning which simply means that ODeL planners must be aware of the critical contingencies facing the system in terms of economic conditions, their competitors, and their customers. You must then attempt to forecast future conditions. These forecasts form the basis for planning. We need to reiterate that as planners, you must establish objectives, which are statements of what needs to be achieved and when. All these should be done in line with the policies in mind. You also must identify alternative courses of action for achieving objectives. After evaluating the various alternatives, ODeL planners must make decisions about the best courses of action for achieving objectives (Gomez-Mejia, David & Robert, 2008). You then formulate necessary steps and ensure effective implementation of plans. Finally, there is a need to evaluate the success of your plans and take corrective action when necessary.

- **Organising:** According to Lamond (2004), organising is the function of ODeL management that involves developing an organisational structure and allocating human resources to ensure the accomplishment of objectives. The structure of the organisation is the framework within which effort is coordinated. The ODeL structure is usually represented by an organisation chart, which provides a graphic representation of the chain of command within the centre. Decisions made about the structure of an organisation are generally referred to as organisational design decisions. Organising also involves the design of individual jobs within the organisation (Lamond, 2004). Decisions must be made about the duties and responsibilities of individual jobs, as well as the way the duties should be carried out in the ODeL campus. You are aware that the school head is at the top of the organisational structure and all ODeL tutors report to the Regional Programme Coordinator, who in turn reports to the Faculty Chairperson.

- **Staffing:** Staffing is an important function which is normally a sub function of the organising function. You notice that all the other functions, including planning, organising, directing, coordinating, and controlling, depend upon the staff within the organisation which are made available through the staffing function (Waring, 2016). Staffing helps in getting right people for the right job at the right time in the ODeL campus. The function of staffing enables the school management to find out as to how many employees are needed and with what qualifications and experience to fill in the post at the ODeL campus as prescribed by the policies. Staffing contributes to improved organisational productivity. Through proper selection, the ODeL institution can enhance the quality of the employees, and through proper training, the performances level of the ODeL employees can also be improved.

- **Directing:** Directing activities is a key function. This entails letting staff know what needs to be done and by when. It is a responsibility of the Faculty Chairperson and other members of the management. However, bosses tell people what to do, while leaders motivate people to contribute in meaningful ways. The directing function requires leaders to do more than simply give orders, even though tasks must be completed for the success of the teaching and learning processes on the ODeL campus. This function begins with supervising subordinates while simultaneously motivating teams through guided leadership communicated in clear ways.

- **Communication:** Directing is built around effective communication. As an ODeL Campus Director, you need to create an environment that supports different communication methods from passing information to exchanging opinions. The important thing is to ensure these different communication channels are not just between the supervisors and subordinates but also between employees and different management levels. You should, therefore, make sure that open channels of communication are opened, and staff communicates in a manner prescribed in the given policies.

- **Motivation:** As we mentioned above, the big part of directing is about inspiring and motivating ODeL staff. You need them to get to know the objectives to ensure there is enthusiasm to achieve the goals. Motivating ODeL staff includes positive and negative feedback, provision of ideas and opportunities to develop skills further. Directing might also have an element of monetary or non-monetary incentives, such as the introduction of bonuses, as dictated by policies.

- **Leading:** According to Waring (2016), leading is the process of influencing or inspiring others to perform as required by the institutional policies. If you are effective ODeL leaders, your subordinates will be enthusiastic about exerting effort to attain organisational objectives. You need to know that to become effective at leading, you should first understand your subordinates' personalities, values, attitudes, and emotions. You need to be good at motivating other staff on the ODeL campus so that they are energised to put forth productive effort in line with the policies.

- **Controlling:** Gomez-Mejia, David, and Robert (2008) assert that in the ODeL campus, controlling involves ensuring that performance does not deviate from policies. Controlling consists of three steps, which include establishing performance standards, comparing actual performance against standards, and taking corrective action when necessary. Performance standards are often stated in monetary terms such as revenue, costs, or profits but may also be stated in other terms, such as units produced, number of defective products, or levels of quality or customer service. When involved in all these, you need to consider what the policy says.

11.17 Principles of ODeL Policy Coordination

Brech (2002) has highlighted the following as the principles of policy coordination:

- **Principle of early introduction:** Coordination must be visualised right from the early stages of planning and policymaking. At the time of preparation of the plan, cooperation, consultation, give and take become the necessity. In case the plan is prepared without coordination, then it becomes difficult to supply the required materials or results in the misallocation of the duties.

- **Principle of continuity:** According to this principle, policy coordination should be followed in the organisation on a continuous basis, and it should be taken as a regular activity. As ODeL managers, you should treat policy coordination as the never-ending exercise.

- **Principle of direct contact:** According to the principle of direct contact, policy coordination can only be established through the direct contact of the parties whose activities are to be coordinated. As through direct contact, the parties can discuss the methods, plans, actions, activities, and work for the achievement of overall organisational goals.

- **Principle of mutual relation:** This principle states that every ODeL employee should understand the problems faced by the other employees and try to solve them. For coordination, there should be perfect adjustment and sense of fellow feeling among the employees.

Now that you are familiar with what is entailed in leadership and policy coordination, we want to focus on the organisational structure of the ODeL system at the provincial level.

11.18. Structure of ODeL Programme Coordination at National Level

The ODeL system has a well-coordinated structure to make sure that its programmes are a success. In most universities, for example, Zimbabwe, you are aware that at the head of the university is the Vice Chancellor (VC). However, the VC may have one or more deputies to take charge of the different aspects of the institution. In Zimbabwe, the VC is deputised by two Pro Vice Chancellors. One looks after the academic affairs of the university while the other oversees research, innovation, and enterprise development. Our focus is on ODeL, and this level of education falls under the jurisdiction of the Pro Vice Chancellor for Academic Affairs. This PVC is there to oversee policy implementation and supervision of all academic related issues. Under the PVC Academic are the Faculty Deans who are in charge of the administration of various faculties. Different Regional Directors who oversee regional campuses also report to the PVC Academic Affairs. This is given so that regional campuses are places where all the teaching and learning takes place, but Regional Directors are mostly concerned with administrative issues of the regional campuses. The Chairperson of the Department comes next, under whose leadership a department falls. Since there are different programmes in the department, these are headed by Programme leaders. However, there is the need to take note that the Chairpersons do not report to the Regional Director, but they do so to the Dean. The Programme Leader oversees programme implementation and works closely with Regional Programme Coordinators to whom he/she provides guidance as to the ODeL programme requirements. Regional Programme Coordinators are responsible for the implementation of department policies and are in the different geo-political regional centres of the country. They are each assigned tasks by the Chairperson in consultation with the Programme Leader. However, the structure varies from one country to the other, but basically what we have presented above is a basic structure for the implementation of ODeL programmes and policies.

11.19. Programme Evaluation Practices

According to Sebba (2004), programme evaluation is an undertaking that uses a range of research methods to systematically investigate the effectiveness of interventions, implementation, and processes, and to determine their merit, worth, or value in terms of improving the social and economic conditions of different stakeholders. From the provided definition, you might have noticed that programme evaluation applies evaluation principles and methods to examine the content, implementation, or impact of a programme. By evaluation, we, therefore, mean an activity through which we develop an understanding of the merit, worth, and utility of a programme.

Once a programme has been implemented, its effectiveness must be evaluated. Research and analysis are again brought to determine if the original problem has been addressed and if there have been any unexpected outcomes (Cummins, 2011). In some cases, cost-benefit analysis can be adopted to determine if the benefits of a programme are worth the expenditure. If the programme demonstrates significant failures, a new cycle may begin with problem definition and agenda setting. It is possible for the cycle to repeat multiple times until a successful programme is implemented. Therefore, you see many programmes being altered or discontinued. It could be that the cost of such a programme initiative outweighs the benefits.

11.19.1. Importance of Programme Evaluation in ODeL

As argued by Brownson et al. (2009), policies are established by those in political power to set forth the guiding principles and rules for various institutions, ODeL institutions included. The policies are meant to assist the institutions, to build the culture that will effectively meet the intended goals through various programmes. There are many components to developing and implementing programmes. Once a programme is implemented, it must be evaluated intermittently to determine whether adjustments are necessary. Most programmes are conceived and then documented in ordinances, memos, or administrative circulars. These documents describe implemented programmes that are considered formal amendments to previous ones and so on. Since programmes are designed to strategically assist society realising their needs, it is important to conduct evaluations on any implemented programme.

Nutley & Webb (2000) argue that organisations need to implement certain policies for the success of their intended strategies. The ODeL programmes need to be both effective and relevant to the community, the ODeL tutors and the period. A programme that was relevant five years ago may no longer be relevant today. Therefore, evaluation is important after a programme is implemented and adopted. They system will not ascertain if a programme requires amendment or change and therefore, there is need for the process evaluation. For example, it was not necessary for the ODeL system to have outdated programmes that used to work years ago. In this modern world, it is not ideal, effective, and efficient to use archaic means to an end. Thus, programmes need to be evaluated for relevance and whether they adhere to current trends. Failure to go with the times may result in ODeL institutions unable to solve societal needs.

Gage & Dunn (2009) assert evaluation as a planned programme with well-developed methodology designed to assess critically all aspects of the policy or legal instrument. Evaluation is carried out to explore whether the intended objectives were met in an efficient way; whether unwanted side effects occurred and to what degree; and whether a high degree of compliance has been reached. The expected result of an evaluation would be information on the possible need for amendments or even the abolition of the legal instrument or policy.

According to Frankel & Gage (2007), evaluation is viewed as the periodic, retrospective assessment of a programme that might be conducted internally or by external independent evaluators. Evaluation, like we have said, refers to a process that seeks to understand specifically why and what changes have occurred after implementation and is, therefore, an impact assessment process. Evaluation aims at assessing the cause-and-effect factor relationships in a bid to identify and utilise the outcomes for new programmes, policies, or projects.

Evaluation is an assessment, as systematic and objective as possible, of an ongoing or completed programme, its design, implementation, and results. The aim is to determine the relevance and fulfilment of objectives, developmental efficiency, effectiveness, impact, and sustainability. We believe evaluation should provide information that is credible and useful, enabling the incorporation of lessons learned into the decision-making process of both recipients and those involved in policy formulation and implementation. Evaluation is, therefore, a systematic and objective assessment of an on-going or completed project, programme, or policy, in relation to its design, implementation, and results. The aim is to determine the relevance and fulfilment of objectives, development efficiency, effectiveness, impact, and sustainability.

Evaluation thus ensures assessment of the programme and its variables in terms of its:

- relevance to expected outcomes
- effectiveness in dealing with identified problems of achieving expected results
- efficiency of the use resources in the process as well as efficiency of the programme, project, or policy in addressing the identified problems
- impact assessment of the programme outcome; and
- sustainability of the programme results.

Given the issues raised above, evaluation is critical to the success or failure of any educational programme. Every educational system, in our case, the ODeL programme, works with educational policies and has programmes and projects which require effective planning and implementation as well as ensuring compliance between expectations and outcomes hence monitoring and evaluation. The processes of evaluation are, therefore, relevant in many areas of education including the following:

11.19.2. ODeL Educational Policy

ODeL institutional policies set the environment in which programmes are planned, implemented, monitored, and evaluated. The process of evaluation, therefore, ensures that the policies are checked in their ability to provide the best institutional and legal framework that promotes the intended objectives. Constant policy reviews and formulation requires critical knowledge of the outcomes of the existing policies, what worked or failed and why and what can be done to improve the policy, which are basic contents of the policy monitoring and evaluation reports. Furthermore, the policy relevance, effectiveness, efficiency, impact and sustainability are key areas of policy consideration, and all of these are possible only through policy monitoring and evaluation.

11.19.3. ODeL educational plans and strategies

Plans and strategies for ODeL teaching and learning cannot be formulated effectively without identifying what needs to be addressed, what has been tried before, which strategies work and which ones do not work, all being outcomes of evaluation. Furthermore, to only implement plans without assessment whether it is an ex-ante or ex-post does not fit into rational planning and may lead to wastage of resources.

11.19.4. ODeL Educational Programmes

This refers to what the ODeL system offers, and its effectiveness entails the failure or success of the entire system since the programmes are directly responsible for educating the ODeL learners. The ODeL educational programmes, therefore, must be monitored and evaluated against the set policies.

11.19.5. ODeL Institution Performance

This is another relevant area for evaluation as it is the execution and result of the ODeL educational programme. The needs to identify the cause-and-effect variables of the ODeL institution performance, measure the actual performance with the expected performance, seek to identify performance problems and solutions all require the processes of monitoring and evaluation. Other areas of evaluation include:

- **Community mobilisation efforts**: ODeL has the community as its beneficiaries and ODeL students as its target groups all of which must be integrated one way or another into the system.

- **Educational research initiatives**: These need to be assessed and evaluated in terms of their outcomes.

- **ODeL tutor policies**: This is inclusive of professional bodies, ethics, conducts and practices of the tutor and their relevance, effectiveness, efficiency, impact, and sustainability.

- **ODeL infrastructure**: This entails building projects, which encompass ODeL campuses, training of tutors, and educational services and general administrative systems.

In summary, therefore, you might have seen that evaluation is useful when meant for the following benefits:

- gaining insight about a programme's operations and its ability to meet the expected results
- improving ODeL practices, performance, and outcomes

- assessing effects in terms of ability to meet outcomes such as ODeL objectives and goals, benefits, effectiveness, and efficiency
- build capacity in increasing funding for ODeL programmes, enhancing skills, and strengthening accountability; and
- determining relevance, effectiveness, efficiency, impact, and sustainability of the ODeL programme.

Further to the above, you might also want to look at evaluation as being critical for building a strong evidence base for assessing the wide and diverse range of interventions being implemented to address ODeL issues and challenges. It is a tool for identifying and documenting successful programmes and approaches and tracking progress toward common indicators across ODeL projects (Gage & Dunn, 2009). Evaluation forms the basis of strengthening understanding around the many multi-layered factors underlying ODeL programmes, and the effectiveness of the response at the service provider, that is the institution in general, community, national, and international level.

According to Frankel and Gage (2007), at the programme level, the purpose of evaluation is to track implementation and outputs systematically and measure the effectiveness of programmes. It helps determine exactly when the ODeL programme is on track and when changes to the programme may be needed. Evaluation forms the basis for modification of interventions and assessing the quality of activities being conducted in ODeL campus.

Evaluation can also be used to demonstrate that the ODeL programme efforts have had a measurable impact on expected outcomes and have been implemented effectively. It is essential in helping ODeL programme planners, implementers, policy makers and donors acquire the information and understanding they need to make informed decisions about programme operations.

Gage & Dunn (2009) have argued that evaluation help in identifying the most valuable and efficient use of resources. It is critical for developing objective conclusions regarding the extent to which programmes can be judged a success. Evaluation together provides the necessary data to guide strategic planning, to design and implement ODeL programmes and to allocate, and re-allocate resources in better ways as dictated by university ordinances in place. For example, it is only after monitoring and evaluation that you can be able to ascertain the numbers of staff required in the ODeL institution.

11.20. Strategies for Evaluation of ODeL Programmes

Several propositions as to what constitutes effective strategies for evaluation have been propounded by different proponents, but we have found the strategies advanced by the World Bank (2002) to be appropriate for the evaluation of ODeL programmes. According to the World Bank Operations Evaluation Department (2002), effective evaluation strategies would include performance indicators approach, the logical framework (LogFrame) approach, theory-based evaluation, and Impact evaluation, among others. Let us look at some of these strategies.

11.20.1. The Performance Indicators Approach

According to the World Bank (2002), when you need to monitor and evaluate a policy or a programme, you need to consider inputs, processes, outputs, outcomes, and impacts of development interventions. For example, you need to ask how much you put into the ODeL programme by way of finances and other resources. You also need to look how you implemented the programme to establish whether the activities you undertook were effective. For ODeL programmes, you may not go it alone without the input of parents and government ministries in charge of tertiary education. You need to look at how each contributed and to what extent the contributions were used. Also, take note of the aspect of outcomes. You need to look at the numbers of ODeL students who are making it after leaving the institution, hence, the aspect of outcomes. This is unlike the aspect of output where you are only concerned with numbers for their own sake where, for example, you take delight in the numbers of ODeL students who are getting out of the system. Therefore, inputs, processes, outputs, outcomes, and impacts are used for setting targets and measuring progress towards them through evaluation.

11.20.2. The Logical Framework (LogFrame) Approach

This identifies objectives and expected causal links and risks along the results chain. It is a vehicle for engaging partners and can help improve programme design. ODeL institutions are, by their nature, afloat with several partners. Each of the faculties in the ODeL institutions are at least, in one way or the other, linked to some partners. The Faculty of Education, for example, cannot be divorced from the relevant education ministries in the different countries that they operate in. Training teachers would require the involvement of the education ministry in the country. The logical framework approach entails such partners who improve the programmes on offer.

11.20.3. Theory-Based Evaluation

The theory-based evaluation strategy is like the LogFrame approach. This provides a deeper understanding of the workings of a complex intervention. It helps planning and management by identifying critical success factors.

11.20.4. Formal Surveys

These are used to collect standardised information from a sample of partners, stakeholders, or even households, depending on the nature of the academic programme of offer. Formal surveys are useful for understanding actual conditions and changes over time. You may go to beneficiaries, current or intended, of the programme, for example, learners attending the ODeL institution, and provide them with questionnaires to fill in on various issues. You can collect quantitative data from employing such methods. From the gathered data, informed decisions are made for the improvement of the programmes.

11.20.5. Rapid Appraisal Methods

These are quick, cheap ways of providing decision-makers with views and feedback from beneficiaries and stakeholders. Using such methods, ODeL programme evaluators may adopt interviews, focus group discussions, and field observations. These data-generating instruments are not new, and scholars and students of research will bear testimony to this. The methods assist in generating huge amounts of qualitative data on programme evaluation issues.

11.20.6. Participatory Methods

In ODeL programme evaluations, participation allows stakeholders to be actively involved in decision-making. Owing to stakeholder participation, these generate a sense of ownership of evaluation results and recommendations and build local capacity. We have seen that different facets of the economy depend, to a large extent, on tertiary institutions. However, this is not to underestimate their potency to influence policy. For example, industry, commerce, and educational institutions are the main consumers of the ODeL programmes, and therefore, ODeL institutions avoid them at their peril.

11.20.7. Public Expenditure Tracking Surveys

These trace the flow of public funds and assess whether resources reach the intended recipients. They can help diagnose service-delivery problems and improve accountability. You are aware that some ODeL institutions are public funded. As such, they need to be subjected to the public expenditure tracking surveys. If the ODeL institution is a result of a legislative process, then it should account for all its processes to the legislative body that gave birth to it. Parliamentary Select Committees on higher and tertiary education within the state can ask the ODeL institution to respond to issues of funds advanced to them for programme implementation.

11.20.8. Impact Evaluation

This is the systematic identification of the effects of an intervention on the institution and the environment using some of the above methods. It can be used to gauge the effectiveness of activities in reaching all clients, including the marginalised in the local community. You need to look at how your programme has affected the lives of the people in the community to gauge its impact.

11.20.9 Cost-Benefit and Cost-Effectiveness Analysis

These two means or tools aim at assessing whether the cost of the programme is justified by its impact. Cost-benefit measures inputs and outputs in monetary terms, whereas cost-effectiveness looks at outputs in non-monetary terms. The ODeL programme needs to subject to both tools to get an objective view of the success or lack of it in the programme.

11.21. Theories of Evaluation of ODeL Programmes

By evaluation theory, we refer to specific practices that ODeL programme evaluators can use to construct knowledge about the value of social programmes, such as ODeL programmes and education (Shadish, Cook & Leviton, 1991).

Many practitioners design evaluations around methodology. However, we argue for a more holistic approach, starting with theory before methodology. Programme evaluators should first consider the purpose of the evaluation to determine its theoretical foundation, and then develop evaluation questions to inform methodology. Oftentimes, evaluators focus on the technical details of the evaluation rather than the overall purpose. Focusing on theory at the onset of a programme ensures the process, that is, stakeholder involvement, methodology, data collection, analysis, reporting, is intentional, purposeful, and more useful for the client.

Let us look at some theories that you need to consider for the evaluation of programmes in ODeL institutions.

11.21.1. Utilisation-Focused Evaluation Theory

Patton (2013) developed the Utilisation-Focused Evaluation (UFE), which is based on the premise that evaluations should be judged by their utility and actual use. This theoretical model should be applied when the end goal is instrumental use (that is, discrete decision-making). UFE focuses on intended use by primary intended users. To engage primary intended users, the evaluator must identify stakeholders who have the most direct, identifiable stake in the evaluation and its results; in other words, the "personal factor" (Patton, 2013). The programme evaluator involves intended users at every stage of the process.

The ultimate purpose of UFE is programmatic improvement driven by a psychology of use. Intended users are more likely to use the evaluation if they feel ownership of the process and its results. Use does not happen naturally; therefore, the evaluator must reinforce utility by engaging intended users, such as the ODeL tutors, learners, and parents at each stage of the evaluation.

11.21.2. Values Engaged Evaluation Theory

Greene et al. (2011) developed the Values Engaged Evaluation (VEE), which is a democratic approach that is highly responsive to context and emphasises stakeholder values. VEE seeks to provide contextualised understandings of social programmes, such as ODEL education, that have promise for underserved and underrepresented populations (Greene et al., 2011). It is considered a democratic approach because it encourages the policy evaluator to include all relevant stakeholder values. Greene et al. (2011) offers three justifications for including stakeholder values: (1) pragmatic (that is, increases chance of use), (2) emancipatory (that is, empowers stakeholders), and (3) deliberative (that is, considers all interests). With this approach, evaluation design and methodology evolve as the evaluator understands the context, needs, and values underlying the programme. VEE is concerned with answering broad and in-depth questions and is more suited for formative rather than summative evaluations. This is to say you can use the theory in the process of policy implementation and not at the end of the programme.

11.21.3. Empowerment Evaluation Theory

In ODeL institutions, empowerment evaluation entails programme improvement through empowerment and self-determination. As developed by Fetterman (2012), the self-determination theory describes an individual's agency to chart his or her own course in life and the ability to identify and express needs. Fetterman (2012) believes the evaluator's role is to empower stakeholders to take ownership of the evaluation process as a vehicle for self-determination. The ODeL programme evaluator engages a diverse range of programme stakeholders and acts as a critical friend or coach while guiding them through the evaluation process. Empowerment evaluation seeks to increase the probability of programme or policy success by providing stakeholders with the tools and skills to self-evaluate and mainstream evaluation within their organisation. Fetterman (2012) outlines three main steps for conducting empowerment evaluation. These are provided below:

- develop and refine the mission.
- take stock and prioritise the programme's activities; and
- plan for the future.

11.21.4. Theory-Driven Evaluation Theory

According to Chen (2015), the theory-driven evaluation approach focuses on the theory of change and causal mechanisms underlying the programme. Chen recognises that programmes exist in an open system, consisting of inputs, outputs, outcomes, and impacts. You can list the inputs, outputs, outcomes, and impacts from the ODeL programme. Chen (2015) further suggests that programme evaluators should start by working with stakeholders to understand the assumptions and intended logic behind the programme. A logic model can be used to illustrate the causal relationships between activities and outcomes. Chen (2015) offers many suggestions for constructing programme theory models, such as an action model, that is, a systematic plan for arranging staff, resources, settings to deliver services and change model, that is, set of descriptive assumptions about causal processes underlying intervention and outcome. ODeL programme evaluators should consider using this approach when working with programme implementers to produce valuable information for formative programme improvement. You need to know that by formative evaluation, we are referring to the evaluation that is on-going as the ODeL programme progresses. This is unlike summative evaluation which is carried out at the end of a programme.

We have looked at the four theoretical approaches that we described above. However, we need to bring to your attention that theories do not advocate a methodology. Programme evaluators can use quantitative, qualitative, or a mix of both methods for collection of data on programme processes. However, before considering methodology, ODeL programme evaluators need to reflect on the theoretical frameworks that guide their practice. Although evaluation is an applied science, it is important for evaluators to be knowledgeable of theory to ensure their adopted and chosen designs are driven by intention and purpose rather than methodological tools.

11.22. Summary

For any successful ODeL programme's implementation, there is a need, to a great extent, for management practices that are amenable to transformational changes because of evaluation practices throughout the process of programme implementation. Thus, there is a need for processes of coordination to direct and oversee implementation of the said programmes to make them deliver outcomes and benefits aligned to the institution's strategic objectives. ODeL institutions, likewise, need to follow available practices, as there might not be any need to reinvent the wheel. This, however, does not mean side-lining innovation, but where existing theories are applicable, ODeL practitioners need not shun these. In this chapter, we looked at the tenets of programme management, implementation, and evaluation practices in ODeL universities.

We provided both theoretical and practical insights into how ODeL institutions ought to be and are involved in programme management, implementation, and evaluation.

11.23 References

Barker, C. & Coy, R. (2004). *The power of culture: Driving Today's organisations.* Sydney: McGraw-Hill.

Brech, E. F. L. (2002). *Organisation: The framework of management.* London: Longman.

Brownson, R. C., Royer, C., Chriqui, J. F., & Stamatakis, K. A. (2009). Understanding evidence-based public health policy. *American Journal of Public Health, 99*(67), 1576–1583.

Brundrett, M. & Crawford, M. (Eds). (2008). *Developing school leaders: An international perspective.* London: Routledge.

Chen, H. T. (2015). *Practical programme evaluation: Theory-driven evaluation and the integrated evaluation perspective.* Thousand Oaks, CA: Sage.

Cummins, L. K. (2011). *Policy practice for social workers: new strategies for a new era.* New York: Pearson.

Fetterman, D. M. (2012). Empowerment evaluation: Learning to think like an evaluator. In M.C. Alkin (Ed.), *Evaluation Roots (2nd Ed.)* (pp. 304-322).

Fligstein, N. & Freeland, R. (1995). Theoretical and comparative perspectives on corporate organisations. *Annual Review of Sociology, 21*(3), 21-43.

Frankel, N. & Gage, A. (2007). *M&E fundamentals: A self-guided minicourse.* U.S. Agency for International Development, MEASURE Evaluation, Interagency Gender Working Group, Washington DC.

Fullan, M. (2001). *Leading in a culture of change.* San Francisco: Jossey-Bass.

Gage, A. & Dunn, M. (2009). *Monitoring and evaluating gender-based violence prevention and mitigation programmes.* Washington DC: US Agency for Development.

Gomez-Mejia, L. R., Balkin, D. B., & Cardy, R. L. (2008). *Managing Human Resources.* Thousand Oaks: Sage.

Greene, J. C., Boyce, A. S., & Ahn, J. (2011). *Value-engaged, educative evaluation guidebook.* University of Illinois, Urbana-Champaign.

Hattie, J. (2003). It's official: Teachers make a difference. Educare News. *The National Newspaper for all Non-government Schools, 144*(3), 24-31.

Johnson, D. W. & Johnson, R. T. (2004). *Assessing students in groups: Promoting group responsibility and institutional accountability.* New York: Corwin Press.

Kivunja, C. (2015). *Teaching, learning assessment: Step Towards creative practice.* Melbourne: Oxford University Press.

Lamond, D. (2004). A matter of style: Reconciling Henri and Henry. *Management Decision, 42*(2), 330-356.

McCrea, N. L. (2015). *Leading and managing early childhood settings: Inspiring people, places and practices.* Port Melbourne: Cambridge University Press.

Nutley, S., & Webb, J. (2000). Evidence and the Policy Process. In Davies, H. T. O., Nutley, S. M., & Smith, P. (Eds.), *What works? Evidence-based policy & practice in public services.* Bristol: Policy Press.

Patton, M. Q. (2013). Utilisation-Focused Evaluation (U-FE) Checklist. *Western Michigan University Checklists.*

Schwalbe, K., & Furlong, D. (2013). *Healthcare Project Management.* Minnesota: Schwalbe Publishing.

Scott, G. (1999). *Change matters: Making a difference in education and training.* St. Leonards: Allen Unwin.

Sebba, J. (2004). Developing an evidence-based approach to policy and practice in education. In Thomas, G. & Pring, R. (Eds.), *Evidence-Based Practice in Education.* Maidenhead: OUP/McGraw-Hill.

Shadish Jr., W. R., Cook, T. D., & Leviton, L. C. (1991). Chapter 2: Good theory for social programme evaluation. In *Foundations of Program Evaluation: Theories of Practice.* Newbury Park, CA: Sage.

The Global Fund. (2009). *Monitoring and Evaluation Toolkit.* (3rd Ed.). http://www.theglobalfund.org.

Truskie, S. D. (2002). *Leadership in high performance organisational cultures.* London: Quorum Books.

Waring, H. Z. (2016). *Theorizing pedagogical interaction: Insights from conversation analysis.* London: Routledge.

World Bank Operations Evaluation Department. (2002). *Monitoring and evaluation: Some tools, methods, and approaches.* Washington, D.C: The World Bank.

Chapter 12

Quality Assurance Practices in Open and Distance e-Learning (ODeL) Institutions

Tichaona Mapolisa

Zimbabwe Open University

Abstract

Quality assurance may relate to a programme, an institution, or the whole higher education system. The chapter focuses on unmasking quality assurance practices in ODeL institutions in the context of Zimbabwe based on how they manifest themselves in other countries. Quality assurance ensures that suitable academic standards are produced, monitored, maintained, and sustained in the areas of programme development and management, teaching and learning, and measurement and evaluation, as well as assessment. Quality assurance practices in ODeL institutions manifest themselves in distinct conspicuous forms that are largely identifiable with ODeL institutions. Universities have quality assurance units. The first benefit of quality assurance practices in ODeL institutions is derived from an e-society of the 21st century we live in. ODeL institutions are offering learning programmes online to prepare people for life in an e-society in which they must fit in without facing challenges. Benchmarking is an important quality assurance practice in ODeL institutions. Notwithstanding the foregoing benefits of quality assurances in ODeL institutions, sticking circumstantial challenges are inevitable. One of the greatest challenges to quality assurance practices in ODeL institutions is financial. Besides the financial challenge, ODeL institutions' quality endeavours are backpedaled by a lack of e-learning facilities. Lack of skilled qualified expert personnel in e-learning is another pitfall of quality assurance practices in ODeL institutions. Appropriate leadership style mitigates quality assurance challenges in the ODeL universities. Use of people-management skills to scale ODeL personnel and institutional performance, among other mitigation measures, combat quality assurance challenges in ODeL.

Keywords: Quality, quality assurance, quality assurance practices, ODeL institutions

***

12.0 Introduction

Open and Distance E-Learning (ODeL) is a buzz concept in the 21st century. Prior to the 21st century, especially before the world was hard hit by Covid-19 in 2020, ODeL was both a luxury and an option. The perception on online qualifications was viewed with a great deal of scepticism in some counties like Zimbabwe, where holders of online diplomas and degrees were regarded as second rate to those who attended face-to-face lectures and tutorials. Such negative regard of online qualifications might have contributed to people's negative perception towards ODeL teaching and learning, as well as its qualifications. Perhaps such unfortunate developments could be a result of discussions in distance education and e-learning are recent (Jung, Wong& Belawti, 2013). In this chapter, the focus is on unmasking quality assurance practices in ODeL institutions in the context of Zimbabwe based on how they manifest themselves in other countries' ODeL countries. In a bid to guide readers, the chapter gives an apt conceptual reflection of quality, quality assurance, and quality assurance practices in ODeL institutions. There is a summary highlighting the key points raised in the chapter.

12.1 Conceptual Reflections

A synopsis of the conceptual reflections providing a proper context to this chapter is necessary. As alluded to earlier on in the chapter, key concepts that ought to be unpacked are quality assurance, quality assurance practices, ODeL, ODeL institutions, and quality assurance practices in ODeL institutions.

12.1.1 Definition for Quality in Higher Education

The term quality assurance refers to "systematic, structured and continuous attention to quality in terms of quality maintenance and improvement" (Vroeijenstijn, 1995a in Kis, 2005). As cited by Watty (2003) in Kis (2005), a further review of the literature around change in higher education reveals two schools of thought:

> The first way that quality assurance practices appear in ODeL institution, according to Kis (2005), citing scholars (Baird, 1988; Fry, 1995; Nordvall& Braxton, 1996) is that it first attaches quality to a context, and as a consequence, quality becomes meaningful. For example, references to the quality of assessment, student intake, academic programmes, teaching and learning, the student experience, and programme designs are not uncommon. Any attempt to define or attach meaning to the term is largely ignored, and one is left to assume that it is 'high' quality that is being referred to as opposed to 'good' or 'poor' quality. A second way of thinking about quality relates to a stakeholder-specific meaning; quality

is considered having regard to a variety of stakeholders with an interest in higher education, each having the potential to think about quality in different ways. In particular, citing the early works of Vroeijenstijn (1992), Middlehurst (1992), and Harvey and Green (1993), and Kis (2005), highlights the importance and value of considering quality from a variety of stakeholder perspectives.

Harvey and Green (1993), as cited in Kis (2005), identify five categories or ways of thinking about quality. Kis (2005) goes on to say, as cited in Watty (2003), key aspects of each of these categories can be summarised as follows:

- *Exception: distinctive, embodies in excellence, passing a minimum set of standards.*
- *Perfection: zero defects, getting things right the first time (focus on process as opposed to inputs and outputs).*
- *Fitness for purpose: relates quality to a purpose, defined by the provider.*
- *Value for money: a focus on efficiency and effectiveness, measuring outputs against input; a populist notion of quality (government).*
- *Transformation: a qualitative change; education is about doing something to the student as opposed to something for the consumer; includes concepts of enhancing and empowering: democratisation of the process, not just outcomes.*

From the preceding scholarly perceptions, one can hardly dispute that quality assurance practices determine the extent to which an ODeL institution is responsive to the needs of its stakeholders. If it is unresponsive to the needs of its clients, then it is dead as an ODeL institution. The quality assurance practices have to an ODeL institution a top-notch learning centre and provider capable of competing with the best in the world. In that regard, quality assurance practices obtain in ODeL institutions in the areas of design, management, implementation, monitoring, and evaluation of saleable programmes that are ably supported with second-to-none resources, facilities, equipment, and human capital.

12.1.2 Quality Assurance

Martin and Stella (2007, p.85), quoted by Saketa (2014, p.1), define "quality assurance" as a generic term used for all forms of external quality monitoring, evaluation, or review. They add that it may be defined as the process of establishing stakeholders; confidence that the provision of education (inputs, processes, and outcomes) will fulfil the expectations of stakeholders. Higher education quality assurance practices at the national, regional, and international levels have been given an enormous volume of attention since the early 1990s.

Originally, quality assurance initiatives were established to assist institutions and individuals in understanding the standards practised in other parts of the same country (Woodhouse, 2004, p. 54 in Saketa, 2014, p.1). As a generic term, quality assurance (QA) can mean different things in different national and regional contexts, and it is used to denote different practices. The generic operational definition from an international network of quality assurance agencies in higher education encompasses many different models. Similarly, Saketa (2014, p.1) cites UNESCO (2005: 56) and NAAC (2007: 12) by remarking that:

> *Quality assurance may relate to a programme, an institution or the whole higher education system. In each case, quality assurance is all of those attitudes, objects, actions, and procedures, which through their existence and use, and together with the quality control activities, ensure that appropriate academic standards are being maintained and enhanced in and by each program. Quality assurance is the responsibility of everyone in an educational institution, though the top management sets the policies and priorities. Thus, assuring quality should be a continuous and on-going process. It should not be considered a one-time activity for accreditation alone.*

From Saketa's (2014) opinion, quality assurance ensures that suitable academic standards are produced, monitored, maintained and sustained in the areas of programme development and management, teaching and learning, and measurement, assessment and evaluation. The appropriate academic standards also apply to the provision and availing pertinent resources and facilities to enhance high quality teaching.

12.3 Quality Assurance Practices in ODeL Institutions: Their Occurrences

Quality assurance practices in ODeL institutions manifest themselves in distinct conspicuous forms that are largely identifiable with ODeL institutions. Universities have quality assurance units. In Australia, ODeL universities occur in the following manner:

> *The first arises from the discourses around online delivery in universities, which I will call the online discourse formation. This modernist discourse formation attempts to demonstrate the educational and institutional advantages of the Internet for the delivery of education. Online technologies have emerged as one of the key mechanisms by which universities have aimed both to modernize their internal operations, through the use of computer-based administrative systems, and to improve the efficiency and effectiveness of their teaching, understood within the massificaction*

paradigm (Scott, 1995 in Reid, 2005, p.4) as an effective way to reach more
students more cost-effectively (Reid, 2005, p.4).

In Australia, universities have:

The second discourse formation is that of quality in university education,
which I will call the quality discourse formation. Quality assurance
processes aim to provide guarantees, not necessarily of quality per se, but
rather of the carrying out of the atomised processes by which particular
'products' are claimed to be produced. Thus, it creates languages and
activities that prescribe and proscribe, while all the time maintaining the
supposed 'independence' of the organizational unit under its gaze: the
university. Implicit in these policy positions is an idealized notion of what
a university is, and consequently of what a good university is (Reid, 2005, p. 4).

12.4 Benefits of Quality Assurance Practices in ODeL Institutions

There are a host of laudable reasons that can be realised as a result of exposure
of personnel, especially lecturers to quality assurance practices in ODeL
institutions. The first benefit of quality assurance practices in ODeL institutions
is derived from an e-society that we as 21st century inhabitants are living in.
Coombs (1970) perceived that educational planning must be responsive to the
needs of the society. In that regard, ODeL attempts to respond to the current
needs of the 21st century citizens. It is common cause that a quality assurance
practice in ODeL institutions is the offering of learning programmes online to
prepare people for life in an e-society in which they must fit in without facing
challenges. Reid (2005, p. 4), citing scholars (Inglis, Ling & Joosten, 1999; King,
2001; Meyer, 2002; Rumble, 2001; Salmon, 2003; Taylor, 2001), effectively enunciates
the benefits of quality assurance practices in ODeL institutions citing other
scholars in this way:

These are some of the ways that online technologies are being used to
enable universities to gain a place at the education marketplace table,
broadening their reach, increasing their visibility, and commercialising
their operations. For distance educators, the advantages of online technologies
are usually portrayed as adding increased interactivity, for example
through the use of online discussion methods, to past delivery techniques.

On the same terrain, Reid (2005, p.5) quoting (Bottomley, 2000; Nunan, 2000)
argues that for teachers of on-campus students, online technologies are promoted
as providing increased flexibility and richness to students' educational experiences,
freeing them from attendance at particular places and times.

ODeL brings along with it benefits of flexibility in terms of attending face-to-
face lectures or tutorials, especially in times of global calamities like the Covid-

19 pandemic. In that way, it complements ODL. Learners can replay their lectures they save, interact with others, write assignments, and have them promptly assessed, thereby, giving them immediate knowledge of results.

A second benefit of quality assurance practices in ODeL institutions pertains to the degree to which lecturers are given conducive work environment to enable them to perform to the best of their ability. Provision of enabling work environment emerged as another cornerstone for retaining staff in the universities. Below is a confirmation to that effect. Case 1 Retained Lecturer participant 1 hinted that at her public university:

> *They have to look at some of the facilities such as printers, photocopiers and make it conducive for us, for our workload too, for us to be able to work.*

Supportive of the foregoing observation, Case 3 Retained Lecturer participant 1 and Case 2 Retained Lecturer participant 1 concurred that an enabling work environment is characterised by the provision of facilities such as office space, computers, internet connectivity, telephones, data analysis software, reputable and comfortable desks, tables and chairs, as well as, toilets and file cabinets.

An apparent revelation in these recommendations is the improvement of the work environment. These findings agree with O'Neil's (2011, p.12) observations that:

> *Unless a leader causes people to share the ambition to prove that most people are really an organisation's most important resource by creating conditions in which they will never be hurt, you can get there. It is not only a measure of greatness, but it is one that I like because it is very hard for people to deny that people should not be hurt at work.*

Based on the above observations, it can be perceived that work environment plays a big part in keeping staff satisfied. Thus, provision of an enabling work environment is an effective staff retention strategy. In the context of this compilation, observations made at the research sites reveal that universities have conditions of service and facilities of varying degrees. While they all report to have good internet connectivity, only one public university (Case 4) and one private university (Case 2) reported that they had reasonably good infrastructural technological facilities to retain staff. Case 1 (public university) and Case 3 (private university), on the other hand, lag behind in infrastructure because they are multi-campus in nature. To catch up with well-resourced universities, the author is of the feeling that other not-so-well-resourced universities could engage strategic partners, donors and well-wishers to mobilise resources. The other ways in which the environment could be made conducive and enabling is through application of appropriate leadership and management styles. With respect to leadership styles, universities have a host of lecturer-centric leadership styles to choose from. They can employ team leadership, transformational leadership, servant leadership, teacher leadership, synodic leadership, consultative leadership, emotional intelligence leadership and ethical leadership (Bush & Glover, 2012; Mullins & Christy, 2017; Northouse, 2016). In line with management styles, universities could reap great staff retention benefits by employing contemporary management innovation facets such as Total Quality Management (TQM), Learning Organisations and Re-engineering (Senge, 1992; Hellriegel & Slocum, 2016; Mullins & Christy, 2017). The outcome associated with the use of this novel management is getting increased production out of workers who have been provided with the right atmosphere to work. Coupled with a possession of the right social intelligence and knowledge to apply the foregoing leadership and management styles, universities retain staff as a result of their capacity to provide a work environment on compassionate grounds.

Another relevant benefit of quality assurance practices in ODeL institutions is continuous professional development of members of staff. Another participant from a public university, Case 4 Retained Lecturer 1, backed the above findings by recommending the need to encourage and facilitate continuous learning and production of knowledge. Funding PhD studies for lecturers is key in two ways. First, it upgrades not only their qualifications but their status in the university and society is enhanced as well. Second, arguably, possession of PhD qualification largely enables one to competently acquire and process academic information more than those with lower qualifications. On the basis of this assumption, the academic profile of the universities is enhanced because it will be presumed that lecturers have polished conceptual, human and technical skills meant to let them execute their professional duties efficiently and effectively. Continuous professional learning is not confined to non-PhD holders alone. Even PhD holders need exposure to a maze and avalanche of learning opportunities, which could range from e-Learning pedagogies, financial management, data analysis software programmes, and research supervision, just to cite a few examples. They should understand that they belong to universities, which are themselves learning organisations. Such organisations hold high expectations for PhD holders and Professors by expecting them to continue learning. This expectation is buttressed by Akinpelu (2001) in Nigeria who argues that a teacher cannot teach effectively do so unless he or she continues to learn himself or herself. In support of Akinpelu's (2001) opinions, by using a multiple regression analysis, Hong et al. (2012) found that training and development through the appraisal system and compensation were significant employee retention strategies. Even though private universities' participants indicated staff development as one of the challenges they face in retaining staff, their Retained Lecturer participants did not suggest solutions. Public university participants aware of their work contractual privileges, like provision of staff development, felt that their employer needs to do more in this area in the search for the right university brand as noted by Botha and Busin (2011) in Mapolisa (2015). If private universities are to effectuate good employee retention exercises using staff development, they then need to adopt Netswera et al.'s (2005) findings in Mapolisa (2015) that recruiting and training the best employees is a major investment. In the context of this compilation, investment in human capital is the key determinant to successful staff retention in public and private universities. Universities stand to be advised by Mullins and Christy (2017) who propound that human capital development of key organisational staff makes them want to affiliate with their organisation more than anything else because they cherish newly acquired status, motivation, and upward mobility they would have earned through continuous professional development.

An almost synonymous strength of quality assurance practices with continuous professional development of members of staff is staff development. Staff development, as established by Mapolisa (2015), emerged as a key staff retention strategy, as was demonstrated by a public university participant, Case 1 Retained Lecturer participant 1 who indicated that:

> ...need to provide adequate funds to support staff development including doctoral studies.

In support of the preceding view, Case 2 Retained Lecturer participant 1 pointed out that:

> .....both junior and experienced lecturers are in dire need of funding to let them pursue and complete their PhD studies.

At Case 4, Retained Lecturer participant 1 from a private university lamented lack of support for PhD studies in this way:

> The university appears to be keen to support and fund lecturers undertaking Masters Degrees at the expense of those in need of PhD studies. Even if you apply for such funding, you will be fortunate to get a response.

In a bid to curtail the preceding career growth let downs, the same participants recommended three noteworthy strategies to curb staff retention challenges. First, they recommended university support for lecturers to attend conferences for academic exposure. This would capacitate them in the area of research and innovation as a result of interacting and networking with tried and tested researchers, scholars and academic. Second, contact leave and sabbatical leave should be supported. Such support enables lecturers to acquire much needed experience, exposure, and experience after learning from what other lecturers do in other universities. They may learn, for example, how to develop and manage programmes, employ e-pedagogy, e-marking, e-supervision and e-registration of students. Furthermore, they acquire higher qualifications and titles that they can use beyond the universities to earn their own money by engaging in part-time work in the universities and other non-education organisations. In a paper presentation made in Ghana about staff retention in Uganda, Tibatemwa-Ekirikubinza in the University Leaders' Forum (2008), as cited in Mapolisa (2015), spoke about, "Makerere University's efforts at staff retention and development with particular reference to gender issues." She described how Makerere's Staff Development Policy and Staff Development (SD) Fund, funded by five percent of tuition from privately sponsored students and a smaller contribution from all students, had reduced depending on external funding for staff development (p.21). The same speaker went on to point out that the allocation of SD funds was based on submissions of priority needs by academic units to the Staff Development Committee. She also said Makerere waived tuition for members of staff and encouraged them to undertake their graduate study at Makerere. She indicated that staff securing full-time training opportunities had to apply for study leave, be bonded, and were required to teach for a period determined by the length of their study abroad. Also, basic salary was paid to members of staff on approved study leave, and the staff retained either the housing unit (for family use) or the housing allowance. The university, she said, assiduously enforced a non-discrimination policy between male and female members of staff (p.21). Thus, when key skilled and experienced ODeL staff members are retained, it stands to benefit ODeL institutions and their stakeholders locally and beyond.

Provision of research funds to ODeL members of staff is another key benefit of quality assurance practices in ODeL institutions. Complementing staff development in retaining university staff was the need to provide research funds for big research. This position was put forward by a public university participant, Case 1 Retained Lecturer participant 1, who said:

There is need for support fund for big research work.

She also suggested that reward and recognition associated with achievement in research undertakings should be a way of the university culture. Underscoring the preceding research sentiment, Case 1 Retained Lecturer lamented that:

On research funding, the Pro Vice Chancellor said he is only able to support patentable research teams...This is an unfortunate development because by and large, the institution has not been supporting research activities financially.

Underlining the foregoing two views from public universities, the following two views from private universities suffice:

Our university is not as dynamic and lecturer research needs-responsive as the Midlands State University which supports each academic on two international conferences per year. Here, it is a dream and a wish (Case 2 Retained Lecturer participant 1).

Our university supports paper publication and international conference paper presentation once in every two years per academic. I feel that when there are no papers for public or presentation before my two years are due, I should be financially supported to undertake my research activities (Case 3 Retained Lecturer participant 2).

These findings agree with Jongbloed (2012) in Mapolisa (2015) who found out that lecturers can be expeditiously promoted through habilitation as a result of their research effort. Such promotions result in recognition and reward which produces staff motivation, commitment to the job and job satisfaction. The author observed that public and private university lecturers were self-motivated to conduct research in various ways. Some were keen to publish research articles in peer-reviewed journals and attend local and international conferences, research workshops and symposia. Others were eager to publish book chapters, books, and monographs. It can be concluded that the use of research support funds is a critical staff retention strategy in the studied public and private universities. It should also be noted that research activities in the university do not only benefit lecturers alone, but the university as well. While these research activities make lecturers more visible, promotable, and impacting in their work, they also enhance university research profile if research outputs are deposited into the institutional repository and research websites such as the Researchgate, Googlescholar, Academia.edu, Ebsco, Jstor, Eric, Scopus, Agora, and the World Bank, just to cite a few examples. Such research platforms would make the researcher or lecturer become conscious of the degree to which their research outputs are making an impact based on their citability, readability and readership they receive globally. On the basis of the preceding positions, we contend that lecturers who are given opportunities for research through support research funds in ODeL institutions tend to go a long way in excelling in their execution of duties using online technologies for e-pedagogy, e-lecturing, e-tutoring, e-supervision of research outputs, and e-marking and e-moderation of online assignments, examination, and research documents.

Benchmarking is also another beneficial quality assurance practices in ODeL institutions. ODeL institutions learn from each other in regard to programme design, offering, management, implementation, review and evaluation. In fact, there are standard practices that ODeL institutions expected of them to follow if ever they are to succeed. One private university lecturer concurred with his public university counterpart in Zimbabwe on the issue that benchmarking ODeL programmes on what other renowned ODeL institutions around the world offer is one of the quickest passports to the accomplishment of quality and accreditation credentials in the universities. ODeL institutions borrow the light from successful institutions and cast the light on dark corners and experiences from non-succeeding institutions (Associations of Asian Universities, 2010; Brown, Kurzweil & Prichett, 2017). All things being equal, benchmarking performance on what best ODeL institutions do and offer arguably one of the contexts bound best quality assurance ODeL practices.

Twinning ODeL institutions ranks top among other quality assurance practices in ODeL institutions. ODeL institutions in different countries can collaborate to implement quality assurance practices that culminate in the offering of quality programmes. They can share programmes, learners, researchers and lecturers; and even embark on collaborative research consortia in which master's and doctoral students can be mentored to undertake applied research meant to provide solutions to real life practical problems in their communities.

Quality assurance practices that are efficacious result in saleable ODeL programmes. In support of this view, Ngubane-Mokiwa and Letseka (2015) contend that the ODeL framework is premised on the assumption that every student learning can be optimally supported by on modern electronic technologies and other digital facilities. The operating term here is 'assumption'. The same writers go on stress that ODeL students are assumed to have access to, and to be able to make optimal use of modern electronic technologies to access their study material and to interact with their lecturers without necessarily being required to make physical contact. After completing the programme, students would easily fit into the e-society and the future world that relies on Information Communication Technology (ICT) in every sector of the economy and aspect of life. In essence, online technologies, as seen by one public university lecturer substantiating the scenario in this manner, an exposure of learners to ICT-enhanced learning opportunities enables to them become impact citizens of the society who will eventually serve their nation well in the present and future because today's world can never run away from the influence of technology in all facets of life.

The other seemingly overlooked benefit of quality assurance practices in ODeL is best seen through the benefit of education in promoting national development in general. This is buttressed by Nekongo-Nielsen (2006, p.1) who nicely puts it in this way:

> *Education, in general, continues to be a crucial means to promote national development, and a well-educated and trained population is found to contribute meaningfully to the socio-economic development of any country (Mapope, 2005). In addition, open and distance learning methods and programmes are known to make valuable contribution to the socio-economic development of countries.*

In the same vein, many countries have recognised that open and distance learning is a powerful tool for achieving the countries' educational and training needs and a potent tool in creating a learning society capable of bringing about scientific, technological, social and economic development (Association of Asian Universities, 2010). While these benefits are realised through open and distance learning, they are most beneficial to a population if they are advanced through ODeL due to its increased limitless access, flexibility, and individualised and communal learning approaches.

12.5 Challenges Associated with Quality Assurance Practices in ODeL Institutions

Notwithstanding the foregoing benefits of quality assurances in ODeL institutions, sticking circumstantial challenges are inevitable. One of the greatest challenges to quality assurance practices in ODeL institutions is financial. According to Nihia et al., citing scholars (CoL, 2004; Lara, 2006; Arinto, 2016 Njihia et al., 2016), these findings are in agreement with others from similar studies. Some of the key individual challenges faced are lack of ICT skills, financial constraints, and work-study-family equilibrium. By the same token, Mapolisa and Tshablala (2013) established that institutions of higher learning inclusive of ODeL ones are yet to put in place mechanisms and resources to enable them to offer quality programmes. By implication the aforementioned resources and mechanisms denote quality assurance practices which ought to obtain in ODeL institutions.

Besides the financial challenge, ODeL institutions quality endeavours are backpedaled by a lack of e-Learning facilities. The individual challenges faced by ODeL students of the UK resonate with those of similar students in other countries (Dodo, 2013; Nyandara, 2012 in Njihia et al., 2016; Kangai & Mapolisa, 2012; Kangai & Mapolisa, 2008). E-Learning facilities are not available in most remote areas of Zimbabwe, although some people have smartphones, iPhones, and iPads, but they are the minority who are economically affluent.

In addition to financial and inadequate e-Learning facilities, limited funds for research, contact, study and sabbatical leave opportunities hinder the implementation of quality assurance practices in ODeL institutions. These challenges are best perceived in the context of staff retention challenges in the Zimbabwe's public and private universities from the point of view of retained lecturers (Mapolisa, 2015). Lack of support for staff development and professional exposure through contact leave and sabbatical leave was perceived as one of the biggest staff retention challenges across the universities. With regards to the provision of contact leave, here is what a public university participant, Case 1 Retained Lecturer participant 1, said:

Contact leave is only given if you are in a senior position; if you are an ordinary lecturer, you are not getting that. That is the point where we will lose people. We don't encourage that.

From the above participant's view, ordinary lecturers are marginalised in terms of provision of contact leave. If they are aware that they are denied contact leave is among their job contractual obligations, they get frustrated and start to search for alternative jobs.

Related to the challenge of contact leave's impact on career growth among public university lecturers, Case 1 Retained Lecturer participant 1 had this to say about sabbatical leave:

Sabbatical leave is supposed to be given to everyone who is a lecturer, a tenured lecturer and that has not happened to a lot of lecturers. Although the university is encouraging people to go local for sabbatical leave, they have only started this year, no, last year. Before... it was not encouraging, there was no money.

In the context of private universities, the following excerpt reflects the challenge of lack of career growth among university lecturers:

First, Case 2 Retained Lecturer participant 1 said:

Lecturers can go for study leave which is unpaid, yet they have family responsibilities to take care of. Issues of contact and sabbatical leave remain a dream for some of us.

From the above comments, it can be perceived that the lack of money in the universities hinders opportunities for lecturers' career growth. Lack of money limits their chances to go for sabbatical leave. The situation could be worse for those in need of contact leave because some tenured and senior lecturers who have served at least five years have not yet gone for sabbatical leave, thereby, depriving lecturers of their opportunities for professional and career growth. In all fairness, going for sabbatical and contact leave are contractual obligations that universities ought to fulfill by providing opportunities to go. While it is the lecturers' responsibilities to apply for contact and sabbatical leave opportunities, universities should provide budgeted funds for lecturers on contact leave to other universities. For sabbatical leave, universities do not pay their lecturers a lump of money, but they will continue paying monthly salaries. However, they will be expected to pay salaries for lecturers who come from other universities for sabbatical leave. Contact leave and sabbatical leave should never be a preserve for only a few academic staff and non-academic staff. These two leaves are a form of retreat exposures in which ODeL lecturers and two might learn best practices from other institutions in two ways. First, ODeL strengths in host universities provide visiting lecturers or scholars with an opportunity to learn how best to reinforce their quality assurance practices. Second, ODeL shortcomings in host institutions equip visiting scholars with mechanisms to monitor and strategies to curb challenges associated with their universities' quality assurance practices.

All the challenges, namely lack of career growth and inadequate resources, are best summarised as human resources challenges. Kiat, Heng and Lim-Ratnam (2017) emphasise human capital as a pillar in human resource development in any education institution. The skills, knowledge, experience, and competence make human capital a driving force for the success of the institution. Thus, Mullins and Christy (2017) regard human capital as the greatest resource in an organisation. By the same token, Mutuva (2012), from a school perspective, likens university managers to principals by suggesting that the success of principals in managing Heads of Departments (who are like lecturers in universities) in schools lies in their competence as school leaders and the provision of lifelong learning to HODs. As principals manage HODs by emphasising human capital development it empowers the team to rise above the ordinary and be in a position to effectively execute their duties. In practice, empowered lecturers are more likely to be retained in the university than their disempowered counterparts. This would be an added advantage to ODeL institutions, especially those intending to compete with the best in the world.

Inappropriate ODeL leadership styles impede the implementation of effective quality assurance practices. In substantiation of this challenge of inappropriate leadership style, two lecturers from private universities and one from a state university put forward the following sentiments:

> *People outside university settings assume that all is rosy in the universities. What they are not aware of is that sometimes, we are subject to toxic leadership styles which work against the attainment of quality assurance practices in ODeL situations. (PU1)*

> *Autocratic leadership styles that characterise the operations of university programmes defeats the whole purpose of putting into effect efficacious quality assurance practices in ODeL. Lecturers are viewed as people who do not know how to think, and therefore, they are told not only what to do but when and how to do it. (SU1).*

> *Vesting effectiveness into a single person who is regarded as a good and effective leader is dangerous. Good and effective leadership is not seen through the power of a single person, but it is exhibited through an appropriate leadership style, which in turn, has a positive knock-on effect on availing quality assurance practices in university settings, particularly, ODeL work settings. (PU2)*

One can perceive that running an ODeL institution is not a preserve of one person, even though there is an adage that an education organisation is either as good as its leader or as bad as its leader. ODeL institutions are efficiently and effectively run by sub-committees rather than by an individual person. The sub-committees bring an element of shared ownership of ODeL programmes by all staff. Hence, they end up having a tendency to pursue quality assurance practices that bring results in ODeL programmes.

Deprivation of academic freedom militates against the effectuation of quality assurance practices in ODeL institutions. This limitation is demonstrated by three excerpts from three state universities in Zimbabwe who have this to say:

> *We have lots of quality assurance practices that we keep holding to our chests, chiefly because we are treated as nonentities in the university. We, as academics, exist to implement decision makers' plans, regardless of their level of academic knowledge. (SU1)*

> *What surprises me is the abundant lack of academic freedom in the Zimbabwean state universities. Lecturers as academics appear inferior to non-academic ODeL personnel such as directors, managers, and administrators. Even Deans as academic leaders of the core business of the university are subservient to directors. In that regard, Deans' inputs regarding quality assurance practices input usually come after directors' decisions. (SU2)*

> *Academic space is remaining a dream rather than a reality in ODeL settings. We are rarely given the latitude to exercise our academic freedom in terms administering our expertise, experience, exposure, interests and background in pursuit of effective quality assurance practices for the benefit of ODeL institutions. (SU3)*

In a sense, ODeL academics who are denied academic space, freedom, and autonomy cease to be creative, resourceful, and imaginative. They become more or less like tools or implements of the management and leaders of ODeL institutions. Their efforts for progress, advancement, and accomplishments are thwarted much to the erosion of quality assurance practices in the interests of ODeL.

Lack of skilled qualified expert personnel in e-learning is another pitfall of quality assurance practices in ODeL institutions. Most of the experienced personnel belong to the digital immigrants. They are not digital natives (Mapolisa & Khosa, 2015; Mapolisa & Chirimuuta, 2012; Nenge, Mapolisa & Chimbadzwa, 2012; Mapolisa, Muyengwa & Chakanyuka, 2008). One public university lecturer remarked that:

> *Lecturers had deficiencies, inadequacies, shortcomings and misconceptions regarding e-learning.*

Such misgivings about e-learning compromised quality assurance practices in ODeL institutions in a big way.

Jung et al. (2013) give six other challenges associated with the implementation of quality assurance practices in ODeL and probably ODeL settings as well. First, according to these scholars, as universities make a transition from the traditional Open and Distance Learning (ODL) to e-learning, there is a huge gap in the faculty capacity to deal with the new delivery modes. Second, Jung et al. (2013) contend that lack of training for staff in internal and external quality assurance standards and indicators is a major stumbling block in developing 'cultures of quality.' Third, another frequently cited challenge is that many Ministry and accreditation bodies use standards and indicators that have been developed for conventional universities and do not serve the purpose of ODL or e-learning well. Fourth, most quality assurance processes cover formal education but do not take into consideration non-formal or informal programmes. Fifth, even in countries with well-established quality assurance processes, there is an increasing challenge for those open universities which are becoming dual mode by beginning to offer face-to-face provision. Sixth, as open universities extend their reach to other jurisdictions, adapting their own quality assurance processes to the new jurisdictions and the corresponding local practices is a significant problem.

Floyd (2008), in Mapolisa and Ncube (2014), give the following challenges associated with the implementation of quality assurance practices in ODeL and ODL settings in the context of collaboration. These challenges are as given below:

- The first risk is that of not getting effective "ownership".

- Another difficulty is that individual academics and departments often have a strong wish to do things in their own way.

- A third problem is that collaborating internationally in teacher education can be difficult because each country has its own curriculum framework and its own regulatory system, and these may be, or at least appear to be incompatible.

- Another major challenge is that of finding the right partners, and even when this is achieved, there can be difficulties in setting up collaborations in an effective way, as well as processes of communication, progress chasing, and so on.

- There may be disagreements over resources and perceptions of unequal contributions, which can be very divisive.

While the five challenges relate more to collaboration applicability in ODL situations, they provide us with the opportunity to ascertain the extent with which they are compatible with possibilities of enhancing quality assurance across ODeL programmes.

Njihia et al.'s (2016) study has established that Kenyatta University e-learning students, through the ODeL programme, face instructional, institutional, and individual (personal) challenges, which have a bearing on their academic progress and on the programme's efficiency and effectiveness. In addition, Njihia et al. (2016) cite scholars (Musingafi, Mapuranga, Chiwanza & Zebron, 2015), that the key institutional challenge was poor administrative services reflected by: delay in delivery of online learning materials, difficulties in registration, lack of ICT technical support, and poor student support services. Also espoused by scholars (CoL, 2004; Lara, 2006; Arinto, 2016), Njihia et al. (2016) state that these findings concur with those of a similar study in Zimbabwe. Regarding instructional challenges, the one key failure was by lecturers who conducted online facilitation. Others were poorly designed instructional materials that were not interactive, inadequate academic support and apathy to ICT by some lecturers.

Mansour (2006), in Njihia et al. (2016), points out that there are three major groups of stakeholders in ODeL: the administration, faculty, and students. Each of these categories of stakeholders brings its own challenges. Consequently, scholars have categorised the challenges facing ODeL programmes into three in tandem with each category of stakeholders, namely: (i) instructional-related challenges, (ii) institutional-related challenges, and (iii) individual-related challenges. The instructional-related challenges have to do with the faculty, whose major challenge is lack of familiarity with ODeL philosophies and the expected ODeL skills since most of them came from the face-to-face mode of delivery (Commonwealth of Learning, 2004 in Njihia et al., 2016). Instructors need sufficient time to gain experience with new technology use (especially in education), to share experience and to effectively use technology for instruction (Ilara, 2006 in Njihia et al., 2016). A study in the Philippines identified resistance to innovation, uneven innovation practice, and lack of standards for innovation as some of the challenges facing faculty in ODeL (Arinto, 2016 in Njihia et al., 2016). Institutional-related challenges mostly revolve around administrative systems that are not designed to address the unique needs of ODeL, funding constraints, development, and deployment of the necessary infrastructure and human resources, among others (Musingafi, Mapuranga, Chiwanza, & Zebron, 2015 in Njihia et al., 2016). Some common documented individual-related challenges are lack of ICT skills, inability to afford necessary ICT hardware and software, high internet costs, and work-study balance, among others (Dodo, 2013; Nyandara, 2012 in Njihia et al., 2016).

Ngubane-Mokiwa & Letseka (2015) bring another dimension of quality assurance challenges to ODeL institutions. They point out that digital illiteracy, inappropriate learning design approaches, and lack of consensus on ODeL approach as topping, among other great challenges. In Zimbabwean settings, it might be inappropriate to assume that all people from all corners have digital literacy to enable them to use online technologies which help them to learn independently and collaboratively. Digital illiteracy begets inappropriate learning design approaches and lack of consensus on ODeL approach.

12.6 Measures to Mitigate Challenges Associated with Quality Assurance Practices in ODeL Institutions

Despite the challenges associated with quality assurances in ODeL institutions, there are some distinct measures to situationally mitigate them. The first measure to combat challenges associated with the implementation of quality assurance practices in ODeL institutions is using appropriate leadership styles (Mapolisa & Kurasha, 2013). It can be argued that best and effective leaders are not seen through the power they hold, but they manifest themselves through the appropriate leadership style they employ in order to get things done (Chikwanda, 2020; Mullins & Christy, 2017; Northouse, 2016). In an ODeL setting, effective leaders reveal themselves in three ways. First, the university managers show political will to commit themselves fully to support the effectuation of ICT-enabled learning strategies. They do so by providing ICT facilities, funds, and opportunities for both lecturers and learners to train in ICT and even hire external agents to train personnel. Second, good leaders constitute ICT expert lecturers themselves. These leaders help others how to learn using ICT gadgets and learning strategies. They show them the best way not only to maximise but to optimise their learning opportunities through e-pedagogy. Third, effective leaders continue to learn themselves so that they inspire, encourage, and motivate lecturers and learners to appreciate the value attached to ODeL. In that regard, such leaders employ transformational leadership style (Mapolisa et al., 2012). In support of the preceding scholarly views, two state university lecturers and one private university lecturer reported that:

> *Real leaders are part of the team. They are practical personnel who experience challenges and successes that are associated with the implementation of ODeL programmes. (SU1)*

On the same wavelength, a private state university lecturer marked in this way:

> *True effective leadership does not reside in the hands of dreamers, but realists. Realists are people-centred leaders, who in actual fact, value the need for them to associate themselves with ODeL quality assurance practices that work. (PU2)*

ODeL institutions need leaders who are visionary, focused, and results-oriented. Such leaders seek for quality assurance practices that continuously improve their staff, learners, and learning resources and facilities. (SU2)

Leadership: excellent leaders develop and facilitate the achievement of the mission and vision. They develop organisational values and systems required for sustainable success and implement these via their actions and behaviours (European Foundation for Quarterly Management, 2003 in Bruson et al., 2014). These three excerpts denote that team leaders, transformational leaders, and felt leaders have the capacity to transform the landscape of ODeL through the great concern they show for their institutions. In that way, they tend to employ quality assurance practices that work well enough to take the ODeL institutions out of the woods.

One other measure to curb challenges associated with the implementation of quality assurance practices in ODeL institutions related to the leadership strategy is the use of the management-based approach to efficiently and effectively run ODeL programmes. Regarding the application of a management-based approach to U.S. higher education quality assurance, Brown, Kurzweil and Pritchett (2017) identify several high-level design principles useful to strengthen ODeL systems all around the world. Their first recommendation pertains to an initial approval and probationary period which should focus on provider track record, programme coherence and value proposition, learner outcome goals, a plan for attaining them, and an exit strategy in the event of failure. The second recommendation according to Brown et al. (2017), is that a more significant departure from the current system is the principle that there should be learner- and programme-defined measures for both original efficacy and learner outcomes which should be peer benchmarked with greater co-ordination around measuring learner learning. This view was echoed by one private university lecturer who pointed out that

benchmarking ODeL programmes enriches both staff and learner performance.

The same scholars also recommend the need for ODeL programmes to be assessed every three years on evidence-based, provider-defined goals for planning implementation and effectiveness of core educational processes with a focus on processes identified as areas for improvement in prior years. In support of the preceding opinion, one public university lecturer accentuated that *monitoring and assessment of quality assurance practices hold the key to success in ODeL institutions.* Brown et al. (2017) further points out that unlike the current system, they recommend an annual review of a small set of learner outcome and financial stability measures that are standard for a peer set of programmes and appropriately account for conditions of operation. Lastly, the same authors contend that results of review should be differentiated, not binary, and conclusions and evidence supporting them should be reported publicly, in an acceptable format, by the reviewer.

> It is honest enough for ODeL providers to exercise a great deal of openness and transparency in their pursuit of quality assurance practices that work. (SUL1).

It sounds academically sound to work with quality assurance practices that do not defeat the intend purposes of ODeL institutions' mandates.

Successful ODeL institutions learn best from what other well-to-do institutions do, as well as what other not-so-well institutions. They do so by benchmarking their performance on the performance of other institutions. Brown et al. (2017) aptly recommend an escalating series of supports and consequences based on institutional performance. In their opinion, the same writers argue that high performance institutions should receive designations of excellence or extend periods between reviews. Institutions that fail to meet benchmarks, as Brown et al. (2017) see it, that implement plans or repeatedly fail to achieve improvement, should receive tailored supports for organisational learning; they may be subject to more frequent or detailed reviews, externally imposed goals, loss of funds, or loss of accreditation for some or all programmes. From the foregoing benchmark benefits, ODeL institutions stand to gain in two ways. First, a knowledge of shortcomings of other institutions often helps other institutions to learn how best to implement ODeL programmes by circumventing other institutions' negative experiences. Second, an exposure to how other ODeL institutions are suceeding inspires others not only to do the same but to attempt to look over the so-called model institutions. Thus, one private university lecturer opined that *benchmarking our performance on standard ODeL practices are the way to go if ever we are going to have world class ODeL universities in this resource-starved country*. In this sense, performance can never be pleasing when ODeL institutions do not have both intra- and inter-competition to raise their performance standards.

Njihia et al. (2016) advance six recommendations. First, it is clear from the results above that in order to enhance the uptake of ODeL programmes in Kenyatta University and elsewhere, there is a need to institute learner support mechanisms to address the institutional, instructional, and individual challenges (Mapolisa, 2012). Second, for a start, there is a need to adequately staff the regional ODeL centres to enable them to fully address the administrative, technical, and psycho-social needs of students. Third, there is also the need to enhance the training given to ODeL students on ICT and instructional technologies to enable them to fully exploit these resources. Fourth, the capacity of lecturers in ICT also requires development to help them develop interactive online modules, as well as engage students online. Fifth, lecturers should also be given the necessary material, technical support, and incentives; for example, tablets and internet bundles. Sixth, the government should also consider extending financial support to ODeL students to enable them to invest in the appropriate ICT gadgets for their studies.

dela Pena-Bandalaria (2011) conducted a study in the Philippines and suggested ways to curb challenges associated with ODeL programmes. They pointed out that in most cases, learning communities in ODeL address concerns like reducing attrition by providing students with that sense of belonging, that is, by making them feel they are part of a structure that aims to help them achieve their goals. In the experience of the UPOU, learning communities in ODeL not only address this concern but also other learning issues, and in the process, also ensure quality education. The Institute of Higher Education Policy (2000) listed 24 benchmarks under seven categories of quality education in ODL. Two are of these are facilitated through the learning communities.

Teaching/learning benchmarks: student interaction with faculty and other students is an essential characteristic and is facilitated through a variety of ways, including voicemail and/or email. These interactions are facilitated by the two forms of learning communities in ODL.

Evaluation and assessment benchmarks: the programme's educational effectiveness and teaching/learning process is assessed through an evaluation process that uses several methods and applies specific standards.

Learning communities are also formed through the shared physical space through the University Learning and Testing Centres. These centres serve as venues for various learning activities and learning assessments that observe the procedure and policies of the university to ensure integrity of the assessment process. Frydenberg (2002) in dela Pena-Bandalaria (2011), on the other hand, listed nine standard domains of quality in e-learning from the point of view of educators. Two of these domains involve the learning communities. These are the student support services and the evaluation domain. Student support services can be further subdivided. They are services needed before students' entrance to a virtual classroom, support during the learning experience, and continued connection between learners and the institution after the course or programme has been completed. All these are provided by the learning communities in the UPOU model. As for the evaluation domain, Frydenberg (2002) in dela Pena-Bandalaria (2011) is of the opinion that "while assessment of student achievement is normally described as part of instructional design and tied to specific course objectives, programme evaluation is a meta-activity that incorporates all the aspects of the eLearning experience". Programme evaluation also checks programme effectiveness, including these indicators: student retention rates, including variations over time, and student satisfaction, as measured by regular surveys (Mapolisa & Ncube, 2014). Learning motivation is another factor that learning communities can provide, such as fellow students motivating one another directly or indirectly. Through the learning communities, students are reminded by the circumstances of others of why they embarked on a programme in the first place.

According to Mukama (2016), ODeL is one of the key components of the ICT in education policy in Rwanda. The fifth strategic objective of the ICT in education strategic plan relates to the use of ODeL as a delivery mode. Accordingly, the policy proposes that ODeL be used to increase access to education at all levels, including basic, secondary, higher education, teacher education, technical and vocational education and training (TVET), and non-formal education. The policy highlights the need to build capacity in ODeL delivery mode, develop appropriate content, including OERs and MOOCs, and adopt quality assurance to meet local and international standards (Mukama, 2016). Given such a preceding standing, the availability of quality assurance practices signifies offerings of ODeL programmes without selecting education sectors in any country.

The Rwanda National ODeL Policy, MINEDUC, developed the Rwanda National Open, Distance and e-Learning Policy, intended to expand access and provide quality education to all learners who may be unable, for any reason, to join the conventional delivery modes (Mukama, 2016). A validation workshop with different stakeholders took place at the Nobleza Hotel in Kigali on 3 February, 2016. The development of this policy and its strategic plan was sponsored by the Commonwealth of Learning (Mukama, 2016). In a bid to replicate the Rwandese experience, Zimbabwe once set up a Ministry of Information Communication Technologies 2009, although conscious intentions to pursue ODeL were rare given the contextual differences between rural and urban areas in terms of resources.

In summing the preceding observations from Australian staff retention challenges' mitigation experiences, Hutchings, De Cieri, and Shea (2009, p. 20) drew three conclusions in the context of measures to mitigate staff retention challenges which are also equally compatible with curtailing hindrances to quality assurance practices in ODeL situations in the following manner:

- Our findings suggest that in response to skills shortages and critical changes in legislation, resource sector organisations utilise at least some 'good' employment practices, such as safe working conditions, high remuneration relative to other sectors and urban locations, and effective communication strategies (p.20)

- However, more needs to be done by employers in this sector to attract employees through offering more flexible work practices for employees and better work-life balance, particularly for firms operating in remote locations. (p.20)

- Environmental conditions, including infrastructure, such as schools and medical facilities, are also considerations for employers seeking to attract a workforce to remote locations.

Skills shortages and environmental conditions are strong determinants of quality assurance practices in ODeL settings. Their availability tends to dictate the pace at which ODeL programmes may be designed, implemented, monitored, and evaluated successfully in search of impact university products that might inscribe indelible marks in their nations.

12.7 Summary

The chapter has highlighted the conceptual reflections of quality assurance, quality assurance practices and quality assurance practices in ODeL institutions. Quality was associated with excellence and improvement. Quality assurance was perceived as the process of enhancement of high standards, enviable, and reputable ODeL programmes and products. Quality assurance practices in ODeL institutions dictate the nature of quality education offered in such educational institutions. Since we are now living in an e-society, quality ODeL education programmes are the way to go. Arguably, any deprivation of quality assurance practices in ODeL institutions spells doom and disaster to the previously looked down upon ODeL education and its qualifications. Benchmarking ODeL institutions on other renowned institutions is the way to go. A knowledge of the ODeL institution's quality assurance benefits gives rise to a situation where universities build on their strength for further enhance their performance, especially, in a globalised university competitive environment.

12.8 References

Akinpelu, J. A. (2001). *An Introduction to Philosophy of Education*. Lagos: MacMillan.

Association of Asian Universities (AAU). (2010). *Quality Assurance Framework*.

Brown, J., Kurzweil, M., & Prichett, W. (2017). *Quality Assurance in U.S. Higher Education. The Current Landscape and Principles for Reform*. ITSHAKA Research Paper.

Brusoni, M. (2014). European Association for Quality Assurance in Higher Education: The Concept of Excellence in Higher Education, AISBL 2014, Brussels.

Bush, T., & Glover, D. (2012a). Leadership development and learner outcomes: Evidence from South Africa. *Journal of Educational Leadership, Policy and Practice, 27*(2), 3-15.

Chikwanda, T. R. (2020). *An Empirical Examination of Leadership Styles' Contribution towards Creation of Conducive Teaching and Learning Environment in Selected Colleges of Education in Zambia* [Unpublished Doctor of Philosophy in Educational Administration and Policy Studies]. Lusaka: University of Zambia.

Coombs, P. H. (1970). *What is Educational Planning?* Paris: UNESCO.

dela Pena-Bandalaria, M. (2011). Ensuring Quality Education in Open and Distance eLearning (ODeL) Through Virtual Learning Communities. *AAOU Journal, 6*(1), 13-23.

Hellriegel, D., & Slocum, J.W.Jr. (2016). *Organisational Behaviour (19ᵗʰ ed.).* London: Longman.

Hong, L., Gu, G., Li, W., Fan, D., Wu, J., Duan, Y., Peng, H., & Shao, Q. (2012). Influencing factors of consumers' willingness to pay for *Crocus sativus*: An analysis of survey data from China. Journal of Medicinal Plants Research, 6(27), 4423-8.

Hutchings, K., De Cieri, H., & Shea, T. (2009). Employee Attraction in the Australian Resources Sector: Australian Sector Employment Practices. *Journal of Industrial Relations, 53*(1), 83-101.

Jung, I., Wong, T. M., & Belawati, T. (2013). *Quality Assurance in Distance Education and E-learning. Challenges and Solutions from Asia.* India: Sage Publications.

Kangai, C., & Mapolisa, T. (2008). Citation Analysis of Research Projects Submitted by Bachelor of Education (EAPPS) Students' (2000-2004) to the Department of Education at the Zimbabwe Open University: Implications for Educators and Librarians. *The African Symposium: An Online Journal of African Educational Research Network, 8* (1), 33-45.

Kangai C., & Mapolisa, T. (2012). Factors Affecting the Bachelor of Education (Educational Management) Success and Completion of the Research Projects at the Zimbabwe Open University. *International Journal on Trends in Education and their Implications (IJONTE), 3*(1), 83-94.

Kis, V. (2005). Quality Assurance in Tertiary Education: Current Practices in OECD Countries and a Literature Review on Potential Effects. https://www.oecd.org/education/skills-beyond-school/38006910.pdf

Kiat, T. H., Heng, M. A., & Lim-Ratnam, C. (Eds). (2017). *Curriculum leadership by middle leaders: theory, design and practice.* Abingdon, Oxon: Routledge.

Mapolisa, T. (2012). Provision of Research Support Services to ODL Learners by Tutors: A Focus on the Zimbabwe Open University's Bachelor of Education (Educational Management) Research Students' Supervision Experiences. *Turkish Online Journal of Distance Education (TOJDE), 13*(2), 58-68.

Mapolisa, T. (2015). *A Comparative Case Study of Zimbabwe's Public and Private Universities' Staff Retention Strategies* [Doctor of Philosophy Thesis in Educational Management]. Harare: Zimbabwe Open University.

Mapolisa, T. & Chirimuuta, C. (2012). Luring them back Home: Strategies to Lure back and Retain Professionals in the Diaspora: A Case Study of the Zimbabwe Open University (ZOU). *International Journal of Social Sciences and Education, 2*(3), 438-445.

Mapolisa, T., & Khosa, T. K. (2015). The Efficacy of Information and Communication Technology (ICT) in Enhancing Quality Open and Distance (ODL) Teaching:

Zimbabwe Open University National Centre's Programme Leaders' Perceptions. *Journal of Global Research and Social Science, 3*(2), 102-111.

Mapolisa, T. & Kurasha, P. (2013). Leader-Member Exchange Theory: A Driver for Open and Distance Learning (ODL): A Case Study of the Zimbabwe Open University (ZOU). *International Journal of Asian Social Science, 3*(2), 321-332.

Mapolisa, T., & Mafa, O. (2012). Challenges being Experienced by Undergraduate Research Students in Conducting Research in Open and Distance Learning. *International Journal of Asian Social Science and Education (AESS), 2*(10), 1672-1684.

Mapolisa, T., & Mubika, A. K. (2013). Total Quality Management: The Pathway to Quality Research Supervision of the Postgraduate Diploma in Education Programme at the Zimbabwe Open University. *International Journal of Asian Social Science, 3*(2), 308-320.

Mapolisa, T., Muyengwa, B. & Chakanyuka, S. (2010). Tutors' Experiences in Supervising in Research Projects for Students on the Master's and Bachelor of Education (M Ed and B Ed) in Education Management: The Case of Mashonaland Central and Mashonaland East Regional Centres of the Zimbabwe Open University. *The African Symposium: An Online Journal of African Educational Research Network, 10*(1), 111-127.

Mapolisa, T., & Ncube, A. C. (2012). Team Leadership: The Engine for Quality Performance and Outputs in the Management in the Open and Distance Learning Programmes. Zimbabwe *International Open and Distance Learning Journal: International Research Conference Special Edition Issue, 1*(1), 101-110.

Mapolisa, T., & Ncube, A. C. (2014). Possibilities to enhancing quality assurance across ODL programmes: A Focus on Zimbabwe Open University's selected unit heads' perceptions. *International Open and Distance Learning Journal 4th ACDE Special Edition, June 2014,* 118-134.

Mapolisa, T., & Tshabalala, T. (2013). An Evaluation of the Impact of the Inadequate Teaching and Learning Resources in Public Institutions of Higher Learning in Zimbabwe. *International Journal of Advanced Research, 1*(10), 739-745.

Mukama, E. (2016). Baseline Study of the Status of Open and Distance Learning in Rwanda. http://oasis.col.org/bitstream/handle/11599/2489/2016_Mukama _Baseline-Study-ODeL-Rwanda.pdf?sequence=1&isAllowed=y

Mullins, L. J., & Christy, G. (2017). *Management and Organisational Behaviour.* London: Pearson.

Mutuva, S. N. (2012). *Challenges Faced by Secondary School Head Teachers in Leadership and Management of Human Resources in Nzaui District-Makueni County, Kenya. MED Project.* Nairobi: Kenyatta University.

Nekongo-Nielsen, H. (2006). The Contributions of Open and Distance Learning in Namibia. A paper presented at the Fourth Pan-Commonwealth of Open Learning. Retrieved from http://pof4.dec.uwi.edu/viewpaper.php?id=351

Nenge, R. T., Chimbadzwa, Z., & Mapolisa, T. (2012). ICT Implementation Challenges and Strategies for ODL Institutions: The ZOU's National Centre Academic Staff Experiences. *Turkish Online Journal of Distance Education (TOJDE), 3*(4), 112-124.

Ngubane-Mokiwa, S., & Letseka, M. (2015). *Shift from Open Distance Learning to Open Distance E-Learning.* https://www.researchgate.net/publication/269875807

Njihia, M., Mwaniki, E. W., Ireri, A. M., & Chege, F. (2016). Uptake of Open Distance and e-Learning (ODEL) programmes: A Case of Kenyatta University, Kenya. https://www.researchgate.net/publication/315688656

Northouse, P. G. (2016). *Leadership: Theory and Practice (7th ed.).* Thousand Oaks, CA: Sage.

O'Neil, P. H. (2011). Truth, Transparency, and Leadership. *Public Administration Review, 72*(1), 11-12.

Reid, I. (2005). Quality Assurance, Open and Distance Learning, and Australian Universities. *International Review of Research in Open and Distributed Learning, 6*(1), 1–12.

Saketa, K. N. (2014). *Quality Assurance Practices in Ethiopian Public and Private Higher Education Institutions* [Doctor of Education Thesis]. South Africa: University of South Africa.

Senge, P. M. (1992). Mental Models. *Planning Review, 20*(20), 4-44.

Index

A

academic advising, 63
accelerators, 134
accountability, 38
accreditation, 92
active learning, 79
admission services, 62
African Virtual University, 14
ambition, 34
appraisal costs, 101
attributes, 144

B

banner advertisements, 49
barriers to university-industry
   links, 137
blended learning, 30
broad perspective, 160
buttons, 49
characteristics, 144

C

climate categories, 152
collaborative research, 132
commitmen, 149
communication, 38, 179
competitive education market, 93
complex linkages, 95
Complexity Leadership Theory, 4
computerised system, 93
confidence, 36
consultation services, 78
continuing education, 84
controlling, 179

conviction, 37
copyright, 80
Corona Virus, 106
course development, 97
COVID 19 era, 22
creativity, 146

D

development dimensions, 150
digital age, 66
digital literacy, 20
digital transformation, 105
direct marketing, 52
directing, 178
distance and e-learning
   organisations, 29
distance education, 2
Distance Learning Library
   Services, 73
distance librarianship, 72, 80
diverse rewards, 94

E

educational policy, 183
e-learning, 30, 97
electronic information sources,
   77
emotional and moral muscle, 151
empathy, 40
employee-centered climates, 151
empowerment evaluation theory,
   189
environment, 161
evaluation, 182
evaluation of ODeL programmes,
   185

experiential learning, 130
external environment, 147

F

faculty entrepreneurship, 131
focused evaluation theory, 188
formalised systems, 93
formative evaluation, 24

G

goal system, 101
goal-setting theory, 90
guidance and counselling
    services, 63

H

holistic innovation system
    framework, 128

I

Industrialisation, 126
information literacy, 79
innovation, 124
innovative leadership, 15
institutional positioning, 45
institutional websites, 54
integrate, 99
intellectual property (IP), 136
internet advertising, 49
interpersonal relationships, 145

L

leaders, 159
leadership, 1, 15
leadership roles in programme
    management, 172
leading, 179

leading by example, 36
librarians, 73
library services, 69

M

management, 148
management practices, 165
managing staff, 11
marketing strategy, 44
massification of education, 18
materials and document delivery,
    77
mechanisms, 146
mission, 160
mobile marketing, 54
mobile phones and access to
    tertiary education, 111
modern trend, 146
monitor, 99
MOOCS, 23
motivation, 156, 179
MyVista,, 21

N

National Innovation
    Systems/Triple Helix, 128

O

ODeL educational programmes,
    184
ODeL in higher education
    institutions, 106
ODeL through radio broadcasting
    of HEI programmes, 114
online student services., 61
online student support services,
    66
online technology, 65

Open and Distance Learning (ODL), 12, 69
open and distance library services, 70
open learning,, 12
open, distance and e-learning, 30
operationalisation, 98
organisational climate, 143
organisational goals, 88
organisational innovation, 94
organising, 178

P

paternalistic leadership style, 100
perceptions, 148
performance indicators, 186
performance management, 88
personal selling, 52
physical barriers, 96
place/distribution, 53
planning, 177
policy coordination, 180
price/tuition, 46
productivity, 96
programme coordination, 180
programme evaluation, 181
programme evaluation practices, 181
programme goal, 168
programme implementation practices, 166
programme leaders, 168
programme management, 165
programme management cycle, 169
programmes implementation, 165, 190
promotion, 48
psychological climates, 152
psychological contract, 153
public relations (PR), 51, 76

Q

quantitative indicators, 91

R

recognition, 150
reference services, 78
registration services, 62
relationship, 154
research mobility, 133
research productivity, 94
revolutionising the HEIs mode of delivery, 106
role, 157

S

sales promotions, 50
science park, 137
segmentation, targeting and positioning, 45
self-improvement, 40
situational leadership, 3
skyscraper advertisements, 50
SMART objectives, 19, 168
social media channels, 54
special needs support services, 64
spin-offs, 136
staffing, 178
standards for distance library services, 75
start-up incubators, 135
stimulating creativity, 156
student advisement, 65
student affairs, 59
student affairs professionals, 65
student services, 60
student support services, 61
students in the rural areas and access to internet, 110

students with disabilities and
      online learning, 116
support, 155
Systems Theory, 5

T

teaching performance, 92
techniques, 156
technology, 147
technology use in distance
      libraries, 80
theories of evaluation, 188
theory-driven evaluation theory,
      190
training, 24
training needs, 21
training of staff, 20
transactional roles, 99
transformation mindset, 39
transformational leadership, 2
transforming, 98
transforming inputs, 92
transparency, 37

U

university-industry partnerships,
      132

V

valence, 90
variables, 158
virtual environment, 29
virtual methods, 5
virtual teams, 6

W

workload model, 96

www.ingramcontent.com/pod-product-compliance
Lightning Source LLC
Chambersburg PA
CBHW072102020426
42334CB00017B/1606